Social Scientists for Social Justice

CRITICAL AMERICA

General Editors: Richard Delgado and Jean Stefancic

Social Scientists for Social Justice

Making the Case against Segregation

John P. Jackson, Jr.

NEW YORK UNIVERSITY PRESS

New York and London

NEW YORK UNIVERSITY PRESS
New York and London
www.nyupress.org

First published in paperback in 2005

Library of Congress Cataloging-in-Publication Data
Jackson, John P., 1961–
Social scientists for social justice : making the case against segregation /
John P. Jackson, Jr.
p. cm. — (Critical America)
Includes bibliographical references and index.
ISBN 0–8147–4266–1 (cloth : alk. paper)
ISBN 0–8147–4267–X (pbk. : alk. paper)
1. Brown, Oliver, 1918– —Trials, litigation, etc.   2. Topeka (Kan.). Board
of Education—Trials, litigation, etc.   3. Discrimination in education—
Law and legislation—United States—History—20th Century.   4. Race
discrimination—Law and legislation—United States—History—20th Century.
5. Discrimination in education—United States—History—20th Century.
6. Race discrimination—United States—History—20th Century.   7. African
Americans—Segregation—Psychological aspects—History—20th Century.
8. Sociological jurisprudence.   9. Social justice—United States—History—
20th Century.   10. Social scientists—United States—History—20th Century.
11. Social engineering—United States—History—20th Century.   I. Title.   II. Series.
KF228.B76 J33 2001
340'.115—dc21   2001004144

New York University Press books are printed on acid-free paper,
and their binding materials are chosen for strength and durability.

c 10 9 8 7 6 5 4 3 2 1
p 10 9 8 7 6 5 4 3 2 1

To Maggie, Jack, and Michele
with all my love.

Contents

Acknowledgments

I would like to acknowledge the support of the National Science Foundation, which supported this work through their Office of Law and Social Sciences.

I have been very gratified by the enthusiasm of Jean Stefancic and Richard Delgado. Their support has been invaluable for me in getting this project in its final form. Stephen Magro and everyone else at New York University Press have been very supportive, and I thank them.

Historians would be unable to practice their trade without archivists and librarians. I was very fortunate to have the help of many able archivists, including Sharon Ochencrist and John Popplestone at the Archive for the History of American Psychology in Akron, Ohio; Michelle Feller-Kopman at the American Jewish Historical Society in Waltham, Massachusetts; Mike Widener at the Tarleton Law Library in Austin, Texas; the staffs of the Harvard University Archives in Cambridge, Massachusetts, the University of Chicago Archives in Chicago, Illinois, and the University of Minnesota archives in Minneapolis, Minnesota. Special thanks need to go to the staff of the Manuscript Division of the Library of Congress in Washington, D.C., who were exceedingly helpful during my extended visit.

A number of people offered advice, encouragement, and support during the course of this project. I thank Fran Cherry, Mary Dudziak, Ellen Herman, Ben Keppel, Paul Kimmel, and Ian Nicholson. Mark Tushnet bought me lunch and shared his vast knowledge of the NAACP-LDEF one pleasant afternoon in Washington. John Galliher graciously shared pages of his then-forthcoming book on Alfred McClung Lee.

Ben Harris introduced me to the professional world of the history of psychology and gave me opportunities to present my ideas publicly. Neil Jumonville first suggested to me that I should try to write this book.

I need to thank many, many friends who helped me in so many ways that I cannot possibly recount them all here. This work would have been much poorer without the help of Pam Andras, Kai-Henrik Barth, Kelly Bennett, Robert Ferguson, Susan D. Jones, Mike Reidy, Shari Rudavsky, Mary Thomas, Chris Young, and John Zelle. And special thanks to Shawn Rounds and Lyda Morehouse for their love of books and for their endless encouragement.

This project began while I was in graduate school at the University of Minnesota. I owe my thanks to Mischa Penn and Sally Gregory Kohlstedt for helping me get this project started. John Beatty encouraged me to enter graduate school and first suggested that I explore the intersection of law and science. Arthur Norberg guided me through the difficult process of writing my dissertation.

This book started a decade ago as a seminar paper for Paul L. Murphy, Regent's Professor of History at the University of Minnesota. My one regret about this project is that Paul did not live to see that paper transformed into this book. Paul continues to be an inspiration to me as a scholar and a human being, and I like to think that he would have been pleased at my effort here.

Finally, I owe profound thanks to my family. My children, Maggie and Jack, are wonderful sources of inspiration and energy. They have enriched my life beyond measure. Michele, my partner in everything, has never wavered in her belief in me or my work. Thank you, my love.

1

Introduction

Framing the Historical Problem

In 1951, when the attorneys of the National Association for the Advancement of Colored People–Legal Defense and Education Fund (NAACP-LDEF) began litigation to desegregate primary and secondary schools in the United States, they called on social scientists for help. Organized by social psychologist Kenneth B. Clark, social scientists testified at several trials and wrote briefs, submitted to the Supreme Court, arguing that segregation was psychologically damaging and that the desegregation process could be expected to proceed smoothly. In 1954, when the Supreme Court found segregation in schools unconstitutional in *Brown v. Topeka Board of Education*, Chief Justice Earl Warren, writing for the unanimous Court, cited social-scientific evidence as one basis for the Court's opinion. The 1954 decision delayed any order regarding remedy, and social scientists continued to work with the NAACP-LDEF through 1955, when the Supreme Court handed down *Brown II*, ordering desegregation with "all deliberate speed."[1]

The year 1979 marked the twenty-fifth anniversary of the first *Brown* decision, and the American Psychological Association asked some of the psychologists involved with the NAACP-LDEF to speak on their experiences in the *Brown* campaign as well as on their hopes for the future. Yet, far from celebrating their involvement with *Brown*, the speakers were defensive about their actions. M. Brewster Smith, who had served as an expert witness and had signed the Social Science Statement, complained, "It is hinted in various quarters and said openly in others that the social science testimony on the cases culminating in *Brown v. Board of Education* was tendentious and ungrounded."[2] Against these charges, Isidor Chein, perhaps Kenneth B. Clark's closest confidant during the *Brown* decision, declared: "Let me state at the outset that I know of no serious reason for retracting anything that was said in the so-called Social Science Brief submitted in *Brown v. Board of*

Education or in the testimony of the expert witnesses called by counsel for the plaintiffs."[3]

Indeed, in the two decades since Chein and Smith made these claims, the idea that social scientists' testimony in *Brown* was unfounded has become the dominant understanding of the case. Within four decades, what was once viewed as psychology's greatest achievement in social engineering has been proclaimed a miserable failure. The psychologists involved in *Brown* are often viewed as liberal reformers who cloaked their political wishes in the guise of social science. In his history of the United States since 1945, James T. Patterson writes that the psychological evidence for a feeling of inferiority among African American children was "dubious and subject to different interpretations . . . . The fact of the matter was that in 1954 there simply did not exist sufficient research that could 'prove' whether any particular racial mix in schools was superior—or in what ways—to any other."[4] Ellen Herman, in her history of psychology in the postwar United States asks "how an allegedly scientific consensus had failed rather miserably to predict the course of desegregation and stand the test of close examination."[5] William Tucker, in his history of "scientific racism," argues, "Neither the infliction of psychological harm nor the intellectual equality of blacks and whites was in any way relevant. . . . In addition, the only empirical data submitted to the court [Clark's doll test] to support the scientific assertions turned out to be of questionable validity."[6] Activist/scholar Harold Cruse claims that "the scientific testimony [in *Brown*] . . . was, to a great degree blind to objective sociological facts. Obscured were webs of causative processes behind public school developments that could not be explained by simplistic methods of historical summation."[7]

In the most extensive critique of the social science in *Brown*, Daryl Scott claims:

> The plaintiffs had to demonstrate first, that black children had damaged psyches; second, that the damage flowed from the schools rather than from their families or social discrimination at large; and third, that the damage to their psyches adversely affected their ability to learn. These issues were more than the literature could handle. [These claims] exceeded the factual knowledge of the social sciences on the relationship between self-concept and learning, strained the methodological approaches to measuring damage, and ran counter to the prevailing assumptions underlying theories about the spatial relationship between dominant and subordinate groups and personality developments among the latter.[8]

The argument that Clark and his colleagues were social reformers rather than objective scientists is not new. Indeed, segregationists in the South proclaimed the social science in *Brown* unscientific as soon as they were presented with it. What is new is the general proclamation by "mainstream" scholars that the South was right so long ago.

Clark and his colleagues were part of the generation that has been characterized by David Hollinger as indulging in "extravagant universalism" that "looked to the species as a whole" to break down the barriers of race and nationalism.[9] To put the argument another way, in the 1950s, almost the only people to argue that "race matters" were segregationists. The integrationist response was that race did not matter, that black people were, as Kenneth Stampp unapologetically claimed in 1956, "only white men with black skins, nothing more, nothing less."[10] Integrationists thus adopted an assimilationist position on cultural and racial diversity, because any argument for cultural pluralism, which allows for a limited form of racial or ethnic separatism, was seen as playing into the hands of the segregationists.[11]

In the 1960s, everything changed. Jim Crow came to an end just as the inner cities exploded. Much of the thinking about race since World War II seemed naive, confused, or just plain wrong.[12] "Racial progress" could no longer automatically be equated with "integration," as African Americans made race central to their place in American society. During the 1960s, as Stephen Steinberg has argued, "no longer was it certain that blacks could be—or *wanted* to be—integrated into the white communities."[13] With this claim came the idea that African American culture was different from European American culture but valuable and worth preserving nonetheless. Being black became a source of pride and strength, and the idea that African Americans should somehow submerge their black identity to join white culture became repellent to many. The pursuit of integration was seen as a trap for African Americans.[14] In 1967, Harold Cruse, one of the most eloquent of the scholars influenced by the Black Power movement, sounded very much like the segregationists when he wrote that "the Negro integrationist runs afoul of reality in the pursuit of an illusion, the 'open society'—a false front that hides several worlds of hyphenated-Americans. Which group or subgroup leaves its door wide open for the outsider? None really."[15]

The view that black culture was pathological and inferior to white culture, an idea that was central to the integrationist arguments of the social science in *Brown*, was seen as another manifestation of white supremacy as the debate on American race relations was transformed in the 1960s.[16] The notion of African Americans somehow "damaged" by white oppression was itself seen as a racist claim. Albert Murray argued that images of the "damage" wrought by discrimination, which "naive Negro spokesmen given to mortal outcry seize upon as evidence of the need for reform— are all too obvious extensions of the process of degradation by other means, and have always functioned as an indispensable element in the vicious cycle that perpetuates white supremacy through the systematic exploitation of black people."[17]

The collapse of the integrationist consensus was not only an ideological shift in American society but also a reflection of new realities about race relations. Six days after President Lyndon Johnson signed the Voting Rights Act of 1965, which drove the final nail into Jim Crow's coffin, Watts exploded. In a political heartbeat, the center of America's racial problems became large cities rather than the rural South.[18] New social problems forced themselves onto the national agenda. The problems created by "institutional" racism became paramount, and the older problems created by *de jure* segregation were quickly forgotten.

In this new political climate, a new series of critiques of *Brown* appeared in the social science literature. In 1978, Walter Stephan published a study that evaluated the predictions made in *Brown* and concluded: "It does appear that the social scientists [in *Brown*] were incorrect in the expectation that desegregation would reduce the prejudice of whites toward blacks and that they were only partially correct in their assumption that segregated blacks would have lower self-esteem than segregated whites."[19] Five years later, Harold Gerard was quite blunt in his assessment of the *Brown* social scientists. Central to Gerard's argument were the conditions for orderly desegregation that were outlined by the social scientists in their 1952 statement to the Supreme Court and later codified by Kenneth Clark in a 1953 article on desegregation.[20] The conditions centered on firm and consistent authority ordering desegregation and on students from different races coming into contact under conditions of relative equality. Writing in *American Psychologist*, Gerard claimed that "it was extraordinarily quixotic to assume that . . . the conditions specified in the statement [submitted to the Supreme Court] would or could be met in the typical school system."[21]

Stephan and Gerard were repeating some of the basic arguments made by the segregationists, namely, that the *Brown* social scientists had skimpy evidence for their arguments and were motivated by moral and political concerns rather than scientific data. Of course, the contexts in which these charges were made differed greatly. No one suggested in the late 1970s and early 1980s that these results argued for a return to Jim Crow. Rather, Stephan and Gerard were testing a scientific hypothesis against newly discovered evidence and circumstances and found the hypothesis wanting.

It is not just new social-scientific evaluations of *Brown* that have shaped our contemporary understanding of the case. While the Black Power movement of the 1960s may not have transformed the U.S. political culture in the way its proponents had hoped, it did have lasting influence on how scholars approached the African American experience. African American historians never again viewed African Americans as mere victims of white racism. Historians began to explore the myriad ways in which African Americans resisted white oppression and created a unique culture that stood apart from white culture. The arguments that Clark and his colleagues made to the Supreme Court, which viewed African Americans as victims of white oppression who existed in a pathological state, became unpalatable to contemporary African American historians. Historians rejected the "victimization model" to describe African American experiences during slavery and, increasingly, during twentieth-century urban life as well. As Earl Lewis wrote, since the 1980s, historians have "used words such as self-determination, agency, and empowerment to name the variations" of African Americans' "lived experiences."[22]

Certainly, this new historiography has led to a much clearer and more accurate picture of the African American experience. But the new historiographical outlook has contributed to a distorted view of social scientists' activities in the *Brown* litigation. I maintain that the common view—that social scientists stepped outside their role as scientific experts when they testified that segregation was damaging—misunderstands the nature of their arguments. The arguments that social scientists made to the courts were both subtle and complex and, unfortunately, easily caricatured. It is these caricatures, rather than the original arguments themselves, that segregationists, social scientists, and historians have criticized. By putting Clark and his colleagues in their proper historical context, and by closely examining the nature of their arguments before the Court, we can discover if their actions as scientists were justified by their standards of "scientific objectivity."

To understand social scientists' actions, I hope to answer three historical questions. First, *how did social scientists choose to study race prejudice and discrimination?* What were the origins of the research that was used in the *Brown* litigation? Second, *how did social scientists define a role for themselves as experts in the area of race prejudice and discrimination?* It is one thing for social scientists to study race prejudice; it is quite another for their studies to gain authority beyond the academy and in American society. Finally, *how did social scientists try to maintain the role of objective scientific experts when drawn into the highly adversarial process of a litigation campaign?* Commonly conceived, science seeks truth through consensus—a rational give-and-take of ideas—whereas the law seeks truth through an adversarial process—there is no possibility of reaching a true consensus between the warring parties.[23] How did the social scientists cope with the very different culture of the law?

Answering these three questions demonstrates how a group of social scientists were able to use their scientific expertise to become "social engineers." As social engineers, they worked hard to make the United States into what they believed to be a more just and equitable place to live. The following sections explore these three questions in detail.

How Did Social Scientists Come to Study Race Prejudice?

Unlike physical or natural sciences, to claim that the social sciences are ineluctably bound to the societies in which they have matured seems rather unproblematic. As Mitchell Ash has written in reference to psychology, "To undermine psychologists' naive pretensions to universalism and rationality by demonstrating the sociocultural embeddedness of this particular science may have shock value to psychologists and their students, but comes as no surprise to others."[24] Perhaps in no other area of the social sciences are the ties to society clearer than in the scientific study of race and race relations. The point is made by Graham Richards in reference to the social psychologists who are the subject of this book: "US Social Psychological work on prejudice and the roots of racism was part and parcel of the wider civil rights movement."[25]

And yet, exactly how social scientists became tied to the civil rights movement is unexplored in the historical literature. The story begins with the rise of the scientific study of race prejudice. In the nineteenth and the early part of the twentieth century, social-scientific thinking on race largely mirrored that of the dominant white society: there was a natural racial hierarchy with Anglo-Saxons on the top and African Americans at the bottom. Among social scientists, this viewpoint nearly disappeared between World War I and World War II and was replaced with the viewpoint that all races had equal intellectual and physical abilities. By 1939, the social-scientific community explained what were previously viewed as *innate* racial differences as only *apparent* differences. For example, the differences in IQ scores between African Americans and white Americans were no longer viewed as proof of racial inferiority but as proof of the cultural bias inherent in the testing procedure.

This shift in scientific thinking about race led to a new social-scientific problem. Antipathy between the races had long been explained by pointing to the natural differences between the races. Whites would "naturally" dislike close contact with an inferior race. Similarly, African Americans would be uncomfortable with close contact with whites— with whom they could not possibly compete. But when social scientists rejected race differences in the 1930s, a new explanation for racial antipathy emerged: what they began calling "race prejudice." By the 1940s, scientists were busy attempting to measure race prejudice quantitatively, to link it with other personality traits, and to identify its origins in child development.

In describing the rise of the study of race prejudice, Franz Samelson argued that the scientific study of race "was enmeshed in the real world from the start, in ways which are more obvious if perhaps not more important than is true of other, seemingly more esoteric problems of psychology."[26] For the social scientists involved in the *Brown* case, the urge to understand race prejudice arose from several areas of the "real world." Many of these scientists were themselves cultural minorities in the United States. Whether Jewish, like Otto Klineberg and Isidor Chein, or African American, like Kenneth and Mamie Clark, their experiences with racism sensitized them to the problems of racial discrimination. Those social scientists who were not cultural minorities, such as Gardner Murphy, Goodwin Watson, and Gordon Allport, were the products of liberal/leftist political tradition, often with an overlay of radical Christian theology that emphasized the equality of human beings. These views substantially changed the concept of how scientifically to study the problems of race relations, particularly problems of race prejudice and racial identity.

Defining Experts in Race Prejudice

Throughout the twentieth century, psychologists have faced the problem of convincing the general public that "scientific psychology offered an understanding of mental events superior to that of common sense."[27] For the psychologists in the *Brown* case to be taken seriously as scientific experts, they had to convince the public that what social psychology had to say about race relations was more reliable than what society believed about race relations.

Social psychologists came to a number of conclusions regarding race prejudice that belied the commonly accepted wisdom of American society regarding the proper relationship between the two races. Indeed, in the decades after the end of World War II most white Americans firmly believed in the "natural inferiority" of African Americans. Yet social scientists went much further in their claims: not only did social scientists preach the equality of all races, but they also preached that segregation was not a natural "instinct"—children had to be *taught* race prejudice. Moreover, scientists claimed that desegregation of the races could be *imposed* on groups who did not wish it—the law did not have to wait for a "natural" societal evolution away from discrimination to social equality. Finally, social scientists claimed that the law could require rapid desegregation—giving no time for any sort of gradual adjustment. None of these viewpoints was reflected in the "common sense" of the postwar citizenry of the United States.

Social scientists gained a foothold as "experts" in society during World War II, when they allied themselves with the war effort. For the first time, social scientists had access to powerful policymakers who seemed to be willing to use their advice. These experiences during the war gave social scientists a new confidence that they could use their scientific expertise to remake society, particularly in the area of race relations. Quelling race riots, boosting morale by building national unity, analyzing Nazi racist propaganda—all these activities served to thrust race prejudice to the center of social scientists' wartime work.

After the war, to convince others that racial change was possible, social scientists took a new approach to legal change. Before the war, social science was often hesitant to recommend legal change to alter society—they often thought that the laws of a particular society were mere reflections of the attitudes held by members of that society. After the war, however, social scientists built an argument that it was not necessary to wait and do nothing while society "evolved" more egalitarian racial mores; rather, the law could change racial attitudes.

To put their new views toward the law into practice, social scientists joined organizations dedicated to fighting race discrimination. The exemplar among such organizations was the American Jewish Congress in New York City. Social-scientific work within a socially active body such as the American Jewish Congress represented a confluence of interests between civil rights workers and social scientists. For the civil rights worker, social science represented the "scientific viewpoint" regarding race—a powerful weapon in the postwar United States. For the social scientist, the civil rights movement was an opportunity to use social science to reshape society. Additionally, the NAACP-LDEF provided the social scientists with a venue through which to change the law, and thereby society's views on the "race problem."

Scientist or Advocate?

Unlike attorneys, community activists, religious leaders, politicians, and others in the civil rights struggle, social scientists were supposed to be apolitical, nonpartisan students of society, rather than active shapers of society. Their involvement on behalf of civil rights, therefore, represented a potential conflict between their role as objective observers of society and that of active participants in society.

This conflict of roles in the social scientists' involvement in the *Brown* litigation underscores a theme prevalent in recent histories of the American social sciences. A glance at the titles of established works in the field reveals a preoccupation with a fundamental paradox concerning the role of social science in American society, that of "advocacy versus objectivity." Indeed, the quest for objectivity has been called the "crucible" of social science.[28] The paradox can be read as follows: presumably, social science draws its authority from the "objectivity" of science. That is, what social science has to say about society can be trusted as accurate because it is "scientific": disinterested, detached, and apolitical. Science is about "facts," not morality, politics, or emotion. And yet, social science has flourished in this country precisely because it is used to solve moral, political, or emotional problems, so much so that historian Hamilton Cravens has suggested it be redubbed "social technology."[29]

If the corollary to technology is not "science" but "engineering," the corollary to social technology would be social engineering. Social engineering has been embedded in the very professionalization of twentieth-century American social science. Psychology is a useful example. For the first half of the twentieth century, psychologists struggled to professionalize psychology by donning the mantle of natural science as objective knowledge. This move, however, was made palatable to American society by claims that the study of psychology could produce knowledge that would be of great use in the efficient operation of society. In other words, the professionalization of psychology in the United States was premised on the utility of psychology to cure various social ills, while simultaneously establishing itself as an autonomous discipline modeled after the natural sciences.[30]

The involvement of social scientists in the *Brown* litigation is a particularly appropriate vehicle to explore issues surrounding social engineering in the social sciences, because it is often seen as the ultimate expression of one side of the equation—historian Walter Jackson argued that the involvement of social scientists in *Brown* meant that "the days in which social scientists vied with each other to establish their objectivity by distancing themselves from public controversy were clearly over."[31] The citation of social science in a Supreme Court opinion was the result of a decade-long effort by social scientists to become, in their own words, "social engineers." Because it is often seen as such a pure expression of activist social science, the *Brown* case offers a unique showcase for the mechanisms by which social scientists took their science and used it to reshape U.S. society into what they saw as a more democratic and egalitarian one. In particular, by tracing the activities of this particular group of social scientists, we can see how they translated their political and ethical beliefs into social science and their social science into social action.

Between 1945 and 1950, social scientists proclaimed themselves social engineers, especially in the area of race prejudice. New organizations gave social scientists new opportunities to study racial prejudice, to recommend methods for combating it, and to work with policymakers and attorneys to enact their recommendations. This work included involving social scientists in court cases as expert witnesses as well as calling for research designed for use in court cases. Social scientists had demonstrated their usefulness to civil rights attorneys by the time the trials of the four cases of the *Brown* campaign started in 1951.

The work in *Brown* is far from unproblematic when considered as social engineering. Social scientists' public pronouncements about the arrival of social engineering masked an ongoing project to define the proper use of social-scientific knowledge. The social scientists were aware that their credibility as experts was predicated on presenting "objective, scientific" evidence. Yet their objectivity could be called into question because of their close involvement with the partisan issue of school desegregation.

The tension between objectivity and advocacy was not an abstract problem; it was a very real problem that arose out of the experiences of social scientists in the litigation. The opposing side in the litigation, as well as commentators on the litigation, leveled charges that the social scientists were merely dressing up their political and social choices in scientific garb. Each time such a charge was made, the response from the social scientists was the same: to claim that they were detached and uninterested investigators presenting the latest scientific findings on race relations. Any charges of subjectivity were denied, sometimes vehemently.

Questions about objectivity were not raised only by the opposing side in the litigation but also by the social scientists themselves. The social scientists constantly struggled to define how they could be objective scientists in the context of their work with the legal team. Different views of the proper role of scientific knowledge can be seen at certain points of the litigation—during the recruitment of social scientists as expert witnesses, in the drafting of legal briefs submitted for the appeals process, during the campaign to gain signatures for those appellate briefs, in the defense of the social science quoted in the first *Brown* opinion, during the work done for the *Brown II* in 1955, and during the attempt to establish the Committee of Social Science Consultants within the NAACP-LDEF. The community of social scientists involved in the litigation debated the proper role of social science in public controversy at each of these points. To justify their actions as appropriate for scientists *qua* scientists, they drew the mantle of objectivity around themselves and embraced the rhetoric of value-free and neutral social science.

The responsible social scientist, the social scientists themselves argued, owed his or her first allegiance to science, and only secondary allegiance to a particular social policy. But in making such a move toward science,

Clark and his colleagues also ensured that their scientific credibility could be used by the NAACP-LDEF to fight for the very social policy that the social scientists desired. It is impossible to separate out the advocacy from the objectivity in their actions.

Organization of the Book

This book is organized into four sections. Part I, "Background," examines two eras of social-scientific thinking about race. These chapters explore how scientists came to study race prejudice as a scientifically interesting topic. Chapter 2 traces the development of a new, racially egalitarian social science that began in the 1920s and 1930s. During the 1930s, new explanations for racial differences and new ways of examining racial attitudes reshaped the social-scientific concepts of race. Explanations of racial differences that argued for the existence of innate racial characteristics were largely displaced by cultural explanations for racial differences. The acceptance of cultural differences made a racially egalitarian social science possible. Many of the social scientists in the *Brown* litigation were leaders in the drive for a racially egalitarian social science. Chapter 3 looks at the effect of World War II on the social-scientific community. The war gave social science unprecedented access to policymakers, making social scientists believe that they could be social engineers. The one aspect of society that they felt needed their attention the most was "intergroup relations" or race relations. Their war work made social scientists believe that they could use their knowledge to reduce or eliminate racial prejudice.

Part II, "Forging the Alliance," examines the specific mechanisms by which social scientists became involved in the legal process. This involvement in the legal process explains how they established themselves as experts on race prejudice in the larger society. Chapter 4 traces how social scientists' wartime concerns for eliminating race prejudice found expression in the American Jewish Congress's new organization, the Commission on Community Interrelations (CCI). CCI brought social scientists into contact with the legal culture, specifically with a group of attorneys who were interested in using social-scientific data in civil rights cases. Chapter 5 shows how social scientists and general use of social science were adopted by the NAACP Legal Defense and Education Fund's (LDEF) campaign to desegregate graduate schools.

Part III, "*Brown* Litigation," examines how social scientists became directly involved in the campaign to desegregate public schools. At each stage of the litigation, scientists constantly had to guard against the perception that they were advocates rather than objective scientists. Chapters 5 and 6 start at the trial level of the litigation. There were four trials in the school segregation cases. Social science played an increased role in each successive trial. In *Briggs*, the first trial, social science was evident in only a few dozen pages of testimony for the plaintiffs. In *Davis*, the fourth trial, the social science testimony ran to hundreds of pages, as each side called expert witnesses. I focus on the recruitment of these social scientists and the arguments they offered in testimony.

Chapters 8 and 9 look at the role social scientists played at the appellate level of the litigation. Social scientists wrote briefs for submission to the Supreme Court. I focus on the drafting of these briefs, the nature of the argument presented, and the campaign to collect signatures for the briefs. There was significant controversy within the social science community over these briefs and over the proper role of social science in the legal arena. I explain how these controversies were resolved.

Part IV, "Dissolution," looks at the failure of the LDEF and the social scientists to formalize their relationship within the Committee of Social Science Consultants (CSSC). The CSSC was meant to be a formal body of social scientists that would work under the auspices of the LDEF. The CSSC was not able to obtain funding for their work, and by 1957, social scientists were so chary of the LDEF that they hesitated to be connected with the organization.

PART I

Background

2

The Study of Race between the Wars

Between World War I and World War II, anthropologists, geneticists, sociologists, and psychologists reconceptualized the study of race. To put the matter simply: at the end of World War I, most scientists were convinced that race was a useful scientific concept and that the races could be placed in a fairly firm racial hierarchy, with whites on top and "Negroes" on the bottom. By World War II, most scientists had abandoned these views. A strong contingent of cultural anthropologists argued that race was a useless scientific construct. Psychologists, for the most part, abandoned the notion that there were innate intellectual differences between different "races" and turned their attention to the study of "race prejudice."

The reasons for this shift in scientific thinking are complex and a matter of some historical dispute. On the one hand, the shift in scientific thinking regarding race coincided with social changes such as American revulsion with Nazi race doctrines in the 1930s and the entry of minority group members, primarily American Jews, into social-scientific ranks, leading some historians to argue that the shift could not have been caused by new scientific data. On the other hand, other historians have found that deep scientific flaws in the older, white supremacist scientific program led to its collapse.[1]

In a carefully nuanced argument, Graham Richards has suggested that *both* accounts are correct: scientific racism's demise can be traced back both to its scientific failings and to a changing social world. The older school of thought simply failed to provide the analytical tools necessary for it to cope with a host of new social problems in the United States. I think that Richard's account is essentially correct, and I hope to follow his model in this chapter.[2]

This chapter sketches the basic contours of this shift in scientific thinking. My survey is necessarily selective and focuses on how aspects of the emerging "scientific antiracism" of the 1920s and 1930s set the stage for the transformation of social scientists into antiracist social advocates after World War II. Once scientists rejected the notion of essential racial differences, new forms of scientific research were needed to answer questions that arose because of that rejection. If the races were not "naturally" different and unequal, why were African Americans so despised in American society? Why did they experience such high crime rates, illiteracy rates, and other forms of "social pathology? These were the sorts of questions that social scientists were seeking to answer during these decades.[3]

Four basic strands of research embodied this fundamental rethinking of race by social scientists. First, social scientists began using the anthropological concept of "culture" to debunk the notion of innate superiority of the white race. Second, social scientists began conceptualizing "race prejudice" as a fundamentally irrational attitude. Third, social scientists began investigating the origins of racial attitudes in children in an attempt to prove that racial attitudes were not "natural kinds" but rather learned behaviors. Fourth, social scientists began sociological investigations of African American culture in order to investigate the "social pathology" of African Americans. To begin the story, it is necessary to understand the revolution in anthropology fomented by Franz Boas and his students at Columbia University.

The Rise of Culture

Franz Boas (1858–1942) received his doctorate in physics with a minor in geography in 1881 in Germany. Following a brief career as a geographer, Boas became interested in anthropology after a cartographic expedition to Baffinland in 1883. Soon after that, he emigrated to the United States and was appointed to the anthropology faculty of Columbia University in 1896, just as anthropology was beginning to establish itself as an academic discipline. During the first third of the twentieth century, Boas trained an entire cadre of professional anthropologists who came to dominate the newly formed departments of anthropology. Among Boas's students were some of the most prominent names in twentieth-century anthropology: Alfred L. Kroeber, Edward Sapir, Robert Lowie, Melville Herskovits, Ruth Benedict, Margaret Mead, and Jules Henry. Many of Boas's students were Jewish, some were African American, and many were women. These groups were perhaps more sensitive to racial and sexist oppression than the WASP males who previously had made their academy their exclusive domain.[4]

Boas came to the United States for a variety of reasons, but a significant one was the anti-Semitism in Germany, which limited career opportunities for a Jew there. By the time he acquired the Columbia position, Boas was a confirmed race egalitarian, both scientifically and politically. His own experiences with anti-Semitism and his observations of Eskimo life during his trip to the Arctic had convinced him of the importance of treating individuals as such, rather than as members of a group or "race."[5]

In a series of works between 1894 and his death in 1942, Boas argued that race, language, and culture should be considered three separate categories of analysis. Race should be viewed strictly as a biological unit and not linked to social or cultural traits. This separation resulted in what Audrey Smedley has characterized as a "radical transformation of the meaning of race," since "physical and cultural-behavioral elements had been cognitively and integrally fused in the term from its origin." According to Boas, *race* should denote only specific physical features, rather than mental or moral ones. Moreover, those physical features were not fixed. Boas's work in physical anthropology showed that physical types could be changed within one generation, which indicated that race was a far more fluid concept than previously believed.[6]

Boas's denial that behavioral traits were "racial" in nature called forth new explanations for human behavior. It was "culture," not "race," that could be used to explain people's mental or moral characteristics. Boas never fully synthesized his scientific views relating to culture. It fell to his students to fully explicate the culture concept. Kroeber, Mead, Benedict, and other former students popularized cultural explanations for human behavior, not only in anthropology but also in sociology, history, and the popular press. By the 1930s, the culture concept had penetrated the other social sciences, essentially replacing the older, racial explanations for differences in human behavior.[7]

Perhaps as innovative as Boas, although ultimately less influential, was the pioneering work of African American scholar and activist W. E. B. Du Bois. The first African American to receive a Ph.D. from Harvard University, Dubois had argued early and often for the separation of race and culture. His work *The Philadelphia Negro* (1896) was one of the first sociological studies that did not resort to crude racial stereotypes to explain African American life. While Boas enjoyed his position at Columbia in New York, Du Bois struggled along at the impoverished Atlanta

University where he continued his study of "the American Negro." Du Bois's work would be slighted by his white contemporaries (though not by Boas and many of his students) because it was widely believed that Negroes could not be objective about the status of "their people." (The white scholars who came to this determination did not see their vested interest in perpetuating a racist society as compromising their own objectivity.) By 1910, Du Bois realized the limitations of what he could accomplish as a scholar and left the academy to become the director of publicity and research at a new organization he had helped found: the National Association for the Advancement of Colored People.[8]

Separating Intelligence from Race

Of particular importance for subsequent social-scientific developments was the use of culture as an explanatory mechanism for group differences in intelligence. A central component of racist ideology in the United States was that there were significant intellectual differences between whites and African Americans. African Americans had long argued against their own intellectual inferiority, both in the public as well as the in scientific realm.

During the 1920s and 1930s, African American scholars took to the journals to dispute the notion that intelligence was distributed disproportionately between the white and black races. These scholars, like Du Bois, often held posts at segregated colleges and universities and lacked the prestigious academic homes of their white counterparts. Nonetheless, scholars such as Horace Mann Bond of Langston University and Howard Hale Long at Paine College in Georgia wrote a series of articles criticizing the use of IQ tests to prove the innate inferiority of African Americans.[9]

The efforts of African American social scientists to debunk the race-IQ link notwithstanding, the most famous attack on the concept was that of Otto Klineberg (1899–1992). Klineberg was born in Quebec, Canada, and received a B.A. and an M.D. at McGill University in Montreal. After earning a master's degree in philosophy from Harvard, he earned his Ph.D. in psychology at Columbia University in 1927.[10] While pursuing his Ph.D., Klineberg sat in on anthropology courses offered by Franz Boas, which, he claimed, affected him "somewhat like a religious conversion. How could psychologists speak of *human* attributes and *human* behavior when they knew of only one kind of human being? . . . What would our field be like if the books had been written by Hottentots or Eskimos rather than by Europeans and Americans?"[11] Klineberg was convinced that most of the racial differences reported by psychologists and other social scientists were, in fact, cultural differences.

Indeed, the title of his dissertation, in its use of quotation marks, signaled Klineberg's suspicion of the very notion of race: "An Experimental Study of Speed and Other Factors in 'Racial' Differences." Here he argued that all psychological tests that claimed to measure intelligence were culturally biased, because previous studies that compared different racial groups failed to control for all aspects of a child's educational experience; while these studies focused on "schooling," they ignored a more important part of a child's education, "what the anthropologists call culture, which includes all the customs and conventions, all the habits of thought and action shared by the community."[12]

Klineberg administered a standard intelligence test to Yakima Indian children at two different locations, African American children in two locations, and white children in three locations.[13] Klineberg noted that the white children consistently outperformed the Yakima and African American children on the completion of a given set of tasks in a given period of time. He explained the performance of the Yakima children, however, by pointing out that they completely ignored any time constraints and moved at whatever speed they deemed comfortable. As Klineberg later recounted, "No matter how often I repeated or emphasized the words 'as quickly as possible,' they paid no attention."[14] A similar situation was found for the African American children. Once the time variable was removed from the analysis, the Yakima and African American children did better than the white children. Klineberg maintained that "speed" was a cultural concept, and in the Yakima culture, it is not valued as it is in white culture. Hence, argued Klineberg, even a seemingly neutral test, such as how quickly a subject completes a given task, was inevitably bound to culture. Klineberg concluded, "The use of speed alone or errors alone as a criterion of excellence may be unfair to one group. The former criterion is particularly unfair to groups which have not been accustomed to hurry."[15]

After he completed his dissertation in 1928, Klineberg joined the Columbia Psychology Department, where he continued arguing for the importance of culture and environment to explain racial differences. In 1935, he took on one of the prizes of those who argued for innate racial differences: the "selective migration" thesis.

In the 1930s, most social scientists were aware that African Americans living in the North consistently outperformed those who lived in the South on IQ tests. Those social scientists who believed that innate racial differences in intelligence had a ready explanation: northern African Americans were a self-selected group. Aware that the North offered better opportunities than the South, the most intelligent and energetic of southern African Americans migrated north. Hence, the better results of northern African Americans on IQ tests owed to this "selective migration" of the best African American stock, and not to the better social and educational environment offered by the North. Klineberg came to the opposite conclusion: that there was no reason to attribute superior performance of northern African Americans to anything but their superior environment.

Klineberg examined a variety of school records of children who had moved north and children who had stayed in the South and found "no evidence of selective migration." He concluded, "The school records of those who migrated did not demonstrate any superiority over those who remained behind. The intelligence tests showed no superiority of recent arrivals in the North over those of the same age and sex who were still in the southern cities." Klineberg did admit, however, that the African American children in the North still lagged behind white children, but this, too, could be explained through environmental factors. As Klineberg noted, "The final and crucial comparison could only be made in a society in which the Negro lived on terms of complete equality with white, and where he suffered not the slightest social, economic, or educational handicap." Such an experiment, given the social and political standing of African Americans in the 1930s, would clearly have been impossible.[16]

By the time Klineberg published his seminal piece on selective migration, the entire notion of innate racial differences in intelligence had fallen into disrepute. For example, in a 1925 survey of the entire field of "race psychology," a graduate classmate of Klineberg and the leading "race psychologist" of his day, Thomas R. Garth, noted, "These studies taken all together seem to indicate the mental superiority of the white race."[17] Just six years later, however, Garth was much less sanguine about what intelligence tests meant. He concluded that "it is doubtful whether or not the intelligence-test results of these groups [of Negroes, Mexicans, and American Indians] are the true measures of their intelligence," and that it was "possible they cannot take the white man's seriousness seriously" when asked to complete an intelligence test.[18]

By 1935, the tide had turned against those who argued for innate racial differences. Indeed, some notable social scientists of the previous generation, notably Carl Brigham, had recanted their earlier racial claims.[19] While not all social scientists were as firmly egalitarian as Klineberg, as a group, social scientists were at least committed to the notion that psychological tests were much more problematic than previously believed.[20]

Abandoning notions of racial superiority/inferiority led scientists to seek out new explanations for racial antipathy. Antagonism between the races was easy for social scientists to explain if the races were fundamentally different. If the races were essentially the same, however, how could social scientists account for racial hostility? To answer this question, scientists turned their attention to the study of racial attitudes, in particular, of racial *prejudice.*

The Study of Race Prejudice

In the interwar years, the study of race prejudice underwent a shift nearly as profound as that regarding innate racial differences: from a rational response to a changing social world to an irrational attitude with no firm basis in reality.

Some of the first measurements of racial antagonism came from the "Chicago School" of sociology.[21] During the 1920s, University of Chicago sociologist Robert Park developed the "race-relations cycle" model to explain the dynamics of racial change. Park viewed race prejudice as one part of this larger cycle of assimilation of minority groups into the larger society. As minority groups strove to increase their status within a society, the majority group reacted against what they perceived as a threat to their higher status. One aspect of this reaction was race prejudice, which Park viewed as a relatively benign method to maintain the "social distance" between different groups in society. Park wrote, "Prejudice is on the whole not an aggressive but a conservative force; a sort of spontaneous conservation which tends to preserve the social order and the social distances upon which that order rests."[22]

While Park's theories regarding the nature of racial prejudice may never have been as widely accepted as he wished, he was still one of the most influential thinkers on race relations before World War II.[23] His sociology department trained many of the more prestigious race-relations researchers.[24] One of these students was Emory Bogardus, who was one of the first researchers to attempt to quantify Park's theories on social distance.

After Bogardus received his Ph.D. from the University of Chicago in sociology in 1911, he joined the Sociology Department at the University of Southern California. Bogardus asked 248 of his students to rank the degree of "racial antipathy" felt for thirty-six ethnic groups, "putting first those races toward which the greatest degree of friendliness was felt, and the others in order."[25] White students found African Americans to be the second most objectionable group, trailed only by Turks.

In a subsequent study, Bogardus had test subjects rank-order different ethnic groups on a "social distance/social contact" scale. For each ethnic group, the respondent had to answer if he or she would accept the ethnic minority as a member of a select group. The groups ranged in intimacy from "Close kinship by marriage" and "To my club as personal chums" to "Visitors only to my country." On this scale, African Americans ranked the third least desirable, behind "Mulattos" and, once again, Turks.[26]

Bogardus, like Park, saw race prejudice as a benign force that served to preserve the present social order. As a sociologist, Bogardus wanted to use the results of his social distance scales to chart various social relations and interactions. When psychologists began measuring race prejudice they were interested in different aspects of the problem such as how race prejudice developed or its effect on the personality. Additionally, psychologists wanted to know how race prejudice could be reduced. This was a question that could not be posed by Park and his students: for them, the race-relations cycle followed a natural progression and was immune to any attempts to modify it. Psychologists were not wedded to the concept that race prejudice was an immutable part of the race-relations cycle.

Goodwin Watson was one of the first psychologists to attempt to measure racial prejudice, in his Ph.D. dissertation at Columbia Teacher's College in 1925, the same year that Bogardus published his studies on social distance. Watson (1899–1976) was a minister in the Methodist Episcopal Church and a student at the Union Theological Seminary (UTS), located near Columbia University. During the 1920s and 1930s, the leaders of UTS were teaching the "social gospel," which maintained that spiritual equality was the core of Christianity and that political and economic democracy were necessary for all to lead a Christian life. Some conservative theologians referred to UTS as the "Red Seminary" because its socialistic teachings were viewed as playing into the hands of Communists and radicals. Watson was deeply influenced by the social gospel's call to work for political and economic equality. It was the democratic ethos of UTS that led Watson to believe psychology was a better means than preaching to achieve the goals of Christianity, and he completed his dissertation in educational psychology in 1925.[27]

Watson's concern for political equality informed the shape of his scientific work. In his dissertation, Watson proposed to use psychological tests to measure something other than "intelligence or practical skills." Watson proposed to measure those "attitudes which are considered most desirable by a considerable group of religious educators . . . called variously, Open-Mindedness, Freedom from Prejudice, Scientific-Mindedness, and Fair-Mindedness."[28] While Watson's tests were designed to measure a number of attitudes, one measured what would later be considered "race prejudice." This test asked if the individual being tested had a tendency "to say that all Jews would cheat, . . . that all Roman Catholics are superstitious or that none of them are, and so on—attributing to all the members of a group characteristics which are true of only part of the group."[29] In Watson's tests of race prejudice, the subjects were also asked how strongly they agreed with statements such as "Colored people should go to schools, hotels, theatres, etc., patronized exclusively by colored people, thus preventing some inter-racial contact," and "'Pure blooded' members of a race are superior to those of mixed stock."[30]

Although not necessarily rational, Watson did assume that race prejudice arose out of some real-world experience: specifically, from unfriendly encounters with members of the race in question. He argued, "It has been rather clearly demonstrated by the testimony of a number of individuals that they acquired some of the race-prejudice in a single instance, or two, and afterwards reacted to all members of the race in terms of the conditioning of the single experience.[31] Watson administered his test of racial prejudice before and after classes in tolerance to see if he could discover the best methods for reducing prejudice. This contrasted with the earlier sociological thinkers, who saw race prejudice as an inevitable part of the process of assimilation; Watson thought that race prejudice was socially undesirable and needed to be reduced or, if possible, eliminated.

The contrast between the sociological and psychological view of race prejudice was even sharper in the work of Floyd Allport, one of the first experiment-oriented social psychologists. Allport (1890–1978) received his Ph.D. in experimental psychology from Harvard in 1919, under the direction of Hugo Münsterberg. After a year's instructorship at Harvard and two years at the University of North Carolina, he arrived at Syracuse

University to establish the first Ph.D. program in social psychology in the United States. Allport was trained in the behaviorist tradition at Harvard and rebelled against what he perceived as the "fallacy of the group mind," as portrayed by sociologists and some social psychologists. He put forth his views in one of the first textbooks in social psychology, published in 1924, where he argued that psychology was the study of behavior and consciousness, and that the only unit that possessed these characteristics was the individual, not the group.[32]

In the early 1920s, the contrast between the psychological and sociological approaches to the study of attitude was underscored by a public feud between Allport and Bogardus on the proper role of the individual and the group in social-scientific research. The two approaches to research are illustrated by the two researchers different uses of opinion research. Bogardus, as we have seen, relied on self-reported behaviors—that is, respondents were required to report what they would do in a given situation. This information was then used to discover information about community structures and movements of groups in society. In contrast, Allport's scale provided insight into the respondent's attitudes by means of their stated opinions on a host of subjects. These opinions were then independently analyzed for their relationships to personality traits.[33]

The different approach to race prejudice can be seen in *Students' Attitudes*, a book-length monograph on the measurement of students' attitudes published in 1931. The book was a project that grew out of a dissertation by Daniel Katz, Allport's first Ph.D. student at Syracuse University.[34] In one section of the book, the authors measured students' "snobbishness." Students were asked if they admitted certain groups into their fraternities or rooming houses. African Americans ranked last, below anarchists, Bolshevists, Japanese, Hindus, and Turks. Katz and Allport noted, "Only 5 percent of 3,408 Syracuse students checked Negroes; and since this 5 percent probably includes the Negroes on the campus, it follows that only a very small faction of white students are willing to live with Negroes."[35]

Allport did not undertake further work into race prejudice; but two years after the published results of the Syracuse study, Katz, who had moved to Princeton, published one of the first attempts to measure stereotypes and their effect on racial prejudice. With his student Kenneth Braly, he had subjects match a list of adjectives to a list of ethnic minorities. Once again, African Americans fared the worst, along with Turks.

An important aspect of Katz and Braly's work is that they defined race prejudice as a matter of *stereotypes* rather than as a reasoned response to any real attribute shared by the members of a group: these "attitudes toward racial and national groups," Katz and Braly argued, "are stereotypes of our cultural pattern and are not based upon animosity toward a member of a proscribed group because of any genuine qualities that inhere in him."[36] In other words, Katz and Braly assumed that prejudice was inherently irrational, because no group's members could possibly share all traits.

Social-scientific thinking about race prejudice had now undergone a complete shift in its stance regarding the rationality of race prejudice. Robert Park and Emory Bogardus claimed that race prejudice was a rational response to the social mobility of minority groups. Goodwin Watson, in his early study, assumed that prejudice flowed from unfortunate contact with individuals of a given group—perhaps not as rational a response as Park had assumed but with at least some basis in actual experience. For Katz and Braly, however, people were prejudiced toward an entire group based merely on the cultural stereotypes of that group, rather than on any experiences of the prejudiced individual. In a second study two years later, Katz and Braly defined "racial prejudice" as "a generalized set of stereotypes of a high degree of consistency which includes emotional responses to race names, a belief in typical characteristics associated with race names, and an evaluation of such typical traits."[37] By 1935, the study of attitudes had taken over social psychology in general, and the study of racial attitudes, specifically race prejudice, came to be widely accepted. Prejudice was, in essence, a *psychological* phenomenon—basically, a problem with people's internal mental states.[38]

Katz and Braly had posited that the origin of race prejudice had to do with matters of racial stereotypes. Yet the origins of racial attitudes were poorly understood. When did racial attitudes begin in an individual's personality? Indeed, when did individuals even become aware of the concept of "race"? To answer these questions, psychologists began investigating the development of racial attitudes in children, in order to discover just how society transmitted racial thinking to the next generation.

The Influence of Columbia University

Many of the psychologists who were trained at Columbia were the students of Gardner Murphy (1895–1966). Murphy was an original contributor to several areas of psychology, perhaps best known for his postwar concept of the "biosocial theory of personality," which served to integrate the many strands of psychological thought regarding personality. During the interwar period, Murphy wrote one of the first books on the history of psychology and was instrumental in establishing the professional organization of social psychology. Further, as we shall see, Murphy was important as a teacher of graduate students, directing dozens of Ph.D. dissertations.[39]

In many ways, Gardner Murphy's life had paralleled that of Goodwin Watson. Murphy was the son of a Methodist Episcopal preacher and as a young man had planned to become a missionary. As an undergraduate at Yale, Murphy began questioning his religious beliefs as he found them challenged by scientific findings. He continued to struggle with theological questions while receiving a master's degree in psychology from Harvard. After brief service in World War I, Murphy came to New York City to pursue his doctoral studies in psychology at Columbia. While studying at the university, he took classes at UTS. Like Watson, Murphy became convinced that the "social gospel" was a way to serve both "God and man." His subsequent career would reflect UTS's call to build a just and equitable society.[40]

Murphy and Watson were only two of several psychology students to be influenced by the social gospel as taught "across the street" at UTS.[41] Lois Barclay was also a student there, taking classes so she could teach comparative religion. By the time Barclay arrived at UTS, Murphy was already on Columbia's faculty, and one of his student's introduced them. They were married in 1926. After getting her degree from UTS in 1928, Lois Murphy entered Columbia Teacher's College program to get a Ph.D. in educational psychology.[42]

Gardner Murphy received his Ph.D. in psychology from Columbia in 1923 and remained on faculty there until 1940. In 1924, Robert Woodworth asked Murphy to take over teaching Woodworth's seminar in social psychology, and Murphy's interest in the field began to grow from that time onward.[43] In 1931, Gardner Murphy and Lois Barclay Murphy surveyed all the available research on racial attitudes in their book *Experimental Social Psychology* and concluded, "The crying need for research on Negro-white antagonisms has, so far as we have discovered, resulted, as yet, in very little exact research."[44] Very soon after the Murphys wrote these words, the psychological study of racial attitudes would take off— for example, in the work of Katz and Braly. More work was to follow, much of it directed by Gardner Murphy himself. Murphy worked with a number of graduate students at Columbia, concentrating on attitude studies and propaganda studies, in the hopes of providing the "exact research" he and Lois Murphy wanted.[45]

"Exact research," however, did not necessarily mean the isolation of independent variables in an experimental setting. Social psychology of the 1930s was marked by a variety of methodological outlooks, many of which rejected the sterility of laboratory experimentation. Not until the 1960s did experimentation come to dominate social psychology. The training and outlook of the social psychologists involved in *Brown* were very different from the experimental reliance of their successors.[46]

Origins of Race Prejudice

Early studies of racial attitudes—for example, those of Goodwin Watson and Daniel Katz—had focused on adult populations in an attempt to measure the existence of race prejudice. Eugene Horowitz, in the dissertation he completed under the direction of Gardner Murphy in 1936, had a different end in mind. Horowitz studied young children to see if he could understand the *genesis* of race prejudice. One of Horowitz's main objectives was to show that race prejudice was a learned behavior and not ingrained in humans at birth.[47]

There had been some earlier attempts to prove that race prejudice was a learned behavior. One of the earliest studies on this question was Bruno Lasker's *Race Attitudes in Children*, published in 1929. Lasker found that children could develop racial hostility toward members of "outgroups" as early as five or six years old. The variations in how children acquired racial attitudes led Lasker to reject an inborn instinct to react against members of another race. Lasker wrote that he could "dogmatically assert that there can be no such inborn trait, and that all the observed responses are the results of acquired habits."[48]

Lasker's work was not systematic, and in his dissertation, Horowitz dismissed it as "a collection of anecdotes and incidental observations." By contrast, Horowitz claimed he would "study, in an objective fashion the development in white children of attitudes towards the Negroes."[49] To do so, Horowitz examined the racial attitudes of "several hundred boys in New York City, in an all-white school (with a retest after six months) and in one grade in a mixed school, and in a small group of Communist children; in urban Tennessee; and in urban and rural Georgia."[50]

One of the tests Horowitz administered was dubbed a "Show Me" test. The children—all boys, to prevent complications arising from gender preferences—were required to rank, in order of preference, a group of photographs of both white and African American children. They then were required to answer a group of questions about those photographs: for example, "Show me all those you want to sit next to on a street car" or "Show me all those that you want to be in your class at school."[51] The results of these tests showed equal degrees of prejudice in northern and southern white boys and in segregated and racially mixed groups. The only group who showed no race prejudice at all was the small group of children raised in a Communist commune in New York City. Horowitz concluded that the "social forces" that gave rise to prejudice operated with equal efficiency in the North and South, but that they "do not, however, penetrate, or are neglected by, the training given to the Communist-trained children." His conclusion was similar to that of Katz and Braly: "It seems that attitudes toward Negroes are now chiefly determined not by contact with Negroes, but by contact with the prevalent attitude toward Negroes."[52]

Horowitz was interested in the racial attitudes of white children; however, his sample included a small number of African American children. He noted that the African American children often identified themselves as white, and he concluded, "Negro boys in the mixed school gave evidence of having accepted, in part, the standards of the white (majority) group."[53] But it was Ruth Horowitz who took up the issue suggested by her husband's conclusion regarding African American children. Where Eugene was interested in discovering racial preference, Ruth was interested in discovering when children were aware of race and of their own racial identity.

Racial Identity

Eugene Horowitz's "Show Me" tests were designed for very young children for whom paper-and-pencil tests would be inappropriate. The Show Me test was one of a number of "projective techniques" coming into psychological vogue at the time. In 1938, Ruth Horowitz and Lois Barclay Murphy published an article on the use of "projective" techniques for "revealing conscious and unconscious layers of motivation and personality" of very young children. Projective techniques were described as the use of toys, pictures, dramatic presentations, and other "unstructured materials" that "invite spontaneous projection of patterns of movement and feelings."[54]

In 1939, Ruth Horowitz published the first article on racial identity in children that used projective methodologies. Her sample consisted of twenty-four nursery-school children in New York City. Horowitz administered two sets of tests to the children. In the first, the "choice tests," children were shown two pictures and asked, "Which one is you? Which one is _____?" filling in the child's name. In the second test, the "portrait series," each child was shown ten pictures in succession. At each picture, the children were asked, "Is this you? Is this _____?"

The two techniques employed gave different results. In the choice test, 66 percent of the African American children made a correct identification, compared to only 40 percent of the white children. On the portrait test, 66 percent of the African American boys made an incorrect identification. Horowitz offered one possible explanation for the incorrect identification as "wishful activity" or a desire to be white. Given the extremely small sample size, Horowitz recognized that the findings were far from conclusive.[55] Indeed, as William Cross has subsequently shown, the number of African American boys making the incorrect racial identification could have been no more than two out of a total of three.[56]

Soon after the Horowitzes completed their studies of racial attitudes, they caught the attention of a young graduate student at Columbia. Kenneth B. Clark, only recently arrived at Columbia, introduced his wife, Mamie Phipps Clark, to the Horowitzes in 1939.[57] Soon the Clarks would embark on efforts to expand on what the Horowitzes had done by greatly increasing the number of African American children in the sample

Kenneth Bancroft Clark was born in the Panama Canal Zone in 1914. When he was seven years old, his mother moved her family to New York City. After he graduated from high school, Clark enrolled in the pre-medical program at Howard University in 1929.[58] During his sophomore year, Clark took a psychology course from Francis Cecil Sumner. Sumner had been trained at Clark University by G. Stanley Hall, one of the founders of American psychology. Although Sumner was a brilliant student, few universities would hire an African American professor, and after a series of temporary appointments, he became the chair of the Psychology Department at Howard. Sumner quickly made Howard's Psychology Department a place of rigorous and disciplined study and one of the most respected programs at Howard.[59]

Sumner's psychology course affected Clark much as Boas's anthropology course had affected Klineberg. Clark later recalled that he said to himself, "To hell with medical school. This is the discipline for me."[60] He went on to receive his bachelor's and master's degrees in psychology at Howard, under Sumner's direction. Moreover, he convinced his fiancée to consider psychology as well.

Mamie Phipps was born in 1917 in Hot Springs, Arkansas. She enrolled at Howard University at age sixteen, and there she met Kenneth Clark. Soon he had convinced her not only to change her major from mathematics and physics to psychology but also to marry him, which she did in 1938. That summer she worked as a secretary in the law offices of William Houston. Houston's brother was Charles Hamilton Houston, the dean of Howard Law School and the architect of the NAACP's strategy against segregated education. While she worked for William Houston, Mamie Clark met William Hastie, Thurgood Marshall, and other lawyers who were laying the foundations for the *Brown* decision.[61]

By the time they were married, Kenneth was in his first year of Ph.D. work in Columbia's Psychology Department, the first African American to be enrolled in the department. One reason Clark had for choosing Columbia was the presence of Otto Klineberg. Klineberg had come to Howard while Clark was a student there and had given a talk on his findings on racial differences. At Columbia, Clark chose Klineberg as his major adviser but also worked closely with Gardner Murphy.

It was at Columbia that Kenneth learned of the work the Horowitzes had done. Knowing that Mamie was interested in the psychology of children, he suggested that Mamie continue the Horowitzes work. She did so, working in African American nurseries in Washington, D.C. The work became her master's thesis at Howard. She and Kenneth went on to publish three articles from the data set collected for her thesis.[62]

The Clarks' subjects were 150 African American nursery-school children in segregated schools. The children were shown three sets of line drawings depicting white children, African American children, a hen, and a clown and were asked, "Show me which one is you. Which one is _____?"[63] Unlike Ruth Horowitz, who presented her data in an undifferentiated mass, the Clarks attempted to control for more refined factors. In their first article based on this data set, the Clarks pointed out how children's choices were affected by their age:

> The ratio of choices of the colored boy to choices of the white boy increased with age in favor of the colored boy. Choices of the lion, dog, clown, and hen were dropped off at the end of the three-year level, indicating a level of development in consciousness of self where identification of

one's self in terms of a distinct person rather than in terms of animals or other characters.[64]

In their second article, the Clarks argued that skin color was not the bifurcated "white or black" assumed by Horowitz. As in the first article, where they divided their sample into age brackets, in their second article the Clarks divided their sample according to complexions. They noted that the children with dark complexions reasonably associated themselves with the "colored boy," as did children with medium complexions; however,

> There would be . . . a definite incompatibility if the majority of light children identified themselves with the drawings of the colored boy, hence the persistence of their identifications with the white boy. It is obvious that these children are not identifying on the basis of "race" because "race" is a social concept which they learn at a higher stage of development. They are however, definitely identifying on the basis of their own skin color which is to them a concrete reality.[65]

In other words, in their interwar work the Clarks took exception to Ruth Horowitz's study that claimed young black children "wished" they were white.

In the third and final article that emerged from this data set, the Clarks compared the segregated children with other children in a "semi-segregated" environment and a "mixed" environment. Their results demonstrated that children in the racially mixed environment "appear to develop a consciousness of self and concomitant racial identification at a later chronological period than either the wholly segregated children or the semi-segregated children."[66] As William Cross has noted, the Clarks were "at a loss to interpret these results"; they seemed unaware that Eugene Horowitz had described the exact same phenomenon in his doctoral dissertation.[67] The Clarks described the delay in racial identification as a "retardation" in the development of children raised in a racially mixed environment.

The studies published by Ruth Horowitz and the Clarks concerned racial *identity*, and yet both Horowitz and the Clarks were concerned about racial *preference*, or the "wishful thinking" postulated by Ruth Horowitz in her original study. The next project that Kenneth and Mamie Clark would embark on together set out to test the "wishful thinking" hypothesis: did black boys and girls actually wish they were white? In 1940, a grant from the Julius Rosenwald Fund allowed Mamie Clark to enter Columbia's Ph.D. program in psychology and to gather another round of data for a second series of articles. Throughout 1940, Kenneth set out to collect data from selected northern and southern states, in order to determine the question of racial preference in African American children.[68] World War II, however, delayed the effort, and the publication of this second data set did not occur until after the war.

Before turning to these publications by the Clarks, we need to explore one more facet of interwar social research. With the rejection of the assumption of racial inferiority, a host of questions presented themselves. As Graham Richards noted, "If innate differences were illusory, some other approach to human cultural and psychological diversity was required."[69] The studies explored below attempted to provide those explanations.

Social Pathology

A group of studies related to those of the Clarks and Ruth Horowitz sought to determine the "social pathology" of African American culture during the 1930s. These studies came from two separate research programs. First were studies conducted by researchers trained at the Chicago School of sociology, notably by E. Franklin Frazier and Charles S. Johnson. Second was a series of anthropological studies that viewed race relations as a function of "caste and class." This group of studies was exemplified by the work of W. Lloyd Warner, John Dollard, and Allison Davis. Both the sociological and the anthropological studies were well represented by a series of books sponsored by the American Council on Education.

In 1937, the American Council on Education (ACE) funded a series of studies to determine the impact of racial discrimination on the personalities of African American youth. The studies were designed to be interdisciplinary examinations of African American children in various regions of the United States, and as such, they reflected a new merging of sociology, anthropology, and psychology in the study of race relations. For our purposes, it is useful to focus on what sorts of "pathology" the researchers found in African American communities and to what extent that pathology could be traced back to the oppressive conditions of the United States.[70]

The first book published in the ACE series was by African American sociologist Ira De Augustine Reid (1901–1968), who had long been director of research and investigations for the National Urban League. In the late 1930s, Reid was teaching in the sociology department of Atlanta University, which was headed by W. E. B. Du Bois.[71] Reid's ACE book was a compilation of sociological data that was to be the keynote for the books that would follow in the series. Reid argued, "Race may not dominate but at least it throws its shadow across every phase of the Negro youth's life in the North and envelops every aspect of it in the South." The problem of race for these children, according to Reid, was a problem of their "outer environment of social and economic problems and adjustments . . . but also an inner environment of being Negro—which in the United States is interpreted to mean inferior, impoverished, and inconvenienced." Both the inner and outer environment, Reid concluded, "determine the status of Negroes [and] also create the Negro personality—a personality that has had to develop in whatever way and to whatever extent it could within the iron ring of race prejudice."[72] The books that followed Reid's study would explore how race prejudice affected the personalities of African American children.

The first large-scale study that emerged after Reid's keynote piece was an anthropological study by Allison Davis and John Dollard. Allison Davis was an African American anthropologist who was doing his doctoral work at the University of Chicago, where he later became a professor. John Dollard had a Ph.D. in anthropology from Chicago and was at the Institute of Social Research at Yale University.

Davis and Dollard examined African American life through two lenses—caste and class. Davis defined their approach as "the view that the relationships of whites and Negroes in the South are systematically ordered and maintained by a caste structure, and that the status of individuals within each of these groups is further determined by a system of social classes existing within each color-caste."[73] Davis and Dollard conducted a series of "life history" interviews with 123 African American families in New Orleans and Natchez, Louisiana.

In their results, Davis and Dollard reported that class, rather than caste, was the more significant variable affecting the personality of African American youth, because "social class governs a much wider area of the child's training than Negro-white controls."[74] Race, however, was still an important variable affecting personality development.[75] Davis and Dollard reported that the caste into which the African American was forced had a marked influence on his or her personality. While Dollard and Davis stopped short of arguing the presence of deep and lasting psychological scars that owed to discrimination and segregation, they did argue that the caste-ordered society of the South led to frustration and aggression in African American youth. The common argument of the white South, that African Americans were happy with the "caste controls" imposed on them because they were "childlike beings with childlike needs," was a ruse to "prevent general human recognition of the basic deprivations and frustrations which life in a lower caste involves. But it is certain that the sting of caste is deep and sharp for most Negroes."[76]

The linking of caste to frustration and aggression was one way in which the ACE studies attempted to show the psychological damage that discrimination inflicted on African American youth. A second way would be to attempt to discover evidence of "self-hatred" in the children. Did African American children wish to be white or accept white judgments about the inferiority of African Americans? This was the question raised, though not necessarily answered by, the Horowitzes and the Clarks in their studies of children.

The third book in the ACE series provided a picture of African American youth adjusting as best they could to a life of racial discrimination. Charles S. Johnson (1893–1956) was an African American who was one of Robert W. Park's prize sociology students at the University of Chicago. He was named the director of the social sciences department at Fisk University in 1928, where he published a number of influential works on race relations.[77]

For his ACE studies, Johnson conducted a series of tests of African American youth in eight southern counties. One of the tests was designed to determine to what degree African American youth "take over the ideas of those very institutions which disparage their physical and mental traits," because "color concepts which stamp the race as innately inferior are, in a vast number of cases, the source of deep emotional disturbance."[78] Johnson designed a test, administered to 2,241 African American rural children, in which

the individual was asked merely to check the color of (a) the most stupid boy (or girl) you know, (b) the most handsome boy (or girl) you know, (c) the smartest boy (or girl) you know, (d) the boy (or girl) you dislike most, (e) the boy (or girl) you like best, and a list of 30 similar value judgments.[79]

The color choice ranges were: black, dark brown, brown, light brown, yellow, and white.

Johnson found that the children tended to reject both extremes of black and white and gravitate toward "light brown," which led him to postulate that African Americans were defining themselves as a new "brown race." In short, Johnson failed to find that African American youth were indulging in "wishful thinking" and desired to be white. Only 4 percent of the tested children agreed with the statement "I wish I were white." Johnson explained:

> The Negro community is built around the idea of adjustment to being a Negro, and it rejects escape into the white world. Community opinion builds up a picture of whites as a different kind of being, with whom one associates but does not become intimate. Without much conscious instruction the child is taught that his first loyalties are to the Negro group. . . . This doctrine is reinforced by stories of the meanness and cruelty of white people. To wish to be white is a sacrifice of pride. It is equivalent to a statement that Negroes are inferior and, consequently, that the youth himself is inferior.[80]

Because the African American youth would prefer not to associate with whites, segregation was seen as a rather minor problem. Johnson wrote, "Most youth feel that segregation imposes only minor deprivations. In most cases the youth expressed themselves as preferring not to associate with whites, and viewed their segregation with indifference."[81]

Johnson's position was consistent with his training at the University of Chicago. The accommodation of minority groups striving to assimilate into majority culture was a central component of Park's race-relations cycle. Johnson noted that the attitudes African American youths held toward segregation were a good example of the psychological adjustment that discrimination necessitated. One area of society in which the African American children failed to adjust adequately, however, was in the school system of the South, with its radically inequitable distribution of resources between the two segregated school systems. Johnson observed that southern African American families were devoted to education and attempted to persevere in the education of their children in the face of the terribly underfunded, segregated school system of the South. He explained that the pressure to get a good education in the face of woefully inadequate schools "has developed in many instances misshapen personalities which, to the casual and busy school administrator, sometimes seem to be evidence alike of the danger and of the meaninglessness of education for Negro youth."[82]

Charles Johnson's name will probably be forever linked to that of the author of the next book in the ACE series, E. Franklin Frazier, if only because both men were African American sociologists trained at the University of Chicago by Robert Park. But whereas Johnson was always viewed as a political liberal, Frazier was a radical. Even before he received his Ph.D. from Chicago in 1929, Frazier was publishing articles on race relations while at Atlanta University. Indeed, it was a 1927 article, "The Pathology of Race Prejudice," in which Frazier claimed that southern race prejudice had "the same intense emotional tone that characterizes insane complexes,"[83] that forced Frazier out of the South and to the relative safety of Chicago. After completing his studies at Chicago, Frazier moved for an uncomfortable five-year stay at Fisk University with Charles Johnson. In 1934, Frazier moved to Howard University, where he stayed until his death in 1962.[84]

Throughout the late 1920s and the 1930s, Frazier concentrated on the study of the African American family. For Frazier, the African American family was moving from the "disorganization" that resulted from slavery to "reorganization" into urban life. He wanted to refute any claim that the social situation of the African American family owed anything to innate racial characteristics. Slavery and segregation, not a racial tendency toward licentiousness, led to a pathological state within the African American family. In 1939, Frazier argued that "the immorality, delinquency, desertions, and broken homes which have been involved in the development of Negro family life in the United States, . . . appear to have been the inevitable consequences of the attempt of a preliterate people, stripped of their cultural heritage, to adjust themselves to civilization."[85]

In his American Council on Education study, Frazier attempted to discover what effect the social disorganization he had documented in the African American family had on the personality of African American children. He conducted a series of studies, including extensive interviews, of African American children in the border areas of Louisville, Kentucky, and Washington, D.C. Unlike Johnson, who found that segregation was a relatively inconsequential factor for his subjects, Frazier found segregation to be a pervasive force in his subjects' lives. Frazier noted that the "pathological feature[s] of the Negro community" owed to "the fact that the Negro is kept behind the walls of segregation and is not permitted to compete in the larger community. . . . Since the Negro is not required to compete in the larger world and to assume its responsibilities and suffer its penalties, he does not have an opportunity to mature."[86]

Like Johnson, however, Frazier found that most of his subjects did not wish to be white. Even in the case of lower-class children, who said "frankly that if they were born again they would prefer to be white," this did not necessarily mean that they rejected their own color. Frazier reported that such responses came from the children only after a few minutes of reflection. By contrast, children usually responded spontaneously that they were satisfied with their present color. This immediate response, Frazier argued, "represented more truly [the child's] feelings, attitudes, and imaginings in regard to being white." It was only after they thought about the advantages of being white that the children claimed they wished to be white. Frazier concluded, "Only when they felt frustrated in their wishes and impulses because of their racial identity and imagined themselves carrying out their wishes and desires as white persons and participating in the white world could we legitimately say that they really wished that they were white."[87] Like Johnson, Frazier found that most interviewed children strove toward a "brown ideal" rather than toward being white. In short, while Frazier found some psychological problems associated with being African American in the United States, he also found these problems did not necessarily translate into the children rejecting of their own skin color.

The viewpoint of the ACE researchers was summarized by the project's director, Robert Sutherland, in the concluding volume of the series. Sutherland argued that the African American youth "cannot be free in the traditional American sense," with "no need for self-proof of his worth, and no need to overstress his achievements in some matters to compensate for lack of others. Psychologically, white freedom differs from colored freedom in America."[88]

All these studies of the 1930s, it must be remembered, were conducted in the midst of the Great Depression. In some sense, they were measures of what African Americans could hope for when the country was facing a profound crisis that threatened many hopes of social stability, not to mention the possibility of a better world. World War II would dramatically alter how African Americans viewed their prospects in the United States, and psychological studies after World War II would reflect the rising expectations African Americans had about the postwar world. Before we turn to the war and its effects, however, one last development of the 1930s needs our attention.

The Society for the Psychological Study of Social Issues

Part of the explanation for the development of new types of scientific research into race prejudice and identity during the 1930s was simply that there were more psychologists being trained. Columbia, Yale, Harvard, and a host of other institutions were producing more doctorates in psychology than ever before. Unfortunately, the Great Depression made employment of these new doctorate recipients difficult. The American Psychological Association (APA), the professional organization for psychology, responded to the abundance of young psychologists with the suggestion of raising Ph.D. requirements, hence shrinking the future supply of young psychologists.[89]

Younger psychologists, not unexpectedly, resented APA's call to restrict the number of doctoral degrees in psychology. In particular, a young psychologist working at the University of Chicago, Isadore Krechevsky, "conceived the idea of stimulating more psychologists to direct their efforts toward the making of a new and better America."[90] In the early 1930s, Krechevsky—later David Krech—was a member of New America, a socialist political organization founded by UTS theologian Harry F. Ward and one of his students, psychologist Goodwin Watson. According to Krech, New America was Marxist in orientation but disapproved of communism, especially as practiced in the Soviet Union. It was, Krech remembered, "compulsively democratic in its public ideology and in its internal structures."[91]

In 1934, faced with the reluctance of the APA to take any action about the employment of younger psychologists, Krech and a colleague, Ross Stagner, began circulating a petition to urge the APA to request funds from the federal government to help the employment situation of psychologists. After a series of attempts to get the APA to respond, Krech finally called on the younger members of the APA to create an organization dedicated to "important contemporary problems of social and economic change."[92]

The situation came to a head at the 1936 APA convention at Dartmouth College. A meeting chaired by Ross Stagner led to the formation of the Society for the Psychological Study of Social Issues (SPSSI). Goodwin Watson was elected president, and David Krech was elected secretary/treasurer. Stagner later recounted that SPSSI was founded as a group to open up job opportunities in Washington, D.C., "to facilitate research on pressing social problems, and to defend colleagues who seemed to be victims of unfair treatment."[93]

Within a year after its founding, SPSSI was a force to be reckoned with—at least within the world of psychology—as one of every six APA members was also a member of SPSSI.[94] Soon, the society began publishing an "SPSSI Bulletin" as part of the *Journal of Social Psychology*, and it produced *Industrial Conflict*, a book on labor conflict.[95] By the time the United States entered the war, SPSSI was an established group of reformers, interested in using their expertise to make American society more just and democratic.

Conclusion

Between World War I and World War II, a transformation took place in American social-scientific understanding of race. Anthropology had cast doubt on the utility of "race" as a scientific concept, replacing it with "culture." Other disciplines, including psychology, used cultural explanations to demonstrate that there were no innate racial characteristics. Moreover, the culture concept had so complicated the picture that ideas of innate racial differences would never have the same resonance they enjoyed in the early 1920s and before.

Concomitant with the decline of "scientific racism" was the rise of the scientific study of attitudes. Two things need to be noted about this area of study. First, race prejudice was transformed from a perhaps conservative but not harmful attitude into an attitude that was not based in reality, or at least not based on real characteristics shared by members of any single group. It was, in essence, viewed as an irrational attitude. Second, race prejudice was becoming a purely psychological phenomenon. Analysis of other causes of prejudice—institutional patterns, economic hardships, power relationships, and other broad sociological explanations—was forsaken in favor of explanations that relied on the attitudes of individuals. Prejudice was viewed as a problem in the hearts and minds of individuals.

During World War II, social scientists would take the study of prejudice and transmute it into a topic that demanded the attention of social scientists, making it, in Franz Samelson's words, "one of the corner-stones of the developing discipline of empirical social psychology."[96] Moreover, events during the war provided the opportunity for social science to move outside the walls of the academy and into the "real world," giving social scientists a new confidence in their ability to become social engineers.

3

The Effect of World War II on the Study of Racial Prejudice

Historian Robin D. G. Kelley has noted, "When thinking about the Jim Crow South, we need always to keep in mind that African Americans . . . did not *experience* a liberal democracy. They lived and struggled in a world that resembled, at least from their vantage point, a fascist or, more appropriately, a colonial situation."[1] In this context, African Americans experienced America's entry into World War II in a profoundly different way from white Americans. For African Americans living under Jim Crow in the American South, the call to fight for "freedom" was something of a joke, since they did not experience freedom at home.

The call to arms, therefore, met with ambivalence at best, hostility at worst, among African Americans in the 1940s. African Americans who did want to join the war effort were frustrated by the segregation of the armed forces and blatant racial discrimination in the defense industries. Using wartime propaganda of freedom to their advantage, African Americans began demanding that the United States live up to its promises of equality and democracy. African Americans' attitudes about the war presented problems for a government that needed to unite the country, including African Americans, behind the war effort.[2] Social scientists were uniquely situated to help the government in this task.

By the end of the 1930s, most social scientists were convinced that the races were, scientifically speaking, equal. Additionally, social scientists were increasingly convinced that race prejudice was an irrational attitude that had no firm basis in reality but grew out of stereotyped thinking. During World War II, these social-scientific themes would take on wartime urgency, and afterward, race prejudice would be considered dangerous and undemocratic rather than merely irrational. This shift was possible because social scientists expressly linked racial egalitarianism to freedom and democracy during the war. In a host of studies, race prejudice was advanced as a barrier to victory and as giving aid and comfort to the Nazi regime.

In addition to bringing attention to the dangers of race prejudice, social psychologists gained new credibility during World War II as "social engineers" by providing unprecedented opportunities for psychologists to work closely with the government. Social psychologists were involved in strategic bombing surveying, propaganda analysis, and analysis of civilian and enemy morale.[3] In all these efforts, psychologists were convinced that their special expertise was necessary to direct governmental power in the most efficient manner possible. Given the importance of the study of race prejudice, it should not be too surprising that social scientists took race relations as the area of society that needed their expertise the most.

In this chapter, I demonstrate how social scientists transformed themselves into experts on race prejudice, not just in the academy but in the larger society. Social scientists made race prejudice into a topic of urgent national concern by expressly linking race problems to democracy and freedom. They also linked these issues of democracy to the discriminatory institutions of society and began arguing that those institutions must be changed. In this way, social scientists became shapers of society, rather than mere observers of society.

Perhaps no single person exemplified the war's effect on social-scientific research more than Harvard psychologist Gordon W. Allport, who was SPSSI president during the 1943–44 term. The younger brother of Syracuse's Floyd Allport, Gordon Allport (1897–1967) received his Ph.D. in psychology from Harvard in 1922. Like those Columbia psychologists who had been deeply influenced by the "social gospel," Allport had a deep religious dedication to social justice. After a brief tour of teaching in Istanbul and at Dartmouth College, he returned to Harvard in 1930, where he remained to the end of his career.[4] Allport's work before the war concentrated on the psychology of personality, and he published what became the definitive book on the subject in 1937.[5]

On America's entry into World War II, Allport quickly became involved in a host of projects for the government, including organizing a seminar at Harvard to aid in the war effort. The seminar would be devoted to whatever topic seemed most useful to the war effort: analysis of rumor, Hitler's character, or rioting behavior. As Allport later recalled, "The seminar had a long-range consequence. It continued year after year, with a gradual focusing on what seemed to be the most urgent problem of national unity, namely, group conflict and prejudice."[6] Allport's published work, as well as his teaching, reflected this new focus on racial prejudice. In the decade after the war, Allport produced a mass of work that ultimately led to his 1954 publication of *The Nature of Prejudice*, which served as the definitive psychological treatment of the subject for a generation.[7]

Allport's work is important not merely because of his stature in the social science community and among the public at large but also because it is a good illustration of the general tone of psychological studies in race prejudice in the decade after World War II. Quite simply, his theme was that prejudice is an affront to democracy. In 1946, Allport wrote that in the world created by World War II, "democracy and the scapegoating of minority groups and nations cannot co-exist. It is for this reason that our battle against scapegoating is an important phase of the battle for democracy within our nation and within the world at large."[8]

There were four areas of research undertaken by social scientists that led to the conclusion that prejudice was not just an irrational, harmless attitude but downright anti-American. First, work in morale underscored the importance of racial harmony and the dangers of divisive racial prejudice. Second, work on the race riots that swept the United States in 1943 saw race prejudice as a genuine threat to civil peace. Third, studies of anti-Semitism linked that particular form of racism to authoritarianism generally, viewing anti-Semitism as a necessary first step in totalitarian government. Fourth, Gunnar Myrdal traced the tension between the country's "American Creed" and its treatment of minorities. The sections below briefly outline these arguments made by social scientists during World War II.

American Morale

Even before America's entry into the war, such prominent social psychologists as Gordon Allport, Kurt Lewin, Gardner Murphy, and Goodwin Watson were exploring American morale. After the Japanese bombing of Pearl Harbor, morale quickly became one of the more popular areas of study and soon underscored that, to maintain an effective fighting spirit during the war, the country must try to eliminate race prejudice.[9]

An example of this work in social psychology is that of Resnis Likert (1903–1981). Likert was another Columbia Ph.D. who had been trained at the Union Theological Seminary. In his 1932 dissertation, directed by Gardner Murphy, Likert developed a new method of scaling for use in opinion polls, in which respondents were asked to rate items on a scale of 1 to 5, where 1 meant they would "strongly approve" and 5 meant they would "strongly disapprove."[10] In 1939, Likert put his innovative survey methodologies to work at the U.S. Department of Agriculture to survey the attitudes of farmers, but in 1942, his program was reorganized into the Office of War Information (OWI) and charged with uncovering the attitudes of the American civilian population about the war.[11]

Likert hired Kenneth Clark at OWI to prepare studies on the morale of African Americans. Likert and Clark argued that it was necessary to tear down discriminatory barriers in order to expect African Americans to join fully in the war effort. In 1942, OWI reported that "[Negro] enthusiasm for the war is dampened by the resentment of discrimination at home. Many feel no burning urge to go 'all out' for a victory that may perpetuate the present way of life to which they are being subjected—a way of life, as they see it, based on the undemocratic premise of white supremacy." The African American community demanded, according to OWI, "the elimination of those obstacles which now prevent their enjoying the many advantages afforded the white man in this country."[12]

Likert would be elected SPSSI president immediately after the war. During the war, his views on morale and democracy were echoed by many other individual members of SPSSI and by the society as a whole, which dedicated its second yearbook to the problem of civilian morale.[13]

The articles in the SPSSI yearbook linked morale to the problem of bringing democracy and freedom to all Americans. For many of these authors, reducing or eliminating problems between minority groups and the majority in society was the key to building national unity. The problem, as these researchers saw it, was not that minorities posed a threat to national security because they were disloyal but that the majority in society did not accept minority members as equals, which prevented minority groups from participating fully in the war effort. In his essay on "ethnic minorities," Otto Klineberg claimed that "the threat against national morale lies . . . in the attitudes which the majority holds toward them. It is the prejudice, not the existence of the minorities, which represents the principal divisive factor."[14]

Writing in the same volume, Kenneth B. Clark wrote, "In a consideration of civilian morale, it is not only pertinent but imperative that one be concerned with the racial tensions of our American society and the dynamic force of those tensions upon the attitude and behavior of Negro and white Americans."[15] Clark argued that, in order to expect African Americans to support the war effort, white attitudes had to change "from those of blind and irrational prejudice with its attendant economic, social, and political injustices, to the wholesome, normal attitudes that stem from understanding and a sincere respect for the rights of every human being."[16] In an essay the next year, Clark expressly linked morale not just to race prejudice but to official expressions of that prejudice—segregation and other forms of discrimination. Contrasting the morale of African Americans in 1943 with their morale during World War I, Clark argued that the "Negro" would not be as willing to "become enthusiastic at minor concessions" from the government as "he" was in 1917. Clark exclaimed, "His morale today is not likely to be appreciably raised by concessions made within the framework of a rigid policy of racial segregation and discrimination." To ensure high morale among African Americans, it would be necessary for the federal government to begin to tear down the barriers of segregation and discrimination. As Clark concluded, "In a democracy this could be done—under Fascism it would not be done."[17]

Gordon Allport also argued in the SPSSI yearbook that it was necessary that the promise of full participation in democratic society not be limited to the duration of the war but that it be a genuine promise that would go beyond the immediate fight: "A [morale] program is good if it stresses the basic tenet of democracy that all persons have equal rights to the pursuit of happiness, to liberty, and to life; and also if it includes, beyond the demand for national defense, a provision of a better world after the war for all peoples, regardless of race and nationality."[18]

Social scientists maintained the wartime linkage between prejudice and democracy well after the war was won. But, during the war, the study of these problems took on a new urgency in 1943, when the country was torn by a series of racial uprisings.

Race Riots

As African Americans searching for wartime employment poured into large industrial cities in the early 1940s, racial tensions grew in these cities and burst into the open during the summer of 1943. In Detroit, a race riot began on a hot June day when thousands of city residents crowded a local amusement park. Small fights occurred all day, finally erupting into a large-scale riot as rumors of racially based atrocities spread across the city. By the end of the rioting, thirty-four people were dead and over seven hundred were injured. Less than two months later, a rumor of an African American soldier being killed by a white policeman caused Harlem to erupt into similar racial conflict. The final toll there was five dead and five hundred injured. Other cities experienced similar rioting during the summer of 1943.[19]

The study of these race riots would bring two researchers, Alfred McClung Lee and Kenneth B. Clark, to each other's attention and mark the beginning not only of a close friendship but also of a close working relationship that would lead the two men into the litigation campaign of *Brown*.

Alfred McClung Lee Jr. (1906–1992) had been raised in a radically egalitarian family. His father was a Pittsburgh attorney who was known for his defense of African Americans and other socially powerless peoples. When Al Lee Sr. unmasked the local Ku Klux Klan (KKK) leader during a raid on an African American church, the KKK repaid the favor by burning a cross on the Lee's front lawn. In 1926, Al Jr. married his hometown sweetheart, Betty Briant, and the two received doctorates in sociology from Yale University—Al in 1933 and Betty in 1937. Because of prevalent sexism in the academy, Betty was unable to secure an academic position despite her scholarly accomplishments.[20]

In 1942, Al Lee was appointed the chair of Wayne State University's Department of Sociology. When the Detroit riot broke out, former newspaper reporter Lee, according to Betty, "beat it out of the house and went to where it was going on. He was busy taking field notes."[21] The book that emerged from his notes was *Race Riot*, written with his Wayne State colleague Norman Humphrey and published in 1943.

Lee and Humphrey claimed that the dangers of rioting went beyond the list of casualties and lost capital: "democracy itself, its very nature and substance, is placed in grave danger by race riots." With America at war with a society trumpeting the "master race theory," Lee and Humphrey argued, race riots could destroy the promise of a government based on freedom, dignity, and equality of all people, leading to "a drive to turn the clock back, as in Fascist Italy and Nazi Germany."[22] To quell this threat to the democratic order, Lee and Humphrey proposed to outline the causes of, and cures for, race riots.

In the immediate aftermath of the riot, city and other government officials posited several, often conflicting causes of the rioting. Agitation—by Axis agents, the Ku Klux Klan, Communists, or "Negro agitators"—was often singled out as the cause of the riot.[23] Lee and Humphrey argued that there was no one immediate cause of the riot that swept Detroit on June 21, 1943; rather, "riots are the products of thousands upon thousands of little events that have affected the habits and emotions of thousands upon thousands of people, both future rioters and future innocent bystanders." Lee and Humphrey attempted to trace the origins of the Detroit riots beyond the immediate precipitating events and to the general tensions that grew from the uneasy race relations in the city. The tension that served as prelude to the riot was the result of social isolation of the races from one another. Lee and Humphrey concluded that "people who live near each other or go to school together feel none of the alleged 'natural animosity,' which so many people claim exists between races—a 'natural animosity' that scientists have disproved a thousand times."[24]

To prevent future riots, Lee and Humphrey claimed it was necessary to do more than create commissions and biracial police forces. It was necessary to strike down discriminatory barriers that cause social isolation, the true root of racial tensions. The three most "practical goals for a long-term program" of riot prevention was to eliminate segregation and discrimination in housing, the schools, and the workplace. Lee and Humphrey argued, "In the Detroit riots . . . observer after observer reported that no noteworthy trouble occurred in mixed districts where white and Negroes had lived as neighbors long enough to get to know and understand each other." This basic argument could be applied to schooling as well: "Through the casual experience of classrooms and playgrounds, white and Negro children and adults can learn to associate with one another without antagonistic racial frictions." Finally, regarding the workplace: "Through the common experiences of shop work and union activity, whites and Negroes learn to appreciate each other's better qualities and recognize their rights as fellow human beings."[25] By linking the general sociological understanding of rioting behavior to the larger issues of segregation and democracy, Lee and Humphrey made those larger issues matters for sociological concern.

Unlike Lee's sociological study of the Detroit riot, Clark's study of the 1943 Harlem riot was of a single individual, because, as Clark argued, "when racial problems and conflicts are seen in the light of their effects upon individual persons rather than in broad, general, detached statistical terms, their psychological significance becomes clearer."[26] The choice to study an individual rather than to attempt a larger-scale analysis reflected Clark's training in social psychology in the 1930s. Both the Murphys and Gordon Allport trumpeted the study of the individual. For these psychologists, psychology should not be about a search for "universal" laws of human behavior. As Katherine Pandora has written, "a commitment to foregrounding individuality signified a resistance to the perpetuating images of scientific method held dear by science's elite."[27]

This view of the preeminence of the individual would follow Clark from his graduate training to his professional career. In 1940, Gardner Murphy left Columbia to chair the Psychology Department at the City College of New York (CCNY). He invited Kenneth Clark to join the CCNY department, and by 1942, Clark was an assistant professor in social psychology there. Clark's study of the Harlem riot, conducted with his colleague James Barker, was an early attempt at the sort of argument that would make him so useful to the NAACP during the *Brown* litigation: an attempt to understand "the impact of racial prejudice and social isolation upon the personality of an individual who is a victim of such circumstances."

Clark and Barker's study of was of a "zoot-suiter." Because of the "wasteful" use of materials, the War Production Board had forbidden the manufacture or sale of zoot suits. African American men in New York (and Latino men in California) continued to wear them as an act of defiance against what they viewed as another constriction on their activities for the white man's war. White servicemen saw the zoot suits as unpatriotic, and in 1943, attacked zoot-suiters across the country, mutilating the suits and injuring the wearers.[28]

Just as it was for Lee and Humphrey, the key for Clark and Barker was the social isolation felt by the zoot-suiter, isolation brought about by racial prejudice. Social isolation led to individuals who lacked any sort of empathy for other individuals or respect for private property. Ultimately, these warped personalities rejected all social authority, leading to events such as the 1943 Harlem race riot. Clark and Barker concluded that "the stability of the individual and the stability of the larger society are inextricably interrelated and therefore the socially accepted dehumanization of an individual or group must inevitably manifest itself in societal disturbances."[29]

In May 1948, Lee wrote to Clark to ask for a reprint of Clark's article. The two men began a correspondence that lasted until Lee moved to New

York to chair the Sociology Department of Brooklyn College in 1949.[30] During the 1950s, when Clark served as the liaison between the attorneys of the NAACP–Legal Defense and Education Fund and the social science community, Lee would prove to be one of his closest confidants and his tie to the sociology community.

Anti-Semitism

Leonard Dinnerstein declared that World War II represented the "high tide" of American anti-Semitism.[31] Underlying many social-scientific studies of anti-Semitism during the war was the idea that the United States could become a Nazi state, just has Germany had. The fear that "it could happen here too" gave special force to the study of homegrown anti-Semitism. Many of these studies were conducted by émigré social scientists who had fled Hitler's dominance of the European continent. For these writers, anti-Semitism was a very real threat to both American society and world peace.

Typical of the rhetoric of studies of anti-Semitism in this period are the writings of the founder of the German Psychoanalytic Society, Ernst Simmel, who left Berlin and came to the United States in 1934. Before the war, argued Simmel, anti-Semitism in the United States was primarily "social": the restriction of elite clubs or summer resorts. However, "during World War II . . . a change in the quality of [American] anti-Semitism began to appear. It has taken on the color of German anti-Semitism. It embraces an ever widening circle of the American population, and the more it expands, the more irrational becomes the defamation of the Jews." For Simmel, the question was, why had anti-Semitism become so widespread in the United States? As he wrote, "The endeavor to find an answer to this question is of far reaching importance, not only because anti-Semitism is a danger to the Jews. It is also a danger to this country. More than that it is a danger to all civilization." Simmel noted that Germany's anti-Semitism not only had brought on the unimaginable horrors of the concentration camps but also had plunged the entire world into war. He concluded, "It would be a fatal error, as well as a form of psychological isolationism, to assume that only in Germany could anti-Semitism have descended to such depths."[32]

Simmel was one of many Jewish psychoanalytic thinkers to have fled European oppression during the 1930s to settle in the United States.[33]

These immigrant thinkers were responsible for the psychoanalytic coloring of much of the research on anti-Semitism during World War II and immediately after. The problem was perceived to be of such importance, however, that even such an outspoken critic of psychoanalytic theory as the ubiquitous Gordon Allport approved of the transplanted Freudianism:

> The inhuman orgies of the past two decades have shocked us into co-operation. No petty doctrinal disputes must be allowed to divide the efforts of scientists in their common determination to preserve their scientific freedom by re-establishing personal liberty and self-respect for all men. Anti-Semitism is so contagious and complex an evil that we welcome all possible aid in combating it.[34]

Allport's characterizing the work on anti-Semitism as cooperation was exactly right, for the European psychoanalysts often joined with American psychologists to study anti-Semitism.[35] The best known and most influential of these collaborations were those funded by the American Jewish Committee.

In 1943, social psychologist Nevitt Sanford at Berkeley was studying American morale. Sanford was attempting to relate personality factors to war morale, in an attempt to find out how "extreme" personalities felt about the war effort. In 1943, two things redirected Sanford to study anti-Semitism. First, he received an anonymous donation to study anti-Semitism. Second, he met Max Horkheimer.[36]

Horkheimer was the director of the Institute of Social Research, or the "Frankfurt School," a group of Marxist and psychoanalytic thinkers who had fled Frankfurt, Germany, to the United States in 1934, after Hitler's rise to power. The Institute of Social Research had, miraculously, fled Germany with its finances intact. On arriving in the United States, the institute entered into a quasi-official relationship with Columbia University, but Horkheimer and other institute members were fiercely independent, refusing to be "assimilated" into American culture. In 1941, an illness forced Horkheimer to relocate the institute to southern California, which made Horkheimer's meeting with Sanford possible.[37]

Horkheimer's institute had long wanted to undertake a comprehensive study of anti-Semitism in the United States.[38] A series of bad investments in the late 1930s had made the institute's finances precarious, and for the first time, Horkheimer was forced to seek outside funding for his work. Aware that the unapologetic Marxism and critical theorizing of the institute were unlikely to secure funding in the politically conservative and empirically oriented United States, Horkheimer sought to combine his school's emphasis on critical theory with the quantitative methodologies common in American social science. Horkheimer got the institute's work on anti-Semitism underwritten by funds from the American Jewish Committee, which then supported the work on the new project at Berkeley.[39]

For the American Jewish Committee's project, Sanford recruited a Berkeley colleague, Else Frenkel-Brunswik, and one of her students, Daniel Levinson. Another refugee scholar, Frenkel-Brunswick had fled her native Vienna after the *Anschluss* and joined her husband, Egon Brunswik, at Berkeley. Her studies of personality were heavily influenced by the logical positivism of the Vienna Circle, as well as by psychoanalysis.[40] The final member of the Berkeley team was Theodor Adorno, a member of the Frankfurt School, brought on board to "teach the American academics some critical and Marxist theory."[41] The team now consisted of two American researchers, Sanford and Levinson, and two European researchers, Frenkel-Brunswik and Adorno.

Less than a year later, the Berkeley group began publishing the results of their work in the professional literature. They argued that anti-Semitism was part of a larger problem that threatened not just Jews but all of American society. Anti-Semitism was viewed as part of a larger personality type—the "proto-Fascist." In reporting the development of their scale for the measurement of anti-Semitism, Levinson and Sanford argued that while Americans profess "rather abstract notions" about democracy and freedom, they also lack "a well-defined, integrated ideological-ethical conception of society and interpersonal relations." This lack allows "many anti-democratic sentiments actively to influence their behavior." Social scientists, Levinson and Sanford concluded, were obligated to discover "the strength of this dangerous 'potential for Fascism'—of which anti-Semitism is an essential part."[42]

Levinson and Sanford's scale measured how anti-Semitic an individual was on the basis of the individual's answers to a series of questions. More in-depth techniques were employed by Frenkel-Brunswik. In her studies, subjects were given a Thematic Apperception Test (TAT) in which they were required to tell stories about a series of pictures designed to elicit their thoughts on racial matters. After the TAT, the subjects were interviewed and given Rorschach tests and lengthy questionnaires. The results suggested that those individuals who betrayed high degrees of anti-Semitism also had "a kind of conservative attitude . . . they tended automatically to support the status quo." Moreover, the individuals were highly "ethnocentric" and displayed "a tendency to hold in high esteem one's own, ethnic or social group, to keep it narrow, unmixed and pure, and to reject everything that is different."[43]

Like the morale work described earlier in this chapter, the work of the Berkeley team raised the stakes in the fight against prejudice by making anti-Semitism part and parcel of authoritarianism. To allow anti-Semitism to spread in the United States would be to surrender to the ideology of Nazi Germany and all it entailed. To surrender to anti-Semitism was the equivalent of surrendering to the authoritarian ideology of the Nazi state. The point was driven home in 1944 when the American Jewish Committee decided to formalize its relationship with Horkheimer's institute by creating a Department of Scientific Research within the AJCommittee auspices.[44] The Department of Scientific Research, under Max Horkheimer, set out to study anti-Semitism scientifically, and to use scientific research "just as American business uses it today, or as the War Department uses it."[45] One of the first functions of the new department was a May 1944 conference on anti-Semitism.

The participants in the conference included not only Horkheimer and Adorno from the Institute of Social Research but also Gordon Allport, Charles S. Johnson, Paul Lazarsfeld, Alfred McClung Lee, Kurt Lewin, Talcott Parsons, and Goodwin Watson—a veritable "who's who" of researchers in racial prejudice during the 1940s.[46] The conclusion of the conference echoed the work of the Berkeley scholars: "anti-Semitism in the USA is tied with Nazism, Fascism, dictatorship, and is a concealed attack on American liberty."[47]

Although it was launched at the 1944 conference, the Department of Scientific Research's work did not come to fruition until after the war. In 1950, it published the Studies in Prejudice series, which consisted of five books on anti-Semitism. The work of the Berkeley team would be the most famous of these, published under the title *The Authoritarian Personality*.[48] The Studies in Prejudice series, and *The Authoritarian Personality* in particular, would be one of the two cornerstones to Kenneth B. Clark's arguments in the *Brown* litigation. The only other work that would figure as heavily would be Gunnar Myrdal's *An American Dilemma*.

An American Dilemma

The impact of the 1944 publication of Gunnar Myrdal's study of American race relations, *An American Dilemma: The Negro Problem and Modern*

Democracy, was not contained merely in the fifteen hundred pages of the final book. In fact, the book's forty-six chapters and six appendixes were not even the entirety of the written work: four "technical monographs" were also spun off from the main book and published under separate cover.[49] Literally every researcher in the area of race relations was involved in Myrdal's project. In the "Author's Preface," Myrdal lists no fewer than seventy-five researchers as members of his staff.[50] Moreover, the book had a tremendous impact beyond the social science community. Arnold Rose, who worked closely with Myrdal in writing the book, brought out a condensed version of the huge work in 1948, titled *The Negro in America*. In a foreword to that edition, Myrdal noted, "The size of the original publication . . . is not deterring many who are not scholars and specialists from reading it, in whole or in part. Up until December 31, 1947, it has sold over 30,000 copies."[51]

Myrdal's notions about race relations quickly spread in the decade after World War II. *An American Dilemma* provided the scientific imprimatur upon many calls for civil rights, ranging from newspaper articles to the Truman administration's report *To Secure These Rights*.[52] Historian Walter Jackson has claimed that Myrdal's book created a "liberal orthodoxy" concerning racial matters. Sociologist Martin Bulmer has called it "the most important single study of race relations to have appeared in the first half of the twentieth century."[53]

An American Dilemma originated in 1935, when the Carnegie Corporation's president, Frederick Keppel, and a Carnegie trustee, Newton D. Baker, decided to sponsor a major study on America's "Negro problem." To ensure that the study would be an objective one, Carnegie's leaders decided to select a foreign scholar who would be untainted, presumably, by any views concerning U.S. race relations. Additionally, the scholar had to be from a nation with no imperial tradition, which Carnegie's leaders also felt would bias the investigation. After a search, Carnegie chose Swedish Social Democrat Gunnar Myrdal.[54]

Myrdal began his study in 1938 with a budget of a quarter of a million dollars and the task of learning about race relations in the United States. To aid in this task, Myrdal assembled a large staff to write monographs on various aspects of race relations. Eschewing better-known researchers on the grounds that their view could be discerned from their published work, Myrdal concentrated on junior scholars. Additionally, Myrdal encouraged African American scholars to join his project. Political scientist Ralph Bunche and sociologists Charles S. Johnson, E. Franklin

Frazier, and Ira De Augustine Reid, as well as Kenneth B. Clark, were on Myrdal's staff.[55]

Much of Myrdal's staff dispersed when the war broke out, and Myrdal returned to Sweden for a time. The project was kept alive in the United States by Samuel Stouffer, a quantitative sociologist from the University of Chicago, who hired a young University of Chicago sociology graduate student named Arnold Rose to assist him. When Myrdal returned to the United States in 1941, he began writing his delayed manuscript with the assistance of Richard Sterner, his Swedish associate, and Rose, both of whom were listed as co-authors.[56] Rose would later become a sociologist at the University of Minnesota and "Myrdal's bulldog" in the United States as the chief defender of the views found in *An American Dilemma.* Additionally, apart from Alfred McClung Lee, Rose would be the sociologist most integral to the *Brown* litigation.

Myrdal's finished effort consolidated several themes that American social science had been sounding for two decades. First, Myrdal's work served to re-enforce the "psychologizing" of race prejudice that originated in the 1930s. The dilemma Myrdal examined was the tension between the professed ideals of the "American Creed" of brotherhood, rationality, and equality, on the one hand, and America's treatment of African Americans, discrimination, and segregation, on the other. According to Myrdal, the problem was a moral one that manifested itself not only between different groups in American society but within individuals' personalities. As Myrdal wrote, "*The moral struggle goes on within people and not only between them.*"[57] Hence, the "Negro problem" for Myrdal was, in fact, a moral and psychological problem of white Americans. This view echoed that of prewar researchers in racial attitudes, as well as that of Klineberg, Clark, and other social psychologists who were working with American morale: the problem was the attitude of the majority group.

The second theme in *An American Dilemma* concerned the proper role of social science as social engineering. As a Swedish Social Democrat, Myrdal was one of the architects of the Swedish welfare state during the 1930s. As a believer in an activist government, he sharply disagreed with the most prominent American social scientists who argued against the efficacy of governmental action regarding race relations.[58]

For example, Myrdal took aim at William Graham Sumner, one of the founders of American sociology, and Robert Park, both of whom argued that natural laws—what Sumner termed "folkways"—could not be altered by artificial laws, that is, legislation—what Sumner termed "state-ways." Myrdal summarized Sumner's views thus:

> If legislation adheres to the "natural laws," it is not exactly damaging but useless; if legislation conflicts with the "natural laws" it will be inefficacious though slightly damaging as it will disturb somewhat the smooth operation of the "natural laws." . . . On this central point, which apparently is much of the political purpose of the whole theory of folkways and mores, Sumner simply expresses a common American prejudice against legislation.[59]

Myrdal had no such prejudice against legislation, especially when it was legislation against prejudice. He wrote approvingly of states experimenting with antidiscrimination laws and criticized the slow federal efforts that were "hampered by pressure from Southern congressmen."[60] Myrdal also praised court action against discrimination and prejudice. He predicted correctly that the Supreme Court would soon declare the white primary (which excluded African Americans from voting in primary elections in the South) unconstitutional and that "the legal foundation for Negro discrimination in the South is dissolving."[61] The ability of the law to change behavior resonated among the social activists of SPSSI, who long had struggled to find a way to use their scientific knowledge to re-create society.

The third theme of Myrdal's work concerned the pathology of African American culture. Myrdal agreed with E. Franklin Frazier, who had argued that slavery and then segregation and discrimination had prevented a genuine African American culture from developing. Myrdal argued:

> The instability of the Negro family, the inadequacy of educational facilities for Negroes, the emotionalism in the Negro church, the insufficiency and unwholesomeness of Negro recreational activity, the plethora of Negro sociable organizations, the narrowness of interests of the average Negro, the provincialism of his political speculation, the high Negro crime rate, the cultivation of the arts to the neglect of other fields, superstition, personality difficulties, and other characteristic traits are mainly forms of social pathology which, for the most part, are created by caste pressures.[62]

Because there was nothing in African American culture worth saving, Myrdal suggested that the solution to this social pathology was to assimilate African Americans completely into white culture.

As we will see soon, Kenneth B. Clark would take the social pathology of African American culture, combine it with Kurt Lewin's concepts of self-hatred, and transform it into a psychological matter. At the end of the war, he and Mamie Phipps Clark had not yet published the data that he thought proved the damage of segregated society on African American children. In 1945, however, he gave a hint of what was to come when he wrote that "K.B. Clark and M.P. Clark obtained [unpublished] experimental evidence which shows . . . that Negro children also learn and accept to a large extent the prevalent unfavorable attitudes toward the Negro."[63] The Clarks would not publish the findings of their second data set until a few years later, however. In 1945, it was *An American Dilemma* that firmly entrenched the social pathology of the American Negro in the public's mind.

An American Dilemma brought into wide currency ideas that had been brewing in the social science community since the early 1930s. Race prejudice was a matter of the attitudes whites held concerning blacks. Race prejudice was an irrational and dangerous attitude that was fundamentally incompatible with democracy. Social-scientific expertise should be used to solve problems of race prejudice. Such a view resonated among the social psychologists of Society for the Psychological Study of Social Issues, for the war had changed how SPSSI conceptualized social engineering.

The Society for the Psychological Study of Social Issues

SPSSI originated in 1936 as a group of "leftists" and "outsiders" who believed that social engineering was best accomplished by the people, or the workers, rather than by a powerful elite, as represented by government or state action. Yet the experiences of World War II linked social psychologists to government to such an extent that even dedicated leftists began writing about how the government could undertake social engineering for the benefit of the people.[64]

Goodwin Watson, the first president of SPSSI, was one of those psychologists involved with war work. Watson served as chief of the Analysis Division of the Foreign Broadcast Intelligence Service from 1941 to 1943 but was forced to resign his post by the House Un-American Activities Committee because of alleged leftist connections and returned to his professorship at Columbia Teacher's College.[65] Despite his unfortunate experience, Watson was convinced that World War II marked the beginning of a new era of "social engineering." In an article published in 1945, Watson noted, "The war lured psychologists away from their cages of white rats into various kind of war jobs in Washington." He believed that social engineering by social psychologists would bring new "insight into factors which change group morale, inter-group relations and mass pressures."[66] Watson's concern for intergroup relations (previously called race relations) was indicative of one of the most important areas the new social engineers claimed for themselves: the reduction of race prejudice.

Most of the research done on race prejudice during the war was conducted by SPSSI members and reflected the organization's interest in socially active social science. A common theme of this research was that social science needed not only to *understand* race prejudice but to work to *eliminate* that prejudice. As World War II came to an end, social psychologists Ronald Lippitt and Marian Radke argued, "The need for an understanding of the dynamics of prejudice has no equivalent in importance in the social sciences. In no other aspects of interpersonal and intergroup relationships is there a more urgent need for social sciences to 'get out and do something.'"[67] Such a view contrasted sharply with prewar views of race prejudice, where prejudice may have been irrational but was never portrayed as a danger to society. Hitler's rise to power, the struggle against Nazi ideology, and the perceived need to unify the nation behind the war effort had transformed the study of prejudice into a struggle against totalitarianism. The social-scientific community began building the argument that not only was race prejudice an irrational attitude, but it was a threat to the democratic order.

After the war, SPSSI began publishing the *Journal of Social Issues*. The first two issues were dedicated to "Racial and Religious Prejudice in Everyday Living."[68] In the third issue, dated August 1945—the month of the bombing of Hiroshima and Nagasaki—Ronald Lippitt issued a call for all social scientists to cooperate in the eradication of prejudice, declaring, "It is now easier to smash an atom than it is to break a prejudice."[69] In the next chapter, I show how the American Jewish Congress provided the opportunity to "break" prejudice, by transforming social scientists into social engineers.

PART II

Forging the Alliance

4

The American Jewish Congress

After World War II, social scientists took a new view toward the effect legal changes in the social system could have on racial attitudes. In *An American Dilemma*, Gunnar Myrdal argued that American social scientists had been too concerned that the law was powerless to affect social change, a view he laid at the feet of sociologist William Graham Sumner. According to Myrdal, Sumner had argued that the "mores" and "folkways" of a society, particularly in the area of race relations, could not be changed by legal methods. The notion of "Sumnerian mores," Myrdal wrote, was "closely related to a bias in social science against induced changes, and especially against all attempts to intervene in the social process by legislation. The concept of mores actually implies a whole social theory and an entire *laissez-faire* ('do-nothing') metaphysics and is so utilized.[1]

Myrdal flatly rejected the notion that race relations could not be improved through legal change, and many postwar social scientists began to adopt his stance—that the law could and should be used to improve race relations. Fundamental to their position was the idea that *legal* change could precede *social* change. The first step to better race relations, according to these social scientists, was not to use propaganda to educate the white public about the "brotherhood of man" and to urge them to accept African Americans as equals. Rather, the first step was to eliminate legal segregation and discrimination, for the legal change would itself serve the educational purpose and lead to better race relations.

This view the power of legal change to improve race relations cut against much of postwar thinking about race. While it was true that, after the war was won, many Americans turned their attention to the elimination of racism and prejudice at home, most organizations believed the way to accomplish this task was to focus on education and moral exhortation.[2]

Hundreds of organizations sprang to life after the war to improve race relations in the United States. The focus of many of these organizations was on education rather than on large-scale institutional changes in society, because such actions were viewed as futile, given that prejudice was a problem of people's personalities. Only through intercultural education aimed at changing people's attitudes toward African Americans, Jews, and other minority groups could society hope to effect changes in discriminatory behaviors of individuals. The intercultural education movement therefore rejected political or legal attempts aimed at combating discrimination. Legal action or other forms of social engineering could not reach people's basic attitudes, which were considered the root of the problem. Typical of this stance is Robert MacIver, a key figure in the intercultural education movement, who wrote in 1944, "What is needed here is not something the government can do for us—no new political credo or even, for the most part, new laws."[3] but rather a change in people's basic philosophy toward minority groups. In a 1951 survey of approaches adopted by these "intergroup relations agencies," H. H. Giles of New York University noted, "Many of them showed a strong concentration on what may be called inspirational talks and pamphlets. . . . Hundreds of thousands of dollars were spent in the financing of these talks and pamphlets."[4]

Many social scientists disagreed with the intercultural education stance toward the utility of legal change. Between 1945 and the start of the *Brown* litigation in 1951, social scientists developed a series of arguments that purported to prove that the elimination of segregation was a necessary first step to better race relations. The leading institution that touted this view was the American Jewish Congress (AJCongress). Indeed, in many ways, the groundwork for the collaboration of social scientists and attorneys in the *Brown* litigation campaign was laid in the AJCongress. Between 1945 and 1950, the AJCongress created new organizations that provided a foundation for collaboration between social scientists and civil rights attorneys.

The American Jewish Congress

After World War II, a host of middle-class Eastern European Jews with socialist/labor backgrounds began to take over Jewish leadership roles in the United States. Contrasted with the older generation of leaders, these men were professional civil rights workers, not interested in placating the WASP elite but eager and willing to join public battle for Jewish rights.[5]

The new militancy in Jewish leadership derived in part from the horrors of Nazi Germany. The dangers of anti-Semitism were now all too real to American Jews. Jewish organizations, including the American Jewish Congress, the American Jewish Committee, and the Anti-Defamation League of B'nai B'rith, formed the National Community Relations Advisory Council (NCRAC) to serve as a clearinghouse for information about anti-Semitism. New funds poured into the coffers of the NCRAC organizations for the fight against anti-Semitism.[6] The AJCongress, however, was unique among these institutions. Unlike the other organizations in NCRAC, and indeed, unlike nearly any other organization in the larger intercultural education movement, the AJCongress was not willing to rely on moral pleading and the process of education to eliminate anti-Semitism. The AJCongress preferred a more direct approach, through litigation and lobbying for legal change.

Founded in 1918, the AJCongress was one of the more militant and confrontational of Jewish organizations. From the beginning, and quite unlike the older and more staid American Jewish Committee, the AJCongress would protest, confront, and publicize anti-Semitism.[7] After World War II, fearing rampant anti-Semitism in the United States, the AJCongress drew on the insights of two innovative émigré scholars, Kurt Lewin and Alexander Pekelis, to launch a "comprehensive program of legal, legislative and social action which would protect and safeguard the rights of Americans . . . by outlawing every form of discrimination on grounds of race, creed, color or national origin."[8] At the heart of their program was the belief that education and moral exhortation against prejudice would always fail if official discrimination continued. For the AJCongress, official discrimination, whether a quota on the number of Jews allowed into medical school or the segregation statutes of the white South, would have to be eliminated in order to eliminate prejudice. Only after these structural changes occurred in society could education to combat prejudice have some hope of success.

To attack official discrimination, the AJCongress created two new divisions concerned with using both the law and social science: The Commission on Community Interrelations (CCI) hoped to translate social science research into social action in order to lead a "scientific attack on anti-Semitism and other minority problems in the United States."[9] They recognized that the law could serve a valuable purpose for their work. The Commission on Law and Social Action (CLSA) was to do for Jewish Americans what the NAACP had been doing for African Americans—litigate to protect their rights. CLSA's attorneys viewed social science as a valuable resource for the creation of new laws against discrimination and segregation.

Commission on Community Interrelations

The Commission on Community Interrelations was the brainchild of Kurt Lewin (1890–1947). Educated at the University of Berlin, he made several fundamental contributions to psychology in Europe, concentrating on worker education and job satisfaction. In 1934, Lewin fled Europe to the United States. Finding himself in a strange new country caused Lewin to turn his attention to issues surrounding group identification, prejudice, aggression, and Jewish identity. After two years at Cornell University, he spent 1935–1945 at the Child Welfare Research Station at the University of Iowa.[10]

While in Iowa, in the late 1930s, Lewin's research with small group settings convinced him that social science could be used to bolster democracy. He began working with a doctoral student, Ronald Lippitt. Lippitt wanted to study how different leadership styles affected behavior of children in small groups. Lewin was intrigued by the idea and suggested that Lippitt study the effect of democratic versus autocratic leadership styles.[11] In these experiments, dubbed the "boys studies," adult experimenters posed as a group leader for a group of young boys. The group leader took the role of either a "democratic" leader, who allowed the children to set much of the agenda for the task at hand, or an "autocratic" leader, who ordered the children to complete the given task. The studies demonstrated that democracy was the road to peaceful cooperation within these groups. Lewin reported, "There was about thirty times as much hostile domination in the autocracy as in the democracy, more demands for attention and much more hostile criticism; whereas in the democratic atmosphere co-operation and praise of the other fellow was much more frequent."[12]

For Lewin, the results of the boys studies suggested the possibility of "democratic social engineering" through the use of small groups of individuals. Lewin expanded his ideas concerning social engineering during World War II. He was enlisted to aid the government to encourage the consumption of more organ meats during the food shortages that accompanied the war. Lewin's work on food habits convinced him that the proper way to inculcate a population was not through a lecture or propaganda but through the use of small groups, where the individuals could discuss the issues under democratic leadership.[13]

Studies such as the "meat study," combined with methods for training democratic leaders, gave Lewin hope for the use of social psychology for social engineering. For example, during the war, Lewin was concerned about the problem of postwar Germany, for he firmly believed that democracy could not be "imposed" on a conquered German people; rather it had to be learned. The way to teach them, he believed, was through small groups, similar to those in the boys studies. In 1943, Lewin wrote that group methods could be used to re-educate the German public in democracy. He claimed, "It seems possible by training democratic leaders and leaders of leaders to build up a pyramid which could reach large masses relatively quickly."[14] By the end of the war, Lewin was firmly convinced that social science could be used for social engineering. He wrote in 1944, "As industrial plants have found out that physical research pays, social organizations will soon find out that social research pays."[15] He began to seek funding for his ideas for linking social science to social action, specifically in the area of minority group relations.[16]

In 1944, some of Lewin's publications came to the attention of AJCongress president Rabbi Stephen Wise. The AJCongress had $1 million earmarked for the creation of a research center for the study of intergroup relations, and Wise thought Lewin should lead it.[17] The AJCongress offer was tailor-made for Lewin's vision of a social engineering organization, and he quickly agreed to undertake the creation of the new commission.

In July 1944, Lewin submitted a plan for the new organization that outlined a vision of lawyers and social scientists working side by side, fighting for democracy. He argued that many existing programs were based on an insufficient understanding of the causes of and cures for anti-Semitism. Lewin's program would be based on two criteria. First, "it has to be objective, i.e. it has to uncover the essential facts in an unbiased scientific manner." Second, the program "has to be practical, i.e. it should lead to coordinated significant actions." To meet both criteria, Lewin envisioned an organization with two main divisions: a research division, which would consist of community sociologists, opinion analysts, group psychologists, individual psychologists, and statisticians, and an "operational division," which would combine two previously existing AJCongress commissions that included numerous lawyers: the Commission on Economic Discrimination and the Commission on Law and

Legislation. In his new Commission on Community Interrelations, re-search workers and operational personnel would be equal participants. As Lewin wrote, "The need for action determines the content of the re-search; scientific requirements determine its technique."[18]

Fundamental to CCI's views on prejudice was the notion that "if we can break down the social segregation and discrimination which defines a racial or religious group as a sanctioned target for prejudice and scape-goating, time will take care of the individual prejudice."[19] CCI's focus on official discrimination rather than the attitude of prejudice is reflected in one of its first projects: a general survey of the state of knowledge about prejudice and discrimination, undertaken by Goodwin Watson. Watson surveyed different techniques for fighting prejudice, including education, moral exhortation, and other methods. He concluded that "*it is more con-structive to attack segregation than it is to attack prejudice.*" Segregation was amenable to public control, unlike people's private prejudices. More-over, education would fail unless official "caste barriers" were torn down, because "habits built around those barriers will silently undo anything we accomplish."[20]

CCI believed that law could do what education could not: break through the irrational attitude of race prejudice. Thus the law became an essential component to fighting discrimination and prejudice. Stuart W. Cook, who would play a pivotal role in the *Brown* litigation, came to CCI in 1948 to serve as co-director along with Lewin. A University of Min-nesota Ph.D. in 1938, Cook had long been interested in the effects of in-tergroup contact on attitude change. Soon after joining the staff of CCI, Cook set forth the CCI's philosophy regarding the relationship between education and legal change:

> Educational programs aimed at reducing discrimination are likely to make slow headway when there are no anti-discrimination laws. But passage of a law changes the atmosphere in which education is carried on. Once legisla-tion exists, an educational program can draw support from the law-abid-ing tradition of most citizens. After a law is passed, an educational cam-paign designed to explain the law's purpose and to encourage compliance with it is no longer an inefficient technique but is in a position to produce a great return for a relatively small investment.[21]

Cook was presenting the key idea for these researchers: that the law is not an *alternative* to education against group prejudice but is best used *in conjunction* with such education.

Isidor Chein, CCI's research director, made a similar point. Like Kenneth B. Clark, Chein had received his Ph.D. in psychology in 1939 from Columbia. Before joining CCI, he worked with one of the first organizations in New York City dedicated to the study of intergroup relations, the Committee on Unity, which was established in the wake of the 1943 Harlem riots.[22] In 1946, while at the Committee on Unity, Chein wrote that legal changes "constitute virtually the only means of breaking into the vicious circle [of prejudice and discrimination]."[23] Hence, he was quite receptive to the AJCongress's program of direct legal action against discrimination. He joined CCI as a research associate and became director of research in 1950.[24] At CCI, Chein continued to maintain that "education and the law . . . go hand in hand; each approach helps to bring out the best potentialities of the other. Either, alone, is apt to be fruitless."[25]

The particular method Lewin developed for CCI was "action research." Lewin envisioned social scientists researching a problem and "actionists" implementing a reform program. Actionists included not just lawyers but also community workers, local leaders, religious personnel, and others who lived and worked in the community under study.[26] From the beginning, CCI personnel saw the difficulties of these two groups of people working side by side. Ronald Lippitt, Lewin's student from the Iowa days, made the issues clear in an internal memorandum. Social scientists, wrote Lippitt, were "likely to feel that action personnel have no appreciation of the problems and requirements of data collection" and were "likely to be put in situations where [their] previous sources of satisfaction—recognition for competence in technical publication, theorizing, etc., are not relevant." By contrast, action personnel were "likely to feel that social research isn't practical enough yet to make improvements on the great mass of experience which has led to certain more or less institutionalized practices" and that "data collection procedures are an unwarranted nuisance when they begin to call for certain modifications of action plans."[27] As we will see, Lippitt's argument would prove prescient, for while CCI created valuable research that would later become important in the *Brown* litigation, social scientists and lawyers would coexist only uneasily within the institutionalized context of the AJCongress.

The first research project undertaken by CCI serves as an example of the uneasy relationship of CCI with the rest of the AJCongress. Kenneth B. Clark was part of a staff hastily assembled by CCI for this project, an investigation of a disturbance at a synagogue at Seaside, a small Coney Island community. Seaside was predominantly a Jewish community but with a large minority of Italians and a smaller number of African Americans. Because the disturbance took place on Yom Kippur, CCI investigators wanted to discover if it was motivated by anti-Semitism in the community. Consequently, Clark and his associates interviewed many Seaside residents to determine their racial attitudes and found that the community was under considerable tension owing to poverty. The disturbance at the synagogue was the result of hostility aimed at Jews because they were conspicuous on Yom Kippur and not because of general feelings of anti-Semitism. The article on Seaside foreshadowed Clark's later work with the NAACP-LDEF in two ways: first, because it was an early demonstration of minority group members accepting the negative evaluations of their group that majority group members imposed on them—an argument that would become significant in the *Brown* litigation—and, second, because it attempted to demonstrate how social scientists strove be social activists while remaining objective researchers.

CCI investigators found that members of Seaside's minority groups often took on unfavorable attitudes about their own race, or what Kurt Lewin had dubbed group "self-hatred." The final report argued, "It may be noted that 30 percent of the Negroes, 21 percent of the Italians, and 14 percent of the Jews express only unfavorable stereotypes about themselves. This illustrates the self-hate factor referred to by Lewin."[28] At the time of Kenneth Clark's involvement with CCI, he and Mamie Clark were busy preparing a new set of articles that would show how African Americans were suffering from a negative self-image. (In chapter 7, I explore this work by the Clarks.)

Another significant thing about the Seaside study was the stance the researchers took toward their role as objective scientists. In their report, the authors were quick to disavow advocacy for the Jewish cause; they wrote that even though CCI was associated with the activist and political AJCongress, "by accepting research responsibility, we necessarily lost the character of a special interest organization and took on the objective role of consultant to the community on its problems." The scientific outlook, the authors claimed, meant that CCI, in researching the problems of minority groups, took those problems "out of the realm of special pleading into the area of social science, where the only possible orientation is that of impartial work toward the common good."[29] This separation of activist organization from social scientific researcher would prove an ongoing struggle for CCI and for Clark during his tenure with the NAACP-LDEF.

Clark's experience at CCI was not a pleasant one. In his resignation letter, he expressed his belief that he was being employed as a "token." Not free to develop his own program of study, nor completely free to write up his own research results, Clark left CCI to work on his own projects.[30]

After Clark's departure, the research sponsored by CCI in the late 1940s and early 1950s demonstrated just how CCI's social scientists believed that education and the law could be partners in the reduction of discrimination and prejudice. CCI attempted to show that a change in the actual physical circumstances of society could precede a change in the attitudes of people. In other words, the law did not have to wait for a change in social climate to be effective; the law could be a causal agent in the attitude change. Two lines of research demonstrate how CCI attempted to merge social science with an attack on discrimination: first, research conducted on the separation of attitudes from behavior, and second, research on the effects of interracial contact.

On the separation of attitudes from behavior, CCI's social scientists built on the work of Richard T. Lapiere.[31] In the 1930s, Lapiere traveled through the United States with a Chinese couple. They stayed in hotels or auto camps and ate in a total of 184 restaurants. With the exception of one hotel, in all cases the three were served without incident. Six months later, Lapiere sent out a questionnaire to the establishments that had served them, asking if they served "members of the Chinese race." Over 90 percent of those responding indicated they did not, despite the fact that they had done just that six months earlier.[32]

In the 1930s, Lapiere's work was noted with approval by the activist social psychologists in New York City,[33] and CCI gave them the opportunity to further his research in the 1940s. Bernard Kutner successfully duplicated Lapiere's research when he sent two white women into a series of New York restaurants. The white women were later joined by an African American woman who was seated without incident. Later, when Kutner inquired as to the racial policies of the restaurants, he was informed that they did not serve African Americans. Gerhart Saenger conducted a similar study on the integration of sales personnel, discovering that customers who, moments earlier, had been assisted by African American sales personnel at a large New York department store would tell a pollster that they would never trade at a store that employed African Americans.[34]

This research into the separation of attitude and behavior was CCI's best-received research in the larger AJCongress, because it fit so well with the AJCongress's program of attacking discrimination rather than prejudice.[35] It was also research on a rather small scale, meaning it could be delivered in time to be useful to the AJCongress's program of social action. In the *Brown* litigation, this research could be used to argue that, despite what the south *said* about resisting desegregation, its actions would probably follow the *fait accompli* of the law.

Within the social science community, of more lasting influence than the attitude/behavior research was the research at CCI on interracial contact.[36] For CCI, interracial contact was the point at which the cycle of discrimination and prejudice could be broken. In 1948, Stuart Cook wrote that interracial contact could cause a rollback of both prejudice and discrimination:

> Insofar as successful action against discriminatory practices brings about a decrease in segregation this will mean increased contact between persons from different backgrounds which will, under favorable circumstances, create a reduction in prejudice. Such a reduction in prejudice should, of course, have the consequences of further reduction of discriminatory practices and hostile behavior.[37]

The notion that contact between differing groups would lead to the reduction of prejudice in those groups became Stuart Cook's life work and one of the most significant contributions of CCI social scientists to social psychology.[38] As soon as he arrived at CCI in 1947, Cook was testifying before city commissions that contact between the races served to decrease racial tensions. For example, before the City Commission of Jersey City, Cook testified that "joint occupancy of the same housing community by Negroes and whites has consistently worked out: Initial, mistaken ideas are soon corrected through day-to-day contact and, in many places, members of the different races have come to share identical responsibilities in a completely democratic way."[39]

As a program of scientific study, CCI researchers attempted to discover the circumstances under which contact between individuals of different races tended to decrease prejudice. The "contact hypothesis"—that contact between different races decreased prejudice—was an open question in the late 1940s. While some unsystematic evidence, such as Lee and Humphrey's book on the Detroit race riot, was available to indicate that racial contact decreased prejudice, there was no firm consensus on the issue; indeed, there was some evidence that contact tended to increase prejudice. In a 1948 survey of various programs designed to decrease prejudice, Cornell University social scientist Robin M. Williams called for further research into the question of interracial contact. Noting that "establishment of the effects of segregation per se will be an extraordinarily difficult task," Williams argued that social scientists should study the effects of segregated and nonsegregated situations in order to answer questions such as "Where is friction greatest? Where are the areas of high and low intensity and incidence of verbal prejudice? How do stable areas of intermingling compare with shifting areas and 'invasion' points?"[40]

Soon, CCI researchers were attempting to answer the sorts of questions posed by Williams. Building on earlier work on the desegregation of the armed forces, CCI's researchers concentrated on interracial public housing and interracial employment situations.[41] These studies were not experimental, as the attitude/behavior studies were, but grew out of the migration of African Americans to New York and the newly desegregated employment and public housing opportunities for them. CCI seized the research opportunities offered by these real-life situations to study interracial contact in a series of field studies. Most often, the results of their work were published in SPSSI's official journal, *The Journal of Social Issues.*

In one of the first studies of interracial housing, two CCI staffers, Morton Deutsch and Mary Evans Collins, conducted interviews with families living in four housing projects. Two of the projects were desegregated and two were segregated. Deutsch and Collins found that in the segregated projects, white prejudice was much higher than in the integrated neighborhoods. Deutsch and Collins posited that the contact possible in integrated neighborhoods gave prejudiced individuals the opportunity to realize that their prejudices had no basis in reality. By contrast, in the segregated neighborhoods, no such opportunity existed for the prejudiced individual to overcome his or her stereotypes about African Americans.[42] Stuart Cook also spent a majority of his research time at CCI on the question of interracial housing, reaching similar results.[43]

A parallel set of studies was conducted on the effects of the interracial workplace. For example, a study by John Harding and Russell Hogrefe dovetailed nicely with the study of customer reaction to the integration of sales personnel. In Harding and Hogrefe's study, the researchers polled the white co-workers of a newly integrated sales floor. Harding and Hogrefe found that, while the basic attitude of the white workers toward their African American co-workers might not have changed significantly, they could nonetheless work peacefully side by side.[44]

CCI and other researchers in interracial contact were attempting to discover the specific conditions under which interracial contact would decrease prejudice. In April 1951, Gordon Allport stated what social science had discovered about the conditions needed for contact to reduce prejudice when he reported, "first, that the contact must be one of equal status; and second, that the members must have objective interests in common." To achieve these conditions, Allport argued that "artificial segregation should be abolished. Until it is abolished equal status contacts cannot take place. And until they take place cooperative projects of joint concern cannot arise. And until this condition is fulfilled we may not expect widespread resolution of intergroup tensions. Hence, nearly all the investigators agree that the attack on segregation must continue."[45] This would be a key point for the social scientists when they became involved in the litigation campaign: that the abolition of segregation was a *necessary* step to better race relations rather than a *sufficient* step. In the case of the "contact hypothesis," for example, social scientists were not arguing that all that needed to be done to reduce prejudice was to eliminate legal segregation but rather that *nothing* could be done to reduce prejudice *until* legal segregation was eliminated. In other words, the elimination of segregation was seen as a necessary first step toward better race relations, not the end of the journey but the beginning.

CCI's research into the contact hypothesis and the relationship between attitude and behavior would become very useful in the 1950s when the *Brown* litigation began. In the 1940s, however, CCI collaborated with another branch of the AJCongress, the Commission on Law and Social Action, to use social-scientific expertise in the creation of new law.

Commission on Law and Social Action

In his memorandum proposing the formation of CCI, Lewin envisioned CCI's operational division as consisting of the existing Commission on Law and Legislation and the Commission on Economic Discrimination. Instead, the AJCongress merged these two existing commissions in November 1945 under the leadership of three attorneys, Will Maslow, Leo Pfeffer, and Alexander Pekelis, to form the Commission on Law and Social Action.[46]

Maslow had come to the United States when he was three years old. He had studied economics at Cornell but switched to law at Columbia when he discovered that universities hesitated to hire Jewish professors. Unfortunately, most large law firms were equally hesitant to hire Jewish attorneys. The newly formed bureaucracies of the New Deal, however, had no such restrictions, and Maslow worked as a trial attorney for the National Labor Relations Board and later supervised the Fair Employment Practices Commission.[47]

In 1945, when Maslow was hired to head the newly formed CLSA, he found Alexander Pekelis employed by the AJCongress with undefined duties. Pekelis had been the director of the Commission on Law and Legislation until it was collapsed into CLSA. Born in Russia, Pekelis spent most of his adult life in Italy and France as a professor of jurisprudence. In 1941, he fled to the United States just before the Nazis entered France. He took a position on the graduate faculty of the New School for Social Research and entered the Columbia School of Law in 1942, where he became editor of the *Columbia Law Review*. Because he was not yet a member of the bar, Pekelis could not serve as a staff attorney for CLSA, but Maslow created a special position for him: "chief consultant."[48] Pekelis's first job for CLSA was to prepare a memorandum that would set out the organization and philosophy of CLSA, just as Kurt Lewin was in the midst of doing for CCI.

Pekelis based his understanding of the law on an older American legal tradition of *legal realism*. There are as many definitions of legal realism as there were legal realists. Generally, the term referred to "that body of legal thought produced for the most part by law professors at Columbia and Yale Law Schools during the 1920s and 1930s."[49] These law professors were following the lead of progressive theorists who rejected nineteenth-century legal reasoning.

At the end of the nineteenth century, American jurisprudence was dominated by the belief that judges discovered, rather than made, law. In this view, law was a deductive reasoning process that took legal rules and case precedents as its major premises and the facts of a particular case as its minor premises. The judge could make a proper ruling in each case by following the formal procedure, which inevitably led to the correct decision. The case method of legal education, pioneered by Christopher C. Langdell at Harvard, perpetuated this formalistic system by teaching that legal precedent, combined with proper reasoning, would lead to a uniform law.[50]

In the twentieth century, the formalistic legal system came under increasing attack as legal theorists and practicing lawyers began to demand that the law pay more attention to how the world actually worked. Columbia law professor Karl Llewellyn was the first to attempt a definition of the new jurisprudence in a 1930 *Columbia Law Review* article, "A Realistic Jurisprudence: The Next Step." Llewellyn called for the findings of the behavioral sciences to be used by lawyers and judges to bring jurisprudence more in line with the way in which the world truly operated.[51] The legal realists, as they came to be known, attacked two major concepts. First, realists denied that judges "discovered" law. Rather, argued the realists, judges *made* law, and the law either helped or hindered certain social policies. Second, the realists argued for new sources of information to replace the abstractions of nineteenth-century jurisprudence. Such sources of information, including social science, began flooding the legal system with facts about how the law operated in society.[52]

At least some of those who could be called legal realists were interested in using some social science in legal proceedings. Progressive lawyers such as Charles E. Clark and William O. Douglas attempted to use social science research to further their progressive reforms. Unfortunately, they found that most social research was much too slow to be of use to the law. In addition, if the results of the research did not suit the needs of the reformers, the research was ignored.[53] The same issues would soon haunt CCI researchers and CLSA attorneys in their attempt to integrate social science and the law.

Pekelis entered Columbia as a mature scholar; for him, law school was almost a formality, needed only to gain access to the American bar. The central notions of realism—that judges make rather than discover law and that information about the "real" world should play a central role in the creation of law—clearly resonated with him. "Similar theories had been developed in Europe long before legal realism became popular here," he wrote in 1943.[54] Pekelis wrote the central doctrines of legal realism into his memorandum for the AJCongress leadership.

At the heart of Pekelis's proposal was the unique nature of anti-Semitism in the United States. In contrast to European anti-Semitism, which was a function of official government action, American anti-Semitism "comes from the forces of society itself. Anti-Semitism here is private or communal, not public or governmental in nature."[55] These social forces, in the form of unofficial quotas on Jews in professional schools, for instance, would be much harder to detect than anything as blatant as a law. Hence, to combat American anti-Semitism, Jews needed the sorts of data that could only be provided by social science. "Contemporary experience," Pekelis wrote, has shown that no political, social, administrative, or legal action can be conducted efficiently unless means are found to narrow the gap between those who devote themselves to the study of social reality and those who, in legislative communities and courts, shape the law of the community. . . . Law without a knowledge of society is blind; sociology without a knowledge of law, powerless.

Pekelis wanted to ensure successful cooperation between social scientists and lawyers by having them work in the "same functional unit." In a line that Lewin might have written, Pekelis urged "a close-knit integration of projects. . . . The same type of integration must be achieved between social and legal action and between research and operational activities."[56]

Although Pekelis did not get his dream of social scientists working within the legal department, his ideas resonated with the working attorneys of CLSA. Just as Pekelis predicted they would, CLSA attorneys found social science materials necessary because of the special problems of American anti-Semitism. Maslow and the other attorneys recognized that the use of social science would be necessary for much of the litigation to be successful. A February 1946 memorandum argued "legal skills, social science training and the capacity for social action must be joined if specific tasks are to be defined intelligently and pursued successfully."[57] In 1949, contrasting the sorts of problems confronted by CLSA, which wanted to eliminate anti-Semitism, with those confronted by the NAACP, which wanted to eliminate discrimination against African Americans, a Note in the *Yale Law Journal* noted, "Discrimination against Jews in the United States is usually non-governmental, non-violent, and extremely subtle," and added that "an organization concerned with Jewish problems must employ sociological research to expose the more subtle discrimination to which Jews are subjected."[58]

The "specific tasks" that CLSA set for itself were those that promised "lasting and desirable results." Maslow noted that "CLSA has the choice of swatting mosquitoes or draining the swamps."[59] CLSA tried to select cases that significantly furthered civil rights not just for Jews but for all minority groups. For the AJCongress, as well as for many other groups interested in fighting racial prejudice in the 1940s and 1950s, prejudice against one minority group was seen as prejudice against all minority groups.[60] To further civil rights on the greatest possible scale. CLSA would take advantage of the freedom offered by the "friend of the court" brief, because "progressive organizations have frequently used such briefs to bring to the attention of the court a broad and general viewpoint transcending the individual claims involved in a given litigation."[61]

The flexibility of the *amicus* brief allowed CLSA to fight for civil rights on a much broader scale than if the commission had been limited to cases concerning only Jews. This was by design, because, although CLSA was primarily concerned with the status of Jews, it recognized that Jewish concerns were tied to those of other minority groups. Will Maslow wrote "One of the Chartered purposes of the American Jewish Congress is to defend the rights of Jews in this country. To be successful that defense requires the elimination of discrimination against all racial, religious and ethnic groups."[62] In civil rights battles concerning African Americans, however, CLSA followed the lead of the NAACP. According to Maslow, this was "Principally because defense of Negroes and their rights is not the basic reason for our existence and we do not like to take action contrary to that of the recognized leader in the fight for Negro emancipation."[63]

Pekelis, like Lewin, had set out a blueprint for collaboration between social scientists and lawyers in the fight against discrimination. Both Lewin and Pekelis had argued that not only would merging the law and social science be advantageous to the battle against discrimination, but that it was vital that lawyers and social scientists actually plan and carry out their projects together. What they envisioned went beyond the citation of a few research results in a legal brief toward the actual partnership of social scientists in the creation of that brief. Moreover, social scientists would not merely study the effects of particular legal changes but would be active agents creating those legal changes. Beyond mere "cooperation," Lewin and Pekelis wanted lawyers and social scientists to work in an almost symbiotic relationship. In reality, however, the lawyers and social scientists would have trouble working as closely as Lewin and Pekelis had hoped. While social scientists did try to design research that would be of use in the legal arena, and while lawyers designed arguments that required social-scientific data, the close collaboration Lewin and Pekelis desired never emerged. In the next chapter, I explore the successes of their ideas, as well as the failure of their unique institutional arrangement.

5

Pre-*Brown* Litigation

By the time the campaign to desegregate elementary and secondary education began in 1951, the NAACP-LDEF was a sophisticated user of social science material in court briefs and had at least some experience with presenting social scientists as expert witnesses in the area of segregation. For the School Segregation Cases that culminated in the Supreme Court decision in *Brown*, the NAACP-LDEF relied on a specific network of social scientists, centered primarily in New York and many with ties to the American Jewish Congress. The School Segregation Cases had their origins in the 1930s, when the NAACP decided to begin a legal campaign to eliminate segregated education.

Background of the Litigation Campaign

In 1896, the United States Supreme Court held in *Plessy v. Ferguson* that laws requiring separate railcars for white and African American passengers were a reasonable exercise of state power and did not violate the equal protection provisions of the Thirteenth or Fourteenth Amendments to the Constitution. The Court held that

> we cannot say that a law which authorizes or even requires the separation of the two races in public conveyances is unreasonable or more obnoxious to the Fourteenth Amendment than the acts of Congress requiring separate schools for colored children in the District of Columbia, the constitutionality of which does not seem to have been questioned, or the corresponding acts of state legislatures.[1]

Though the Court was simply affirming a long line of lower court decisions that upheld the constitutionality of segregated facilities, the status of the Supreme Court entrenched the doctrine of separate-but-equal in

American constitutional law.[2] By 1927, Chief Justice William Howard Taft found the state's power to segregate education long since settled as reasonable.[3] This legal doctrine of separate-but-equal was the target of the NAACP campaign against segregated education.

The roots of the NAACP campaign against segregated education began in 1930, when the NAACP hired a young lawyer, Nathan Margold, to draft a legal strategy that could be used to secure adequate educational facilities for African American children. In his report, Margold counseled against a futile campaign of litigation aimed at the equalization of facilities in the separate-but-equal world of the South. Such a campaign would entail a separate lawsuit for each of the thousands of southern school districts in order to prove that facilities in each of those districts were unequal, quickly sapping the NAACP's meager resources. Margold argued, however, if the NAACP "boldly challenge[d] the constitutional validity of segregation if and when accompanied irremediably by discrimination," the organization could eliminate segregated schooling in one stroke. By eliminating segregation completely, African American children would be guaranteed adequate educational facilities. The Margold report was the blueprint for the NAACP's challenge to segregated education, providing a simple but powerful strategy for the elimination of Jim Crow schools.[4]

Margold's legal strategy arrived just as the NAACP's legal staff was undergoing significant changes, the most important of which was the arrival on staff of Charles Hamilton Houston, dean of the Howard University School of Law, who would be responsible for the planning and execution of the litigation envisioned by Margold. A 1922 graduate of Harvard University School of Law, where he was an exceptional student, earning a doctorate in Juridical Science rather than the more conventional J.D., Houston had come to the attention of two of the most famous and demanding of Harvard's faculty, Felix Frankfurter and Roscoe Pound. Frankfurter, one of Harvard's legal realist professors, became Houston's doctoral adviser. He taught Houston that the law was a tool of social engineering and that an attorney needed an understanding of the law's social setting in order to be successful. Pound, one of the founders of the earlier school of "sociological jurisprudence," believed that the law must include an understanding of the social sciences in order to operate effectively.[5] As dean of Howard Law School, Houston brought the realist emphasis on the use of social science to an entire generation of African American attorneys who would lead the fight for civil rights.[6] In part, the

NAACP's reliance on social science during the School Segregation Cases could have been expected, given that much of the legal staff had received its training at Howard, an important center of legal realist thinking and its concomitant reliance on "real-world" factual data.

Beginning in 1933 under Houston, the NAACP focused on suits to eliminate segregated graduate and professional schools, because Houston felt that these schools were the most vulnerable to a direct attack on segregation. Segregated states seldom made a pretense of offering equal opportunities for African Americans who desired a graduate education. Seventeen of the nineteen states that required segregated education had no graduate schools whatsoever for African Americans to attend. Only three states, West Virginia, Missouri, and Maryland, offered out-of-state scholarships that would pay the tuition for African American students who wished to pursue graduate education. Houston thought that this near-absolute absence of opportunities for graduate education would enable him to demonstrate easily the inequality of segregation.[7]

Five years after the Margold report, Houston was joined in his effort by a former pupil, Thurgood Marshall. Marshall was born in Baltimore, which he described as the "most segregated city in the United States." He was raised in the heart of Baltimore's African American middle class and attended Lincoln University in Pennsylvania in 1925. On graduation from Lincoln, he attended the newly accredited Howard Law School. At Howard, Marshall excelled under the strict hand of Houston and, after graduation, moved into what turned out to be a brief private practice. In 1936, Marshall joined the NAACP staff, with an initial commitment from the NAACP to pay his salary for six months. He quickly moved up in the NAACP hierarchy, however. Houston left the NAACP in 1938 to return to private practice, and Marshall took charge of the NAACP legal activities. In 1939, the NAACP, concerned about the tax-exempt status for its legal work, established a separate organization, the NAACP–Legal Defense and Education Fund, Inc. (NAACP-LDEF), and Marshall became the director of this new organization.[8]

Under Marshall's direction, the NAACP won a major Supreme Court victory in 1938 when the Court decided that the state of Missouri had a constitutional obligation to provide a legal education to Lloyd Gaines, a young African American represented by Marshall. The Court left open, however, the question of whether, if Missouri had a separate law school for African Americans, the state could have fulfilled its constitutional requirements.[9]

World War II interrupted the litigation campaign, and further suits were suspended "for the duration." As the war drew to a close in 1945, the NAACP had one Supreme Court victory: *Gaines*. It was a limited victory, however, because the Supreme Court left open the possibility that separate graduate education for African Americans would be constitutionally permissible. Southern states quickly went about setting up separate graduate programs for African Americans. After the war, the task of the NAACP would be to prove that these hastily assembled programs could not possibly be equal to the long-established programs that existed for white students, a task the NAACP assumed would be relatively simple. In fact, proving any two schools unequal was extraordinarily difficult for the NAACP.[10] It was for this task that the NAACP turned to social science— as one way in which to prove that separate systems of education would be unequal and, hence, discriminatory.

That the NAACP-LDEF would turn to social science shows the influence of the legal realism that Houston brought to Howard Law School. For the legal realists, in order for courts to make good law, they had to be aware of the social consequences of their rulings, even in a rarefied field such as constitutional law. The NAACP-LDEF used social-scientific data to demonstrate the "reality" of school segregation and argued that the court must be aware of these social realities to make good constitutional law.[11] Immediately after World War II, the NAACP-LDEF saw an opportunity to put their legal realist training to the test. The NAACP-LDEF and the AJCongress both joined a California segregation case that was being appealed to the Federal Ninth Circuit Court of Appeals. The California case arose independently of either organization, so each filed an *amicus* brief as a friend of the court. This case would serve as the proving ground for the use of social-scientific data in segregation cases.

Westminster v. Mendez

Segregation of Mexican American schoolchildren had been a common practice in California since the 1920s, when immigration made Mexicans the state's largest minority. Although not sanctioned by California law, the white, or "Anglo," populations of many communities insisted that the local school boards create separate schools for Mexican American children, ostensibly because of language problems.

On March 2, 1945, five Mexican American parents filed a suit in federal district court to enjoin the segregation of their children on the grounds that such segregation constituted a violation of Fifth and Fourteenth Amendment equal protection guarantees. The school districts argued that such segregation was not based on race but served sound educational purposes involving bilingual education. Moreover, they argued that control of the schools was a local matter and hence outside the jurisdiction of the federal courts. Finally, the districts claimed that the separate facilities were in any case equal and therefore constitutional under the separate-but-equal doctrine of *Plessy v. Ferguson*, the 1896 U.S. Supreme Court case that had entrenched segregated facilities in constitutional law.

The federal district court's ruling came nearly a year later. Because California had no segregation statues, the court ruled that there was indeed a violation of equal protection clauses of the U.S. Constitution. The court found that, in the absence of such segregation statutes, the separate-but-equal doctrine did not apply. Finally, it found no sound educational reason for the segregation of Spanish-speaking pupils; in fact, the district court argued that assimilation would proceed more rapidly in integrated schools. The school district quickly appealed the case to the Ninth Circuit Court of Appeals.[12] During this appeal, the case came to the attention of the NAACP-LDEF and the AJCongress.

The NAACP-LDEF Westminster *Brief*

The NAACP-LDEF brief was prepared by Robert L. Carter, Thurgood Marshall's second in command in the organization. A graduate of Columbia Law School, Carter had joined the staff of the NAACP-LDEF in 1944, when he was released from active duty from the U.S. Air Corps. He soon became responsible for the day-to-day running of the office during Marshall's frequent absences. Carter also quickly gained a reputation for rather abstract theorizing about law and took the freedom that Marshall gave to his staff to develop new strategies to address old problems.[13] The California case *Westminster v. Mendez* is a good example of Carter's penchant for creative legal thought.

The brief that Carter prepared for the *Westminster* case made three arguments, two of which presented straightforward legal points. First, he argued that classifications on the basis of race and color were unconstitutional. Carter pointed to a series of Supreme Court cases that held racial classifications suspect and argued that these, not *Plessy*, should control in this case. Second, Carter argued that no U.S. Supreme Court decisions actually upheld racial segregation in education, and the distinguished *Plessy* as a transportation case, not an education case. Both of these arguments were broad attacks on *Plessy*, but they were also traditional constitutional arguments that did not need social science or any other sort of extralegal materials to be effective.

The third argument was not based on previous court cases or on a rule of law but on sociological and psychological materials Carter had assembled. He titled the argument "The requirements of due process and the Equal Protection of the laws under the Fourteenth Amendment cannot be achieved under a system of segregation."[14] Carter argued that, to be a constitutional exercise of state power under the *Plessy* doctrine, equal facilities must be provided. But, Carter claimed, this in itself proved that the very act of separation necessitated inequality. In this way, Carter hoped to give the court a way to move against segregation without directly confronting the Supreme Court precedent.

Carter employed three different lines of reasoning to prove his argument that inequality was a necessary consequence of segregation. First, racial segregation was an instrument of public policy that ensured African Americans remained second-class citizens. True equality in facilities was impossible to achieve, because communities could not afford to maintain two school systems that were truly equal—a position the NAACP had consistently taken since the Margold report in 1931. Carter argued further that the existence of a few isolated equal facilities was irrelevant to the more general point that segregation resulted in a system of discrimination to enforce inequality. He presented sociological data assembled by Ambrose Caliver, the first African American to be employed by the U.S. Office of Education. Caliver was appointed a "specialist in Negro education" in 1930. His office produced bibliographies of African American education, bulletins on various aspects of African American education, and surveys of the state of African American education.[15]

In the *Westminster* brief, Carter used Caliver's data from the seventeen states and the District of Columbia that practiced racial segregation to argue that the "best single index to the quality of education" was expenditures, and he pointed out that general expenditures per white pupil in nine southern states were "almost 212% greater than the average expense per Negro pupil."[16] The result of this inequality in expenditures was the deprivation of educational advancement that African Americans needed to function as effective citizens. Carter also used Caliver's data to point out that states practicing segregation "in 1939–1940 provided one teacher for every 28.6 white pupils, but one teacher for every 36.1 Negroes. And the average salary for a white teacher was $1,046 a year, while the average Negro teacher's salary was only $601."[17] Carter argued:

> The result of such educational inequities brought about as a consequence of the policy of segregation has been to deprive the individual Negro citizen of the skills necessary to a civilized existence, the Negro community of the leadership and professional services it so urgently needs, and the nation as a whole of the full potential embodied in the intellectual and physical resources of its Negro citizens.

For example, Carter drew on U.S. government statistics during World War II, "when the nation was crying for manpower," to demonstrate that African Americans were rejected from military service for educational deficiency almost four times as often as white draftees. He maintained that such educational deficiencies proved the discriminatory effects of segregation.[18]

Carter amassed all this statistical evidence in an attempt to demonstrate the existence of a pattern of discrimination wherever segregation was permitted. In this way, he attempted to sidestep the issue of whether a *particular* facility was equal in a *particular* case. Such equality of facilities was irrelevant to the fact that segregation gave the *power* to discriminate. Carter argued, "Since all available experience, all existing data prove conclusively that where the power is granted it is uniformly used for the purpose of discrimination, it is important that such power not be granted freely."[19] Carter's second line of reasoning paralleled arguments the NAACP–LDEF made in the restrictive covenant cases that were being litigated at the same time as *Westminster*. In the restrictive covenant cases, the NAACP-LDEF was convinced that its attack "must be supported by a full sociological presentation" of the "social ills caused by restrictive covenants."[20] Between 1945 and 1947, the NAACP-LDEF held a series of planning meetings with lawyers and sociologists from the American Race Relations Council of the University of Chicago to build an argument that demonstrated the harms of restricting African Americans from certain neighborhoods.[21]

In the *Westminster* brief, Carter took the argument that the NAACP-LDEF was using in the restrictive covenant cases and presented it to the Ninth Circuit Court of Appeals as an argument against segregated education. Carter argued that, even granting for the moment that separate-but-equal schools were possible, such equal facilities would not ameliorate "the most important inequalities of all," namely, "the effect of such a policy on the attitudes of those whom it most directly affects, the minority citizen, be he Negro, Mexican, Latin American, or Japanese." Segregation created "a feeling of 'second-class citizenship' which expresses itself in criminality and rebellion against constituted authority."[22] Carter's argument here was a variation on the first: segregation was poor public policy because it caused crime and civil unrest through the promotion of antisocial attitudes in minority individuals. Racial segregation "promotes racial strife by teaching the children of both the dominant and minority groups to regard each other as something different and apart."[23] Carter argued that if citizens of the nation were to be tolerant of each other, it was vital that these things be taught by example in the schoolroom.

To support this argument, Carter cited the most famous sociological work of his generation: Gunnar Myrdal's massive project in race relations, *An American Dilemma*. The only other two works he cited were Richard Sterner's *The Negro's Share* and Charles Johnson's *Patterns of Negro Segregation*, both of which were outgrowths of Myrdal's project. Carter's reliance on these works indicates a problem faced by the civil rights attorney interested in using social science evidence in litigation. No work cited by Carter addressed segregated education as the cause of any social problem; rather, the works addressed a *system* of segregation. In fact, Myrdal went as far as to comment that "no studies have been made which quantify the extent of social segregation in any of its different forms or local variations."[24] The two chapters of Myrdal's Swedish associate Richard Sterner cited by Carter were on urban and rural housing conditions and did not mention segregated education, nor any deleterious effects of segregation on the citizenship of African Americans.[25]

The problem of isolating segregated education as a variable affecting African Americans is highlighted by examining the third work relied on by Carter for his argument, Charles S. Johnson's *Patterns of Negro Segregation*. Johnson had published a number of works on race relations, including work he undertook for the American Council on Education (examined in chapter 2). *Patterns of Negro Segregation* was based on a series of studies into the rural and urban South, the border-state cities of Baltimore and Indianapolis, and the cities in the urban North—Chicago and New York. Johnson and his staff based their results on observation of everyday life in these areas and extensive interviewing.

The section Carter referred to was a chapter on "Personality and the Racial Role." Johnson argued there that African Americans responded to segregation in four broad patterns: "*acceptance, avoidance, direct hostility, and aggression.*" Which behavior pattern an individual fell into depended on "(a) the regional and cultural setting, (b) the social stratification of the Negro population, (c) the situation factors involved in a given response, and (d) the basic personality type of the Negro involved in a given racial situation."[26] The most common response to discrimination, Johnson found, was avoidance. Johnson claimed that "segregated institutions and discriminatory treatment have some discernible influence on the personality development of Negroes." African Americans, however, were "aware of the damaging effects on personality and shield themselves as far as possible against situations involving segregation and discrimination. Negro parents are particular in many instances to have their children avoid situations offering any opportunity for sensing the inequalities of the racial system."[27]

While Johnson's cited work did support Carter's claim that segregation could promote unhealthy societal attitudes, it also demonstrated how the broad strokes being painted by social science fit uncomfortably into the detailed world of the law. Carter's brief addressed only segregated education—a sociological variable that Johnson did not attempt to isolate for any special treatment. Indeed, Johnson discussed segregated education for only seven pages, the majority of those recounting the *Gaines* decision and the NAACP's other legal challenges to segregated education.[28] Moreover, Johnson did not isolate segregation *as required by law* as the contributing factor in the personality development of African Americans. Finally, Johnson did not pose an argument for the elimination of segregated education, claiming, "The most desirable solution would be equalization with federal aid."[29]

If the *Westminster* brief demonstrated the difficulties posed by social science for the NAACP-LDEF, it also showed the variety of uses the NAACP-LDEF had for social science material. The "psychological damage" argument was developed in only a few paragraphs; the vast bulk of the material was Caliver's sociological data, used to prove inequality in facilities. The inequality of facilities would become the focus of the NAACP-LDEF's use of social science in the years after the *Westminster* case.

Carter's argument for *Westminster* was an important innovation in the use of social science material in the legal fight against segregation. An even more radical step was the argument developed in the brief filed by CLSA for the AJCongress.

The CLSA *Westminster* Brief

Although not a member of the bar, Alexander Pekelis wrote the CLSA brief for the *Westminster* case, and it was submitted over the signatures of Will Maslow and Pauli Murray. It also bore the name of Carey McWilliams, as local counsel.[30]

Carey McWilliams (1905–1980) was a Los Angeles attorney and journalist. In 1939, Governor Culbert Olson appointed him head of the state Division of Immigration and Housing, where he worked for the welfare of California's alien immigrants. McWilliams held this position until 1943, when his longtime political opponent, newly elected governor Earl Warren, fired him.[31] As a journalist, McWilliams had been writing on race prejudice for a number a years, publishing several books on the subject of California's racial minorities.[32] In 1946, the year of *Westminster*, McWilliams was busy with a new book on anti-Semitism, which is one reason he could serve as the local contact in California for the CLSA.[33] Another reason was a 1945 article he wrote for the Marxist journal *Science and Society*, in which he suggested that "both law and the social sciences seem to share a number of assumptions as to the nature and origin of racial discrimination. I want to call attention to certain of these assumptions for the purpose of stimulating active collaboration between lawyers and social scientists in this field."[34]

McWilliams argued that both law and social sciences had been operating under the Sumnerian dictum that the law was powerless to change the mores of society. He called attention to the law's power to change the behaviors of individuals in society and to the power of the law to inculcate values in society. This was precisely the argument put forth by both CCI and CLSA in their programmatic statements. Clearly, the CLSA had found a kindred spirit in Carey McWilliams.

In his introduction to the CLSA brief, Pekelis noted that CLSA firmly agreed with the central point the NAACP had made in their *amicus* brief: "If facilities were really duplicated, financial ruin of the local bodies of the states would ensue. If financial disaster is to be avoided, the facilities granted to minorities are bound to be physically inferior." So as not to duplicate the argument made by the NAACP in the case, however, rather than attempting to show that the facilities provided to the minority students were inferior, Pekelis predicated all his arguments on the assumption that facilities were "identical." To prove that even identical facilities were inherently unequal, Pekelis relied heavily on sociological and psychological data.[35]

As all attorneys arguing against segregation were obliged to do, Pekelis had to deal with the *Plessy* precedent, the 1896 case that had declared separate-but-equal facilities to be constitutional.[36] Pekelis's strategy was to accept the *legal* doctrine propounded in *Plessy*, that separate-but-equal facilities were, in fact, constitutional. Pekelis analyzed the findings of the 1896 case, however, as firmly anchored in "factual" rather than "legal" grounds. He noted that the *Plessy* case found segregated railroad cars constitutional because "it proceeded on the factual and sociological assumption that such segregation did *'not necessarily imply the inferiority of either race to the other.'*"[37] Pekelis then argued that the legal "fiction" of *Plessy*, that segregation does not connote inferiority of one race to another, was belied by nearly all social-scientific knowledge available. Pekelis asked starkly:

> Will any court today, in the light of the sociological and psychological findings made in the last fifty years, prove so lacking in candor and so blind to realities as to subscribe to the fiction of benevolent segregation on which *Plessy v. Ferguson* relies? That is the issue. Not the legal doctrine of *Plessy v. Ferguson* is in question but the factual fallacy on which it rests.[38]

To prove his point that *Plessy* was grounded in a "factual fallacy," Pekelis argued:

> Whenever a group, considered "inferior" by the prevailing standards of a community, is segregated by official action from the socially dominant group, the very fact of official segregation, whether or not "equal" physical facilities are being furnished to both groups, is a humiliating and discriminatory denial of equality to the group considered "inferior" and a violation of the Constitution of the United States and of treaties duly entered into under its authority.[39]

Pekelis first noted that all parties agreed that separate facilities had to be equal if they were to pass the constitutional test of *Plessy*. Second, he maintained that "equality" was defined not by "mere identity of physical facilities" but on "identity of substantial similarity of their *values*." Pekelis then defined "values" by their "social significance and psychological context, or in short, on the community judgment attached to them." For example, Pekelis maintained that a probate court would not hold two physically identical houses as equal if one were in a slum and the other in a fashionable neighborhood.[40]

Having established that the law recognized the reality of what he called "social inequality," Pekelis then showed how the segregation of a group previously deemed socially inferior in and of itself constituted a legal inequality. The act of segregation, according to Pekelis, was tantamount to an official declaration of inferiority of the segregated group. Once "legal inferiority" of segregation is adopted, it reinforces and intensifies the "social inequality," leading to a vicious circle of discrimination and prejudice.

Such problems were especially acute in segregated education, according to Pekelis: "The official imposition of a segregated pattern based on notions of inferiority and superiority produces its deepest and most lasting social and psychological evil results when applied to children." He went on to argue:

> Since segregation reinforces group isolation and social distance it helps to create conditions in which unhealthy racial attitudes may flourish. By giving official sanction to group separation based upon the assumption in inferiority it helps to perpetuate racial prejudice and contributes to the degradation and humiliation of the minority child. The crippling psychological effects of such segregation are in essence a denial of equality of treatment. In this sense segregation is burdensome and oppressive and comes within the constitutional prohibition.[41]

Pekelis contended that the internal psychology of schoolchildren should be a constitutional issue, regardless of the effect on the larger society. This is the "damage" argument that would underpin the *Brown* decision eight years later. Pekelis supported the argument with a wide variety of social science materials on segregation and discrimination.

On April 14, 1947, the Ninth Circuit Court of Appeals ruled unanimously that the segregation of Mexican American schoolchildren in California schools violated the Fourteenth Amendment. The basis of the opinion was not the far-reaching legal case made by the CLSA or the NAACP-LDEF but a narrow legal ground: segregation was unconstitutional because California law had no provisions for the segregation of Mexican American schoolchildren. Governor Earl Warren made any further litigation a moot point when, on June 14, 1947, he signed a repeal of

California's education segregation statutes, which ended *de jure* segregation in the state.[42]

This case showed that the existing social science literature was not adequate to support Pekelis's argument. With a dearth of psychological studies specifically focusing on segregated education, Pekelis had relied on studies of general childhood development and general studies of segregation. Except for an article by Howard Hale Long, these studies did not directly address segregated education.[43] Neither did the social science literature isolate segregation as required by law as a separate variable from segregation that arose by custom. Finally, there was no social science that could distinguish the psychological effects of segregation in general from the psychological effects of being segregated to inferior facilities. CCI researchers could have begun research projects designed to fill these holes in the social science literature. These projects, however, would have been tremendously difficult to design, and CLSA might have had to wait months or years before the results would have been reported. Nonetheless, the case had important ramifications for the battle against segregation.

The Social Science Survey

The *Westminster* case was too narrowly decided to be of much use to the NAACP-LDEF in their legal campaign against segregation in graduate education. After all, southern states, unlike California, had official policies authorizing segregation of African Americans. The Ninth District Court of Appeals rejected the broad arguments about segregation being discrimination per se. In a press release, Robert Carter noted that while the *Westminster* "case brings the American courts closer to a decision on the whole question of segregation," unfortunately "the Circuit Court in affirming the decision did not go as far as requested in the brief of the NAACP."[44]

While the legal ramifications of the *Westminster* case were rather narrow, it did have repercussions for the NAACP-LDEF's use of social science materials in future litigation. During the litigation, the NAACP-LDEF sent a copy of their brief to William Hastie, who, along with Houston, was one of the founders of the campaign against segregated education. Hastie wrote to Marshall, telling him to develop the social science portion of the argument "with as little delay as possible" and that "we will be able to sustain it only when we make an exhaustive presentation." Hastie suggested that the LDEF assemble and organize "practically the entire body of available material." To emphasize his point in the strongest possible manner, Hastie urged that the task was "important enough for the Association to spend some money on it."[45]

Marshall agreed with Hastie that assembling more social science materials was necessary to make further inroads against *Plessy*. In December 1946, Marshall wrote, "We are now working on the problem of having a complete study made of the evil of segregation to demonstrate that there is no such thing as 'separate but equal' in any governmental agency. . . . When this is completed, it might then be possible to make an all-out attack." He admitted, however, that "I do not know how long it will take to complete this study or whether we can raise sufficient funds to do it."[46]

Annette H. Peyser, a young staffer with a sociology degree from New York University, was responsible for most of the work done on the NAACP-LDEF study. Peyser came to the NAACP after political scientist Harold Lasswell recommended her as a propaganda analyst. In 1945, soon after arriving at the NAACP, she transferred to the LDEF to work on assembling sociological materials relating to the LDEF campaign against restrictive covenants in housing.[47] After *Westminster*, she expanded her efforts in an attempt to give Marshall the "complete study" he wanted.

Throughout 1947, Peyser assembled "all possible data" from "such accredited sources as government and scientific publications." At the end of the year, however, the LDEF discontinued the operation due to lack of funds.[48] In the end, the NAACP-LDEF effort to assemble a "complete study" of the effects of segregation would be limited to assembling existing materials that demonstrated that segregated facilities were always unequal in terms of facilities and expenditures. It did not undertake any new studies or seek to uncover materials proving psychological damage to minority group children.

The NAACP-LDEF effort was limited to a demonstration that segregation was always accompanied by inequality of facilities because they wanted to argue that segregation led to a broad pattern of physical inequality. The NAACP-LDEF simply thought it too soon to argue—as Pekelis had in *Westminster*—that equality in physical facilities was irrelevant to their case. Even Robert Carter, the most outspoken advocate for the use of social science, believed that the argument that "segregation per se amounts to discrimination . . . will be most difficult to prove to the majority of American courts, including the United States Supreme

Court."[49] No such reservations seemed to exist at the American Jewish Congress, and the *Westminster* case had very different ramifications for that organization.

In their *Westminster* brief, CLSA's argument was predicated on the assumption that segregated facilities were physically identical; hence, it made no sense in the AJCongress to gather social science materials demonstrating that segregated facilities were unequal. CLSA's position was that, even given equal facilities, segregation was psychologically harmful, especially to children. But, as we have seen, there was a dearth of psychological studies to prove the point. Pekelis had relied on studies of general childhood development and general studies of segregation and, except for Long's exploratory piece, did not directly address segregated education. Neither did the social science literature isolate segregation as required by law as a separate variable from segregation that arose by custom. Finally, there was no social science that could distinguish the psychological effects of segregation in general from the psychological effects of being segregated to inferior facilities. Strictly speaking, it seemed that each of these issues would have to be addressed to make social science directly relevant to the legal issues presented in desegregation litigation.

To make a more authoritative social science pronouncement on the issue, CLSA turned to CCI's social scientists. Isidor Chein, through consultation with CLSA, decided to poll a wide range of social scientists on the issue of psychological damage of segregation.[50] The results of this survey, designed explicitly for use in legal proceedings, would become one of the most cited articles of social science in subsequent briefs by CLSA and by the NAACP in cases against segregation.

The survey was mailed to 849 social scientists in May 1947. Respondents were asked if they agreed that "enforced segregation has detrimental psychological effects on members of racial and religious groups which are segregated, even if equal facilities were provided." A parallel series of questions asked about psychological effects on "groups which enforce the segregation." The respondents were also asked to state the basis of their opinions. They could choose four options: "My own research findings. Research findings of other social scientists. My own professional experience. Professional experiences of other social scientists which have been made available to me." The cover letter was explicit on the motivations for the research, stating in part: "For the purpose of providing legislative bodies, courts and the general public with a consensus of responsible scientific opinion, we are asking social scientists to indicate their position in this issue."[51]

Chein presented the results at the 1948 Eastern Psychological Association meeting. He reported that 90 percent of the respondents believed segregation to be psychologically damaging to the segregated group, and 83 percent believed segregation also damaged the group enforcing the segregating. All but 10 percent of the respondents checked one of the four alternatives for the basis of their opinion. "All in all, then," Chein concluded, "we may not only say that there is widespread agreement among social scientists that enforced segregation is psychologically detrimental despite equal facilities, but we may add that the majority of these social scientists believe that there is a factual basis for such agreement."[52]

Chein noted that there were problems with the existing research regarding the questions he posed in his survey. "Since equal facilities are in fact not provided," he explained, "the proposition that enforced segregation does have detrimental psychological effects, even under conditions of equal facilities, seems impossible to prove." Indeed, Chein found "virtually nothing in the published literature that is explicitly devoted to this problem." That did not mean, however, that his respondents had no basis whatsoever for their opinions, for there was a large literature on segregation "from which one may cull a great deal of information pertinent to [the problem]."[53] Chein called for social scientists to turn their attention to research designed to prove psychological damage even given equal facilities.

Chein's survey was a curious piece of social-scientific research. As a document for a legal trial, however, it would be tremendously useful. Attorneys fighting segregation could now make part of the legal record the fact that the vast majority of social scientists found segregation to be psychologically damaging. That no study specifically isolated *de jure* segregated education with equal facilities would not be immediately relevant in a court of law. An expert witness was often called to provide an opinion rather than give the reasons for holding the opinion. Hence, the opinion of social scientists, as discovered in the social science survey, would be relevant. How they came to their opinions would not be that important for the lawyers.[54]

The results of Chein's survey were published in May 1948. With statistician Max Deutscher, Chein explained that the survey was inspired by the recent Ninth Circuit Court of Appeals decision in *Westminster.* "According to the Court," they announced, "the basic evidence for this decision consisted of studies in race relations made by anthropologists, psychologists, and sociologists, demonstrating that legal segregation does in reality imply the inferiority of one 'race' to the other and implements such status." The characterization of the Ninth Circuit Court decision as primarily based on social science material was, in fact, completely inaccurate. As noted earlier, the *Westminster* decision was decided on a relatively narrow point of law. Nevertheless, Deutscher and Chein announced that the present study was designed for use in the legal arena. They continued:

> Final decision on the legality of enforced segregation, regardless of equal facilities, has not yet been rendered by the Supreme Court. Here too, social science may be a significant if not crucial factor. For social scientists interested in "social engineering" this represents a concrete opportunity to apply the relevant findings of social science data.[55]

More than any other single work, the Deutscher and Chein survey represented a confluence of interests between social scientists and attorneys. For civil rights attorneys, the social science survey represented a terse, nontechnical presentation of social science opinion that could add authority to legal briefs. For social scientists, the survey represented an opportunity for research to be meaningfully translated into legal action. The social science survey was particularly well timed to be used in the battle against legalized segregation. By 1948, CCI social scientists were beginning to attract the attention of the NAACP-LDEF just as it was attacking segregated graduate education in earnest.

Sweatt v. Painter

Beginning in 1946, the NAACP-LDEF picked up where they had left off in their attack on segregated graduate education. The prewar *Gaines* decision of 1938 was an important victory but had left open the possibility of the creation of separate graduate schools for African Americans. The NAACP-LDEF's postwar task was to show that this was a constitutionally impermissible option for the state to pursue: that a separate school could never be an equal school. One way to do so was to rely on social-scientific data.

In a 1947 case to desegregate the University of Texas Law School, *Sweatt v. Painter*, the NAACP-LDEF sought social science data and social scientists as expert witnesses. The NAACP-LDEF turned to CLSA for the names of likely social scientists who could testify at the *Sweatt* trial. Will Maslow sent a copy of the social science survey to Thurgood Marshall, even though it had not yet been published, and asked if "it can be used in any form in the University of Texas suit." The survey would be of some use, but what the NAACP really needed was a prominent social scientist willing to testify to the evils of segregation. If possible, the social scientist should be at a southern institution, minimizing the appearance of northern hostility toward the South. Unfortunately, Will Maslow had to inform Marshall, "CCI believes there are no nationally known psychologists in the South."[56]

The NAACP did have University of Chicago anthropologist Robert Redfield testify in Texas. Robert Redfield was a rare resource for the NAACP. The son of a prominent Chicago attorney, Redfield entered the University of Chicago Law School, receiving his J.D. in 1921. After a brief practice, he found himself dissatisfied with the law and returned to the University of Chicago, receiving his Ph.D. in anthropology in 1928. His conversion from the law to social science may have been encouraged by his wife, Margaret Lucy Park, the daughter of University of Chicago sociologist Robert Park. For whatever reason, Redfield was much happier as an anthropologist than as a lawyer and published several influential books on Latin American folk culture.[57]

If his almost unique credentials of degrees in both law and anthropology had not been enough to bring Redfield to the attention of the NAACP, then his concern for racial justice would have been. During World War II, Redfield proclaimed that African Americans were the victims of a society that treated them as "half-citizen[s]." The problems of African Americans, Redfield declared, were in the "mythology of the modern man" that proclaimed the natural inferiority of the African American race. Redfield argued that this was nonsense:

> A child of one skin color starts even with a child of any other skin color, if you let him. We don't let him, and we entertain a false biology which seems to justify us. I say again that race is of consequence because of what men think and feel about it and not because of anything that race is of itself.[58]

Between 1947 and 1950, Redfield served as the director of the American Council on Race Relations (ACRR). ACRR was founded in 1944 to "bring about full democracy in race relations through the advancement of the knowledge concerning race relations."[59] The NAACP had been working extensively with two ACRR sociologists, Robert Weaver and

Louis Wirth, on amassing sociological data on the effects of racially restrictive covenants on housing.[60] It is undoubtedly through the work on racially restrictive covenants that Redfield came to the attention of the NAACP. While Redfield had no formal connection to CCI, he was aware of their research on integrated sales counters and interracial housing.[61]

Redfield's testimony in *Sweatt v. Painter* demonstrates how the social-scientific ideas that were at the heart of CCI's research program could be used in a court of law to argue against segregation. Redfield testified that segregation was inimical to "public security and general welfare." Drawing on his experiences at the desegregated University of Chicago, he argued that "segregation policy, and the stigma which segregation attaches to the segregated increases prejudice, mutual suspicion between Negroes and Whites and contributes to the divisiveness and disorder of the national community, contributing to crime and violence." The final point that Redfield addressed was that desegregation could be expected to proceed smoothly—that the "abolition of segregation in education, is likely to be accomplished with beneficial results to public order and the general welfare."[62]

When cross-examining Redfield, Attorney General Price Daniel turned to an issue that would prove to be one of the dominant themes of the litigation concerning educational segregation: whether or not desegregation could be "imposed" on a community that did not desire it. In other words, could legal change precede attitude change in race relations? Daniel pressed Redfield to admit that it was "impossible to force the abolition of segregation upon a community that has had it for a long number of years." Redfield refused to admit the point, arguing, "Segregation in itself is a matter of law, and that law can be changed at once." Daniel refused to give up and questioned Redfield about the speed of attitude change within the community—wasn't it true that this change could not be forced on a community? Redfield then admitted that, depending on circumstances, the attitudes of the community could resist desegregation, but he emphasized that "in every community there is some segregation that can be changed at once, and the area of higher education is the most favorable for making the change."[63]

The arguments that Redfield made in Texas underscore the importance of the research undertaken by CCI. The idea that segregation increases racial tension, and that integration would decrease it, was at the heart of CCI's research into the contact hypothesis. Moreover, the empirical studies that CCI undertook would add to the credibility of witnesses in *Brown*, who would be arguing, as Redfield did in the Texas case, that segregation could be imposed on an unwilling populace.[64]

A month after Redfield's testimony, the court ruled against Heman Sweatt and the NAACP-LDEF.[65] The NAACP-LDEF immediately began the appeal process that would lead the case to the Supreme Court. In the meantime, another opportunity was brewing in which social science data would play a role, in a case against the University of Oklahoma School of Law.

Sipuel v. Oklahoma State Regents

The University of Oklahoma case actually started before the *Sweatt* case. Ada Lois Sipuel attempted to enter the University of Oklahoma School of Law in 1945 and was denied on the basis of race. She enlisted the help of the NAACP-LDEF and sued for entry in April 1946. A series of legal hearings ensued, and the case was finally heard by the U.S. Supreme Court during the first week of January 1948. A mere four days later, the Supreme Court decided in favor of Sipuel and proclaimed that "petitioner is entitled to secure legal education afforded by a state institution." The Supreme Court's decision, however, relied on the *Gaines* rationale, which allowed for the establishment of a separate law school for African Americans. On January 19, 1948, the State Regents for Higher Education decided that, rather than admit Sipuel to Oklahoma's law school, they would create a separate law school just for her. The NAACP-LDEF quickly brought the case back before the U.S. Supreme Court, arguing that Oklahoma was contravening the Court's direct order. The Court, however, ordered a new trial to determine if the new law school was, in fact, equal to the established University of Oklahoma law school.[66] The new trial eventually took place in May 1948.

Just as they had a few months earlier in the *Sweatt* case, the NAACP-LDEF found themselves in a position of proving that a law school created quite literally overnight could not be equal to a long-established law school of some repute. The NAACP-LDEF chose a strategy quite similar to that in the Texas case. Law school deans would be put on the stand to testify that the impromptu school could not possibly have the equal facilities that the University of Oklahoma school possessed. Additionally, to push the desegregation issue further, the NAACP-LDEF would attempt to incorporate Pekelis's *Westminster* argument that "separate but equal must be overruled because of bad effects on both Negro and white children psychologically and sociologically."[67]

To do this, Marshall decided to use psychologists as expert witnesses to testify to the psychological damage inflicted by segregation on minority and majority group students. There was a problem, however, in choosing this strategy. Legally speaking, and unlike the *Sweatt* case, the NAACP-LDEF's original challenge to Oklahoma's segregated law school had not directly challenged the separate-but-equal doctrine. In ordering the new trial, the U.S. Supreme Court had noted that the case as submitted did not demand an end to segregation but merely that the state of Oklahoma establish an educational opportunity for Ada Sipuel that was equal to the one it provided for its white citizens. Hence, the *Sipuel* trial would be strictly on the merits of the impromptu law school—was it equal to the established school? The effects of segregation generally and the constitutionality of segregation were not at issue. Hence, the NAACP-LDEF's arguments on segregation would likely be ruled irrelevant to the proceedings.

Marshall was well aware of this problem. In April 1948, he wrote to the dean of the University of Pennsylvania Law School (who was serving as a witness at the trial) that he planned to put on the stand "two anthropologists" and "one or two witnesses on the question of the effect of segregation on both the segregated group and the majority group." These witnesses, Marshall noted, would "have to get over the hurdle of objection by the Attorney General and there is a good possibility that the objection will be sustained." Marshall would attempt to get portions of the testimony made part of the record in a written form, he explained, so that it could be examined on appeal.[68]

The final list of social-scientific witnesses consisted of Robert Redfield and Robert C. Weaver of the ACRR in Chicago; Charles H. Thompson of Howard University, also editor of the *Journal of Negro Education*; and Stuart W. Cook, director of the CCI of the American Jewish Congress.[69] The first day of the trial, May 24, 1948, Marshall's fears about the expert testimony were realized. The press release written by the NAACP's local correspondent recounted the events as follows:

> Issues were joined in grim earnest on the question of segregation when in the afternoon Miss Sipuel's attorneys called to the witness stand Dr. Charles H. Thompson, the purpose of whose testimony was announced as being an attempt to show the wide discrepancy offered Negroes as against whites under Oklahoma's segregated higher education system. The state's objection to the testimony was sustained by the court, whereupon Dr.

Thompson's testimony was read into the record as narrative testimony. The testimony of Dr. Robert C. Weaver, attempting to show the economic and social consequences of segregation, met a like fate, as did the testimony of Dr. Erwin E. Cooke [*sic*], eminent psychologist, who sought to show the psychological effects of segregation on the segregated.[70]

The next day, Redfield's testimony was similarly disallowed by the court. The legal issues were formed in such a way in the *Sipuel* trial as to render the social-scientific testimony irrelevant to the proceedings. If the *Sweatt* case had demonstrated the usefulness of social-scientific witnesses to the NAACP-LDEF, the *Sipuel* trial had shown them that they needed to frame the legal questions in a manner that allowed the testimony to be heard. Because segregation itself was not on trial in *Sipuel*, what social science had to say about its harms was irrelevant to the case.

For their part, the social scientists seemed undaunted by the court's refusal to hear their testimony. Robert Redfield, who had been to two NAACP-LDEF trials in the past year, merely confided to Thurgood Marshall that he thought he "could learn to be a pretty good carpetbagger."[71] Stuart Cook of CCI was similarly pleased with his trip. As Cook recounted to AJCongress executive director David Petegorsky, he was not permitted to testify but was allowed to submit a brief written statement: "Under these circumstances I offered as my testimony the Deutscher-Chein paper THE PSYCHOLOGICAL EFFECTS OF ENFORCED SEGREGATION: A SURVEY OF SOCIAL SCIENCE OPINION." According to Cook, the NAACP-LDEF was "very enthusiastic about the potential effect of our survey . . . on the psychological effects of segregation."[72]

The trial judge ruled against Ada Sipuel, denying her entrance into the University of Oklahoma Law School. A further appeal of her case was overtaken by events at the university. On January 28, 1948, six more African Americans applied to various graduate programs at Oklahoma. When they were denied entrance, the NAACP-LDEF took up their case, centering the attention on the application of George W. McClaurin, a sixty-eight-year-old man who wanted to get a Ph.D. in education. With this case, the regents of Oklahoma took a different approach. Rather than attempt to create a graduate program in education out of whole cloth, they admitted McLaurin to Oklahoma on a "segregated" basis. McLaurin would sit in an anteroom, adjacent to the main classroom. He had a table reserved only for him at the library. He was to eat his lunch in the school cafeteria by himself, when it was not open to other students.

The NAACP-LDEF took up McLaurin's case and appealed it to a special three-judge panel of the federal district court. After hearing McLaurin's testimony, the presiding judge, Alfred P. Murrah, dismissed all the assembled witnesses. The case was decided on the basis of the lawyer's briefs alone. On November 22, 1948, the federal district court ruled in favor of the state and against McLaurin.[73]

Graduate School Cases on Appeal

The trial portions of *Sipuel, Sweatt,* and *McLaurin* were all in 1948. The trials demonstrate that the NAACP-LDEF was beginning to show considerable interest in the use of social science data and conclusions in the legal arena. A good summary of the NAACP's position on social science was provided the same year by Annette Peyser. The sole social scientist on the NAACP staff, Peyser began a "public relations attempt at compensating for the fact that the NAACP does not have a counterpart to the Commission on Law and Social Action, such as CCI."[74]

The announced purpose of her presented paper was an attempt to "effect a better relationship between the legal expert and the social scientist." Peyser recounted the use of social-scientific data and expert witnesses in *Westminster,* the graduate school cases, and other cases. She noted that the NAACP had emphasized sociological data to prove that segregation leads to inequalities in facilities because there simply were no studies regarding psychological damage. The NAACP had, "in the absence of specific scientific studies relating to the psychological effects of segregation, emphasized the factual aspects of segregation." Peyser looked to the AJCongress to bridge this gap. While the NAACP had neither the funds nor the personnel to undertake original research, the same was not true of the AJCongress, with their two divisions of social scientists and lawyers: "The CCI works independently of but in cooperation with the Commission on Law and Social Action of the American Jewish Congress. It may be that AJCongress, because of its physical structure, will be able to perform some of the necessary research on the psychological effects of segregation." Peyser also noted that CCI had already been an invaluable source of social-scientific materials for the NAACP. In an obvious reference to the social science survey, Peyser claimed that the "American Jewish Congress has been instrumental in reprinting articles that have appeared in scientific journals as well as preparing and writing these articles for the purpose of eventually having them 'planted' in such journals." Peyser closed her address with a call for further cooperation between social scientists and lawyers.[75]

In the same year as Peyser's presentation, the NAACP-LDEF appealed *McLaurin* and *Sweatt* to the Supreme Court. Because of various legal maneuverings, the Supreme Court did not hear the cases until 1950, when it heard the two graduate school cases together with *Henderson*, a case concerning a segregated dining car on a railroad. All three cases were heard on the same day.

The issues in *McLaurin* and *Sweatt* were essentially the same, and the briefs filed by the NAACP-LDEF were very similar. The briefs demonstrate a new mastery of social science material. The *Sweatt* brief, for example used social scientific material to make two points. The first was that there was "no rational basis for a legislative assumption that different races have different intellectual potentialities and should therefore be educated in separate schools." The NAACP-LDEF relied on Klineberg's 1935 work on selective migration and on Arnold Rose's sociological works that he produced on the heels of his work on *An American Dilemma*.[76] As its second point, the NAACP-LDEF argued that segregation "needlessly penalizes Negroes, demoralizes whites and tends to disrupt our democratic institutions." Here the NAACP-LDEF cited Lasker's work on racial identity in children, Long's piece on segregated education, and a host of sociological works, including Myrdal, Johnson, and Frazier. They also relied on Deutscher and Chein's survey to demonstrate that their assertion was supported by a broad consensus in the social science community. While referring to an entire page of footnotes, the NAACP-LDEF argued, "Probably the most irrevocable and deleterious effect of segregation upon the minority group is that it imposes a badge of inferiority upon the segregated group. . . . A definitive study of the scientific works of contemporary sociologists, historians, and anthropologists, conclusively documents the proposition that the intent and result of segregation are the establishment of an inferior status."[77]

Clearly, the NAACP-LDEF had acquired a new sophistication when it came to the use of social science material, and it demonstrated a new willingness to use them. The LDEF's confidence could only have increased when the Supreme Court ruled in their favor in both *Sweatt* and *McLaurin*.[78] The Court based both decisions on ineffable and intangible factors that were denied African Americans by segregation. In the case of Heman Sweatt, those intangibles included the opportunity to attend a law school of the repute of the University of Texas. In the case of George McLaurin, it was the opportunity to exchange ideas with his fellow graduate students. While the Supreme Court stopped short of directly overturning *Plessy*, the door was now wide open to do so.[79] Moreover, passage through that door could be through pointing out "intangible factors."

When they turned their attention to elementary and secondary education, the attorneys of the NAACP-LDEF would attempt to articulate some of those ineffable factors through the use of social science. And social scientists were waiting for them, willing and eager to be enrolled in the cause. The NAACP-LDEF could not, however, merely turn to CCI to find social scientists; for on the eve of the campaign against elementary and public school segregation, the social scientists at the AJCongress were dispirited and in disarray.

The Crisis at CCI

Civil rights attorneys and socially minded social scientists were both dedicated to the same end: the elimination of prejudice and discrimination. The methods employed by each, however, were fundamentally different. The law worked on a strict timetable, and lawyers had to adhere to that timetable. To be persuasive to judges and juries, a good legal argument was forceful and unambiguous, leaving no room for opposing interpretations. In contrast, social science proceeded at a much more leisurely pace, since professional publications usually enforced no strict deadlines. To be persuasive to social-scientific peers, a good social-scientific argument would be provisional and filled with careful caveats. The possibility of other interpretations often would be left open. The differences by which each community produced its arguments against discrimination eventually doomed the institutionalized merger of law and social science at the AJCongress.

Isidor Chein's survey of social science opinion was by far the most successful example of social science research designed to be used as a legal argument. More typically, CCI's social-scientific research did not fit in with the AJCongress's larger campaign against discrimination. Despite the fact that the CCI social scientists quite deliberately directed their research priorities in a manner that would be useful to the CLSA and other activists at the AJCongress, social science never made a significant contribution to the AJCongress's struggle against discrimination.

A tension always existed between the CCI and the rest of the American Jewish Congress. On the one hand, CCI was to be an objective, scientific research agency. On the other, it was funded by, and worked within, the American Jewish Congress—an avowedly political and activist organization. This tension was recognized by Stuart Cook, who told a colleague:

> First, CCI must be an active functioning participant in the general [American Jewish] Congress program. Second, within the framework of [the American Jewish] Congress—which to the outsider's eye is a partisan, political organization—it must be a scientific research group holding the complete confidence of non-Congress organizations and individuals. As you know, we have waged an up-hill fight for this dual objective.[80]

Despite the optimistic tone of much that was written by CCI social scientists, the organization never fit comfortably within the AJCongress framework: the production of social-scientific materials was necessarily slower than for the other branches—the real world, it was argued, moved too fast for the slow social scientists of CCI. The result was that, beginning in 1948, soon after Cook had assumed control, he faced a series of budget and staff cuts that eventually decimated CCI. Cook tried desperately to hold the organization together, but by 1950, he had had enough and accepted an offer to go to New York University (NYU). In his resignation letter, he wrote that he was unhappy with the AJCongress leadership: "What made me accept [the NYU offer] was that no meaningful assurances were really possible; that [CCI's budget of] $240,000 had not really shrunk to a stable $78,000 but rather that no one could really know where the end of the path was to be."[81]

With Cook's resignation, Isidor Chein became CCI director and faced further staff reductions and budget cuts. By 1952, the situation had come to a "crisis," and Marie Jahoda, a distinguished social psychologist, was called in to take stock of the situation. Jahoda surveyed both CCI staffers and American Jewish Congress leaders in an attempt to discover the source of the friction. CCI staff members argued that the AJCongress neither understood nor respected what they were attempting to accomplish. One staff member, John Harding, complained that the AJCongress's position on any issue was decided "ideologically"; that is, the AJCongress had its agenda, and if social science happened to agree with that agenda, well and good. But social science could never actually *guide* AJCongress's position. "Empirical research *is* seen by Congress leadership as serving a useful function in providing evidence from time to time of the correctness of the Congress stand on various issues," Harding wrote to Jahoda. "However this use of research is a dispensable luxury, since the correctness of the Congress position is always clearly evident . . . before the research is done."[82]

Isidor Chein took the opportunity provided by Jahoda's assessment to announce that the situation at CCI was "inherently unstable and similar crises, with all the incident demoralization, must inevitably recur. In other words, regardless of the outcome, I shall be looking for another position."[83] Soon after this, Chein and a number of other CCI staffers would join Cook at NYU.

Jahoda's survey revealed that, while CCI was roundly criticized by the other branches of the American Jewish Congress, there was no clear consensus as to what exactly was wrong. In her final report, Jahoda noted that the criticisms leveled at CCI by the other branches often were contradictory:

> CCI's scientific standards were said by some to be too high, by others too low. On the one hand, CCI was presented as being too perfectionist and too much concerned with meeting scientific requirements when the needs of Congress might have been satisfied with a less thorough job. On the other hand, jobs whose usefulness were recognized . . . were criticized as not really representing a scientific contribution.

All these criticisms could be true, she admitted, because "there exists . . . no generally recognized and defined standard against which the functioning of CCI could be measured and judged adequate or inadequate. CCI's function as a social science department within Congress is undefined."[84]

The fundamental problem confronting CCI, Jahoda claimed, was that "science proceeds at a lower speed, with less flexibility in tackling new problems and with different standards of success than [other] organization activities."[85] Social scientists had little to contribute to an attack on discrimination until they had completed a study on the specific problem in question. Until then, all a social scientist can report is "the analysis of the data continues." Jahoda noted that this report could be regarded as "unsatisfactory and even annoying. A more exact content report [however] . . . might have been even more annoying: it might well have read thus: 'a code was developed and applied. Reliability checks proved that it was inadequate. The code was revised with better reliability checks.' Many of the processes which enter into research are . . . boring and unrevealing."[86] Jahoda recommended that the American Jewish Congress continue to fund CCI but more clearly define what it expected from social-scientific work. CCI did continue, but as a shadow of its former self—it conducted no more serious research into intergroup relations. Many of the CCI social scientists followed Cook and Chein to NYU, where they continued their research in a more academic setting.

The social scientists who had worked at CCI, however, most notably Cook and Chein, would become key players in the litigation campaign against segregated elementary and secondary schools. With the victory over segregated graduate schools, the NAACP-LDEF's attorneys were ready to take on the rest of the South's public school system. And social scientists would be ready and able to assist them.

PART III

Brown Litigation

6

Recruiting Expert Witnesses

CCI may have been in the process of disintegrating just as the school segregation trials were starting up, but it had left behind a well-developed plan of attack that social scientists could use in the court trials. Social scientists, in their published writings, had made a social-scientific case against segregation and discrimination that dovetailed with the legal case of the NAACP-LDEF.

There were three basic arguments that the social-scientific community could make for the NAACP-LDEF. The first was that no differences existed between the races in terms of intelligence or ability to learn. This was the argument Otto Klineberg had been attempting to prove since his dissertation in 1928.

Second was a group of arguments about the psychological damage that flowed from segregation. Although the Clarks' projective tests would be the most readily recognizable form of the damage argument, a theoretical underpinning also came from Lewin's theories of self-hatred in groups. Added to the empirical and theoretical ideas about self-hatred was a basic attitude toward the role of law in society. Although they would not be asked by the NAACP-LDEF necessarily to prove that *legally segregated education* caused psychological damage, social scientists believed for a number of reasons that they could isolate just that variable, at least in theory, as the cause of damage.

The third group of arguments advanced by the social scientists during the *Brown* litigation addressed problems of desegregation. Social scientists believed desegregation could be expected to proceed smoothly, even though the South might vehemently deny that desegregation would ever be possible. The force of the law, appeals to democracy, the nature of the prejudiced personality, the nature of contact between different groups— all these things, the social scientists would argue, meant that desegregation would indeed be possible, even in the South.

The task for the NAACP-LDEF was to enlist social scientists into the litigation campaign in order to introduce these arguments into the legal record against segregation. The year 1950 brought the NAACP-LDEF significant Supreme Court victories against school segregation in the *Sweatt* and *McLaurin* decisions. The LDEF was now ready to attack segregation in elementary and secondary schools, which was a much more ambitious program. There were four separate cases that the NAACP-LDEF was litigating against school segregation in 1951 and 1952. The cases came at a dizzying pace: the South Carolina trial, *Briggs v. Elliot*, was in May 1951; the Kansas trial, *Brown v. Topeka Board of Education*, was in June 1951; the Delaware trial, *Belton v. Gebhart*, was in October 1951; and the Virginia trial, *Davis v. Prince Edward County*, was in February 1952.[1] In this chapter, I explore how social scientists had positioned themselves to serve as expert witnesses for these court cases.

The NAACP-LDEF faced two sets of issues in their recruitment of expert witnesses for the four trials of the School Segregation Cases. The first set of issues revolved around the qualifications of the recruited social scientists. Ideally, the expert witness would be a person of high prestige who had familiarity with and had published on the issues surrounding segregation and discrimination. The second set of issues was perhaps more mundane yet equally important and dealt with the mechanics of getting the witness onto the stand. The expert witness had to be willing to testify. Moreover, he or she should be located close to the trial site—both to give the witness added credibility to the court and to save the NAACP-LDEF's scarce travel funds.

The task of recruiting social scientists and coordinating their activities fell to Robert Carter, who had originated the NAACP-LDEF's use of social science material in the *Westminster* case in 1945. Carter enlisted Kenneth Clark, who became the liaison between the attorneys of the NAACP-LDEF and the social science community. What initially generated the NAACP-LDEF's interest in Clark was a report he had prepared for a government task force called the Mid-Century White House Conference on Children and Youth.

The Mid-Century White House Conference on Children and Youth

Every ten years since 1919, the U.S. government had sponsored a White House Conference on Children and Youth. In 1950, the conference was dedicated to the theme of "personality development and adjustment." In keeping with the postwar emphasis on racial unity in the United States, the conference organizers decided to include a paper on the effects of prejudice and discrimination on the personalities of children.[2]

The organizers started a search for someone to write a technical report on the effects of prejudice on children and finally came to the American Jewish Committee's Department of Scientific Research. The AJCommittee had recently published their "Studies in Prejudice" series of books, which had originated in the research they began during World War II. Since Horkheimer and the rest of the Frankfurt researchers had returned to their native Germany, the department was now headed by Samuel Flowerman. The AJCommittee hired Kenneth Clark to write the report for the Mid-Century Conference. While Clark would technically be employed by the AJCommittee, he would be placed "on loan" to the conference for the duration of his employment. Flowerman's strategy was that Clark could prepare the work for the Mid-Century Conference, and after the conference was over, the AJCommittee would publish it as part of their "Studies in Prejudice" series.[3]

Clark's report, which would be the first source cited by the Supreme Court in its 1954 decision, was a summary of three broad trends in prejudice research: how prejudice affects the personality of the minority group members, how prejudice affects the personality of those who hold the prejudice, and various techniques to reduce prejudice. According to Clark's report, prejudice had the following effects on the "personality of Negro children":

1. There is a pattern of personality disabilities which seems to be associated with the inferior and rejected minority status of the Negro.
2. This pattern includes not only subjective feelings of inferiority, low self-esteem, ambivalent attitudes toward his own group, but also either overt or indirect hostility against both whites and Negroes.[4]

Clark qualified these effects, noting that not all African Americans experienced them in the same manner and that other factors, such as family life or class, could affect the development of an African American's personality.

On the personality of the prejudiced person, Clark relied heavily on the American Jewish Committee's "Studies in Prejudice" series, and one volume, *The Authoritarian Personality*, in particular. *The Authoritarian*

Personality was the final version of the studies conducted by the Berkeley group of social scientists during the war. In the final book, the Berkeley team had devised a number of scales to quantify personality traits. The subjects of the study were rated on anti-Semitism (AS scale), ethnocentrism (E scale), political-economic conservatism (PEC scale), and fascism (F scale). This quantitative information was then supplemented with qualitative data gained through extensive clinical interviews and projective tests. Much of this material had been in circulation in the social science community before the final book was released—for example, in the articles discussed in chapter 3, above, and in a chapter of a volume issued by SPSSI.[5]

The Berkeley team argued that racial prejudice was tied to a host of other personality traits that made up the "authoritarian personality." By tying racial prejudice to a more general personality type, especially such an unfavorable one, the Berkeley team succeeded in portraying racial prejudice as something beyond the merely irrational—racial prejudice made someone deeply disturbed.

Clark, in the White House Conference paper, described the authoritarian personality as "an emotionally maladjusted individual who has achieved social adjustment by taking pleasure in obedience and subordination. He has a blind belief in authority. He admires strength and is ever-ready to attack those he regards as weak and of little account." Clark contended further that the authoritarian personality was deeply prejudiced against other groups. According to Clark, the authoritarian personality's "need to stereotype them, results not from a conventional way of identifying in-groups and out-groups, but from deep emotional need. He must have somebody to punish, for his own overstrict conscience holds him to such severe account."[6]

Clark admitted that the authoritarian personality was manifest only in those individuals who scored on the extreme end of the various scales designed by the Berkeley researchers. Nonetheless, he argued, the authoritarian personality the researchers had studied underscored the fundamental tension between racial prejudice and notions of American democracy and freedom. The moderately prejudiced individual could seek to relieve the tension in a number of ways, all of them the cause of "emotional maladjustment." Clark concluded, "These prejudices inhibit social progress, defined in humanistic terms; they are a manifestation of man's more primitive propensities to debase and harm his fellow human beings . . . and they distort, constrict, humiliate, and, in extreme cases, destroy the personalities of the victims."[7]

Clark's Mid-Century White House Conference paper ultimately was two things. First, it was a relatively comprehensive survey of the psychological literature on racial prejudice. Second, and perhaps more important, it was a tract against racial prejudice that used social science materials. Clark did more than present a "state of the research" paper. He fashioned the existing research into his own synthesis that was more than the sum of its parts. Clark created a powerful argument against racial prejudice that demonstrated that racial prejudice harmed minority and majority group individuals, and that used the form of a scientific research paper while making a moral, political, and social point. As such, it was nearly tailor-made for the NAACP–Legal Defense and Education Fund.

The Mid-Century White House Conference on Children and Youth was held in Washington, D.C., in the first week of December 1950. Two months later, in the first week of February 1951, Kenneth Clark received a visitor, Robert Carter of the NAACP-LDEF. Carter told Clark that the NAACP-LDEF was preparing their case for *Briggs v. Elliot,* a case in South Carolina to test the constitutionality of segregated elementary schools. They were searching for information on the harms of segregation to schoolchildren. Carter explained to Clark that the NAACP-LDEF had first gone to Otto Klineberg, and Klineberg had referred them to Clark. Clark gave Carter a copy of his White House Conference manuscript. A few days later, Carter called Clark and exclaimed that the manuscript was "perfect" for the NAACP-LDEF. Clark later recalled that Carter asked him to do three things for the NAACP-LDEF: "(1) be a witness in the *Briggs* case, (2) enlist other social scientists, as prestigious as possible to testify, and (3) work directly with the NAACP lawyers in going over the briefs as they deal with the social science material. And he wanted me to get started yesterday."[8]

Clark never questioned the wisdom of getting involved with the NAACP-LDEF. As he recalled, Robert Carter and Thurgood Marshall "dragooned me. I mean, they just took for granted that I was going to be with them from that point on—and that, by the way, was true. I just was brought in, as a functioning member of their staff.[9] Clark and Carter began to recruit other social scientists to join the litigation campaign.

Enrollment of Experts

That social scientists would be used at all in the School Segregation Cases was far from clear when Carter and Clark began to recruit experts. Robert Carter was always the most enthusiastic about the use of social science data in the segregation suits. Others in the NAACP-LDEF were less so. William Coleman, one of the assistant attorneys in the litigation, later described himself as "the most debunking" of the doubters. Of particular concern to Coleman was the use of Clark's projective tests, or as Coleman put it, "those damned dolls! I thought it was a joke."[10] Thurgood Marshall, however, wanted to use any and all resources that were available and told Carter to build the social-scientific data into the first of the trials: *Briggs v. Elliot.*[11] The subsequent cases followed the pattern established by *Briggs.*

The *Briggs* trial was set for May 1951, giving Clark and Carter less than four months to arrange for other social scientists to serve as expert witnesses. Immediately, the problem of finding experts who would be willing and able to testify began to present itself. For example, Clark's first suggestion was that the NAACP-LDEF enlist his CCNY colleague, Eugene Hartley, who was one of the editors of *Readings in Social Psychology*, the book in which the Clarks' doll studies had appeared. Eugene Hartley was formerly Eugene Horowitz, who had launched racial identification studies with his 1936 dissertation. Horowitz had changed his name during World War II when he suspected that his "Jewish-sounding" surname was costing him a commission.[12] Unfortunately, Hartley was leaving the country in March, making it impossible for him to testify.[13]

Carter then asked Clark about the possibility of getting Gardner Murphy to testify. As one of the most prestigious social psychologists in the country, Murphy's name would give the roster of expert witnesses some professional weight. But Murphy, who had just returned from an extended trip to India, and who suffered from a series of debilitating illnesses throughout his New York years, felt "unable to assume the responsibility." Carter thought it just as well; too many social scientists from New York City might have hindered rather than helped the NAACP-LDEF cause.[14]

Clark then supplied a list of "real top-notchers and who have published material that would be pertinent to the case."[15] Clark's list, with one or two changes, became the final list of witnesses who appeared at the *Briggs* trial. The list also demonstrated how social scientists had built arguments against segregation into their social-scientific work, making that work the ideal preparation for them to serve as expert witnesses against segregation.

Clark's "first choice" was Theodore M. Newcomb (1903–1984) of the University of Michigan. Newcomb was yet another product of the combination of Union Theological Seminary (UTS) and Columbia University. The son of a Congregational minister, he had received his undergraduate degree from Oberlin College and had come to New York to get a divinity degree from UTS. There he met Lois Barclay, and he transferred to Columbia after a year of divinity school and worked under both Gardner Murphy and Goodwin Watson. After receiving his Ph.D. in 1929, Newcomb taught at Bennington College and worked on the second edition of the Murphys' *Experimental Social Psychology*.[16] Newcomb was a charter member of SPSSI and co-edited their first yearbook on industrial conflict.[17]

During World War II, Newcomb succeeded Goodwin Watson as the principal psychologist of the Foreign Broadcast Service, after Watson was forced to resign because of his leftist connections. Newcomb's own leftist inclinations almost disqualified him from the post.[18] He served as the president of SPSSI immediately after the war and settled down at the University of Michigan to establish one of the most prestigious psychology departments in the United States.[19]

In 1950, Newcomb published a textbook in social psychology where he argued that segregation was both a source and a consequence of prejudice but that the way to break the "vicious circle" of segregation and prejudice was by changing the conditions in which individuals found themselves. One way to do this was through changes that eliminated legalized segregation and discrimination. In the short run, "many people's attitudes of approving segregation . . . are supported mainly by observing the practice of segregation. . . . If this support is removed, their attitudes are likely to be weakened." Newcomb argued that the problem of segregation was especially acute if the segregation was enforced by law. He claimed, "If, in addition to the removal of this support, the opposed attitude is now supported by the prestige of 'the law,' many people's attitudes toward segregation will be changed. In these *indirect* ways legislation may serve to change attitudes, almost as soon as it begins to be enforced." In the longer run, Newcomb argued that "the stopping of segregation means that a new generation of children will be less likely to acquire such attitudes. Here, as elsewhere, an ounce of prevention is worth a pound of cure."[20] He concluded that, while legal change was only a first step, it was a necessary one in the elimination of prejudice.

Clark also suggested that Carter try to enlist David Krech (1909–1977). Krech, previously Isadore Krechevsky, was a moving force behind the founding of SPSSI in 1936. In 1951, Krech was the outgoing president of SPSSI and had a temporary appointment at Harvard; he had a full-time appointment at the University of California at Berkeley but had been "hiding out" as a visiting professor at other institutions to avoid the California loyalty oath.[21] Krech was an eclectic psychologist who, in 1950, was working with Harvard psychologist Jerome Bruner on new theories of perception. It was his 1948 textbook in social psychology, co-authored with Richard Crutchfield, that would make him useful to the NAACP-LDEF. Like Newcomb, Krech argued that segregation, especially segregation with the force of law, was a major factor in forcing a sense of inferiority onto minority group members. The force of law, according to Krech,

> means that the possibility of any specific Negro's . . . escaping the differentiating stigmata is very low. In addition, these stigmata are saturated with acceptability for many people. That is, anything that is legal, written into state laws, official contracts, and land deeds . . . is seen as "good" and "is as it should be." These sociological differentia, in other words, are not seen as happenstance attributes of the minority group members but as necessary and appropriate attributes.[22]

Krech argued against the notion that the law could not change attitudes. He exclaimed, "The use of legal force in changing beliefs and attitudes is frequently a psychologically sound procedure." Moreover, he argued that "even where genuine and significant resistance does appear, legal force in abolishing segregation may be effective." Krech summoned up studies of the forced desegregation of labor unions and the armed forces to prove his point. Even though the elimination was met with stiff resistance, the forcing of desegregation upon these groups was accomplished with a minimum of friction. Moreover, psychological testing showed a decrease in racial prejudice after desegregation.[23]

Krech noted that the studies were limited, at best, proved only that desegregation could be eliminated in certain situations and under certain conditions. Nevertheless, this did not deter him from making the more general point that "any step which can be taken to break down segregation" would "make a significant contribution to the removal of racial prejudice in this country," because the "environmental supports for prejudiced beliefs and attitudes" would be removed.[24] This argument for the effectiveness of legal change would serve the NAACP-LDEF well, and they asked Krech to appear in South Carolina. Krech was only too happy to testify.

Clark had three other suggestions for expert witnesses for the NAACP-LDEF. Krech's co-author Richard Crutchfield was rejected because he was in California, and Carter felt that Crutchfield was "a little too far away for us to bring him to the hearing." Clark also suggested Stuart Cook. Carter admitted that Cook "was a wonderful person" but rejected him because the NAACP-LDEF felt they could not have another New Yorker on the stand. Clark's final suggestion was Gordon Allport. Carter had tried to get Allport before enlisting Clark, but Allport, according to Carter, thought "he would not make an effective witness" and refused to join the effort.[25]

The final list of witnesses scheduled to appear at the *Briggs* trial was as follows: Clark, Newcomb, Krech, Klineberg, Helen Trager, and Robert Redfield. Trager was a psychologist at Vassar who had done work similar to that of the Clarks in racial identification.[26] Redfield was brought in at the last moment by Thurgood Marshall to testify, as he had in *Sweatt* and had attempted to do in *Sipuel*, "on the one point concerning unreasonableness of segregation insofar as school children are concerned and the point that given a similar learning situation, the Negro child will do as well as the others."[27] Redfield's pretrial notes indicated that he was up on the latest literature on intergroup relations. He had prepared an argument that the "law itself is education.... Laws not only affect outward behavior: they also help men to make up their minds in accordance with a major trend or ideal of their society." CCI's research figured heavily in Redfield's argument, as he relied on Gerhart Saenger's studies of integrated sales staffs and Deutsch and Collins's studies of interracial housing.[28]

In the end, Carter and Clark had managed to recruit some of the top names in the field of intergroup relations to testify at the *Briggs* trial. Most of these individuals had taken a stand against segregation in their published works, making them natural candidates for expert witnesses to testify against segregation and discrimination. Finding expert witnesses for the subsequent trials followed the pattern established by *Briggs*.

The second trial was scheduled for the end of June 1951. It was NAACP-LDEF attorney Jack Greenberg's responsibility to arrange for expert witnesses for the Kansas case, *Brown v. Topeka Board of Education*, which came soon after the *Briggs* case. Greenberg faced special problems enlisting scholars for the Kansas case. First, he had been assigned the task only a month before the trial, leaving him precious little time. Second, it was June, one of the busiest times of the year for academics, which made recruiting experts that much more difficult. Third, the trial was in Kansas, and the NAACP-LDEF could not afford to pay travel expenses for a host of East Coast scholars to make the trip to the Midwest. Moreover, because of the location of the trial, Kenneth Clark did very little to help organize witnesses, and the task fell to Hugh Speer, a professor of education in Kansas City, whose local connections would be more useful. These three conditions meant that the expert witnesses in Kansas would be much different from those who testified on the East Coast.

Greenberg approached Robert Lynd, a Columbia sociologist of some repute. In 1939, Lynd had published one of the classics of activist social science, *Knowledge for What?* which was a powerful argument for social scientists to become involved in the society in which they were living. Lynd was a close friend of Gardner and Lois Murphy, and through them, Lynd's views of social activism had a heavy influence on the cadre of social psychologists trained at Columbia in the 1930s.[29] Lynd, however, turned down the opportunity to testify.[30]

Given the expenses of having Lynd travel to Kansas, his loss probably was not felt too deeply. The same cannot be said for Arnold Rose, co-author of *An American Dilemma* and sociologist at the University of Minnesota. After the war, Rose popularized Gunnar Myrdal's notion that the law should be an active agent against discrimination and that the entire notion of Sumnerian folkways should be abandoned. Rose declared that "the sociologists have misled us with their notions of 'mores,' 'folkways,' and the 'inevitable' slowness of social change." He repeated the now-familiar argument that prejudice often arose by observing the actual practice of segregation, especially legal segregation. Thus, according to Rose, "it has been thus demonstrable for a long time that law and power could create or increase attitudes of prejudice." Pointing to the studies emerging from CCI on the separation of attitude and behavior and the nature of interracial contact, Rose concluded that "it should not be surprising from newly-available evidence that law and power would also decrease prejudice. . . . Now we know that law and authority can reduce prejudice."[31]

On June 4, Greenberg wrote to Rose, asking if he could serve as an expert witness on June 25 in Kansas. In a coals-to-Newcastle sort of letter, Rose wrote back and agreed to serve as a witness and asked Greenberg if he was familiar with the study by Deutscher and Chein that addressed this very issue. Rose also believed that the Deutsch and Collins study on interracial housing might be of use. Rose thought it was "important to show how, in a sociological way, segregation *inevitably* results in discrimination."[32] Given his professional reputation and his obvious familiarity with the issues, it was a great blow to the NAACP-LDEF when Rose eventually decided he was too busy to participate.[33]

The one scholar whose name is conspicuous by its absence is Karl Menninger, the founder of the Menninger Clinic in Topeka, a nationally known psychiatric clinic. Menninger himself was a member of both the NAACP and the American Civil Liberties Union (ACLU). The NAACP-LDEF had asked Menninger to testify, but Menninger considered such activity to be a breach of his professional objectivity.[34]

The final list of witnesses to appear at the *Brown* trial reflected the problems the NAACP-LDEF had experienced in getting testimony. While the *Brown* witnesses were all competent scholars, they were not the "top-notchers" who were recruited for the *Briggs* trial—no SPSSI presidents, no nationally renowned scholars appeared at the Kansas trial. Perhaps the biggest name to appear at the *Brown* trial was Horace B. English, professor of psychology at Ohio State University. English had been on the initial council of SPSSI in 1936 and had been one of Gardner Murphy's professors in the 1920s.[35] Others on the final list of witnesses were Wilbur B. Brookover, social psychologist, who was professor of social science at Michigan State University; social psychologist Louisa Holt, who had worked at the Menninger Clinic briefly and was at the school of clinical psychology at Kansas University; John J. Kane, instructor in sociology at Notre Dame University; and Bettie Belk, a Ph.D. student in human development at the University of Chicago.

The third trial was *Gebhart v. Belton*, scheduled for October 1951. This trial was in Delaware, a mere two-hour train ride from New York City. Consequently, it was possible for the NAACP-LDEF to draw from the large contingent of social scientists available on the East Coast. Greenberg began assembling experts in August, which gave him a little more lead time to gather a good group. Again, there were social scientists who, for one reason or another, could or would not testify. Ira De Augustine Reid, who had conducted the ACE studies before World War II, agreed to testify but then backed out. Another disappointment was R. Nevitt Sanford, co-author of *The Authoritarian Personality*, who had moved from Berkeley to Vassar, making him locally available. A third person who backed out was Hadley Cantril, a propaganda analyst from Princeton and longtime SPSSI mainstay.[36] Despite these losses, the cast was impressive: Kenneth Clark; Otto Klineberg; Jerome S. Bruner of Harvard's Department of Social Relations; John K. Morland, professor of sociology and anthropology at the College of William and Mary; George Gorham Lane of the University of Delaware; and Fredrick B. Parker of the University of Delaware. All of these witnesses testified to the familiar issues on the relative learning ability of African American and of white children and the damage inflicted by segregation on the personalities of African American children.

Perhaps the most notable of those testifying at the Delaware trial was Fredric W. Wertham, a psychiatrist educated at Kings College in London and at the University of Munich. He came to the United States to become the chief residential psychiatrist at Johns Hopkins University Hospital. Wertham became friends with the great trial lawyer Clarence Darrow and, through Darrow's influence, began testifying at criminal trials on the mental states of murderers when they committed their crimes. It was also through Darrow's influence that Wertham became interested in issues revolving around social justice. After World War II, Wertham founded the LaFarge Clinic in Harlem, dedicated to helping low-income African Americans who suffered from psychiatric problems.[37] Wertham was nearly tailor-made to be an expert witness for the NAACP-LDEF: a social scientist with near-unimpeachable academic credentials, deeply concerned with social justice, and with vast experience as a witness in a court of law.

The fourth and final trial was *Davis v. County School Board of Prince Edward County*, scheduled for February 1952. For this trial in Virginia, the NAACP-LDEF enrolled more social scientists, and ones of a higher caliber than they had presented at the two previous trials. Once again, the trial was close to New York City, allowing the NAACP-LDEF to draw from the large pool of social scientists there. Once again, however, there were disappointments. For example, Stuart Cook had agreed to testify, but then circumstances prevented his appearance.[38] The NAACP-LDEF did, however, arrange for the testimony of Horace English, who had testified for the NAACP-LDEF in the Kansas case; Kenneth Clark; Mamie Phipps Clark; Alfred McClung Lee; M. Brewster Smith; and Isidor Chein. It is useful to examine how Smith and Chein had positioned themselves to be expert witnesses for the NAACP-LDEF, for it illustrates both the network of activist social scientists that existed after World War II and how social scientists had built arguments against segregation into seemingly esoteric studies.

At first glance, M. Brewster Smith (b. 1919) seems an unlikely candidate for the NAACP-LDEF. A young scholar, he had no significant publications in the area of segregation and discrimination. Yet Smith had an impeccable pedigree. In 1947 he received the first Ph.D. from Harvard University's Department of Social Relations. This department, created after the war, was a mixture of "activist" social scientists led by Clyde Kluckhohn in anthropology, Talcott Parsons in sociology, and Gordon Allport in psychology.[39] Smith's graduate career had been interrupted by World War II, when he briefly worked with Stuart Cook on test development for officer candidates; he also worked during this time with Arnold Rose, for nearly two years. Smith later described his work with Rose as his real education in race relations, although he was uncomfortable because he outranked Rose, whom he regarded as "my professional senior."[40] At the time of the *Davis* trial, Smith was the chair of the Psychology Department at Vassar and editor of SPSSI's official journal, *The Journal of Social Issues*. In short, he was at the center of the postwar activist social science establishment—well positioned to be recruited by the NAACP-LDEF.

If M. Brewster Smith exemplified the junior scholar who was in the right place at the right time, Isidor Chein demonstrated how activist social scientists took a stand against segregation and discrimination despite working in seemingly unrelated areas of social science. In February 1952, the time of the Virginia trial, Isidor Chein was still with the American Jewish Congress. He had been brought down to testify on the survey of social science opinion that had been a mainstay of the NAACP-LDEF's use of social science since its publication in 1948.[41] Yet Chein brought more than the social science survey to the trial, because he was the leading theoretician working on Kurt Lewin's concept of group self-hatred.

The concept of "Jewish self-hatred" had a long history in European medical and anthropological circles. Jews had long been viewed as particularly susceptible to mental illness and social pathology—a tradition that dated back to the Middle Ages. Moreover, German Jews had an equally long history of self-criticism—a concept that was looked on by the German Jewish community as one of their great strengths. In the late nineteenth century, the two popular images of the "mad Jew" and the "self-critical" Jew were combined in German Jewish discourse to create the image of the "self-hating Jew." The rise of the self-hating Jew was a response of German Jews to popular anti-Semitism that primarily was directed at Eastern European Jews. For German Jews, the Eastern European Jew quickly became the "bad Jew," which led to a series of German writings in the first half of the twentieth century describing the self-hatred of Jews.[42]

Kurt Lewin brought this conception of self-hatred in Jews and recast it in terms of his model of group dynamics. For Lewin, the key to understanding Jewish self-hatred was to view it as primarily a *social* phenomenon. Self-hatred was the result of a tug-of-war between social forces—one force that pulled the individual into a group and one that pulled the individual out of the group. Members of an underprivileged group gained status by distancing themselves from their own group. But the privileged, majority group would not permit them to make this movement. Hence, Lewin argued, "in an underprivileged group, many of these individuals are, nevertheless, forced to stay within the group. As a result, we find in every underprivileged group a number of persons ashamed of their membership. In the case of the Jews, such a Jew will try to move away as far as possible from things Jewish." According to Lewin these individuals began to identify with the views of the majority as much as possible, which led to an inferiority complex. As Lewin wrote, "The feeling of inferiority of the Jew is but an indication of the fact that he sees things Jewish with the eyes of an unfriendly majority." The ultimate solution to the problem of Jewish self-hatred, Lewin argued, was to eliminate the social forces that hindered underprivileged group members from leaving the group. In this way, negative forces would be replaced with a healthy "group loyalty." In a key passage, Lewin argued that "Jewish self-hatred will die out only when actual equality of status with the non-Jew is achieved. Only then will the enmity against one's own group decrease to the relatively insignificant proportions characteristic of the majority's group's. Sound self criticism will replace it."[43] Lewin's theory made a deep impression on Chein, as well as on Kenneth B. Clark.

Chein developed Lewin's ideas on building positive group identification, and he did this within a context of the battle against discrimination, legal and otherwise. Chein had tied Lewin's ideas on group self-hatred specifically to the elimination of barriers to free movement between groups—barriers such as legally imposed segregation.

Chein's belief that the law could be a powerful tool against prejudice has been noted in chapter 3. When Chein began to turn his attention to problems of group self-hate in the 1940s, he faced the same conundrum that Lewin had: how does one distinguish healthy group identification, such as racial or religious pride, from unhealthy group chauvinism, such as race prejudice?

One way of making such a distinction, argued Chein, was to examine how groups establish boundaries around themselves: "The groups in which individuals must ... hold membership should have sufficient vitality so that the group boundaries do not have to be set in physical space (i.e. through segregation) or defended by the development of hostility toward other groups."[44] Consequently, Chein argued, building healthy group membership required the removal of these barriers. The primary battle was against society's discrimination. On a panel he shared with Bruno Bettelheim, in which Chein contrasted Bettelheim's theories on group self-hatred with Lewin's, Chein made the point explicit:

> For in the larger perspective it becomes apparent that the most effective thing that can be done in our efforts to secure our children against prejudice and discrimination is to band together to wipe the latter out. The basic disease is in our society, not in our children. The basic remedy, therefore, must be social not individual. Every gain on this front adds to the security of our children. Let us not forget this.[45]

Chein's argument that the elimination of segregation was necessary to build healthy group identification underscores a fundamental point about the role of social scientists in the School Segregation Cases. Clark and the NAACP-LDEF were successful in recruiting socially conscious social scientists to testify at the trials because social scientists had been attacking segregation in their published works for several years.

Not only was there in place a group of social scientists who argued against segregation in their work, but these social scientists were connected through a network of institutions. For example: Columbia University (and to a lesser extent, Harvard), the Society for the Psychological Study of Social Issues, and the Commission on Community Interrelations all provided social scientists with opportunities for social activism. Hence, when the opportunity arose for these scientists, to testify at a trial attacking segregation, many were eager to do so. Recalling his involvement twenty years after his testimony in the *Briggs* case, Krech claimed that "*this* was precisely the sort of thing I had always hoped the SPSSI could do. . . . And I was to be among the first to bear witness to bring forth social psychology to confound the Forces of Repression!"[46]

Their willingness to testify against segregation, however, does not explain the methods by which these scholars translated their social-scientific writings into expert testimony. The NAACP-LDEF needed social-scientific testimony to prove specific legal arguments. As demonstrated in the previous chapter, social science did not always mesh perfectly with legal points that were at issue in a court trial. The next chapter explores how social scientists attempted to be effective witnesses for the NAACP-LDEF while maintaining what they viewed as high scientific standards.

7

Testimony of the Experts

The NAACP-LDEF generally, and Robert Carter especially, had a lot of experience with social-scientific materials by the time of the school segregation trials in 1951 and 1952. Consequently, Carter was able to fashion an argument against segregation that took into account the limitations of scientific knowledge regarding the effects of segregation on schoolchildren.

Many recent histories and commentaries on the social scientists' role in *Brown* have focused on the projective tests conducted by Kenneth B. Clark, the "doll tests." The common claims made about the doll tests—that they were the "only empirical data" submitted to the Supreme Court, that they were referenced in the *Brown* opinion, and that they were the key to the social-scientific testimony—are simply erroneous.[1] To fully understand how social scientists framed their arguments for the court, we must turn our attention away from Kenneth Clark and the doll tests and look to the testimony of *all* the social scientists.

In this chapter, I do several things: first, I sketch the trial strategy that Carter developed for the social scientists to follow during their testimony, Second, I look at how social scientists coped with two key questions: how to isolate segregated education as the cause of psychological harm, and how to isolate *legalized* segregation as the cause of psychological harm. Third, because it came to be the focal point of later criticism, I examine the trial testimony of Kenneth Clark in some detail. Finally, I look at the few social scientists who testified on behalf of segregation, especially the testimony of Henry E. Garrett.

Trial Strategy

Briggs, the first of the four school segregation trials, served as the exemplar for the other three. In the strategy he devised for *Briggs,* Robert

Carter planned to use his experts to prove two points to the court: first, that the educational opportunities available to African American children were not equal to those of white schoolchildren; second, that regardless of the facilities provided, the act of segregation was psychologically damaging and hence unconstitutional.

To prove his first argument on the equality of facilities, Carter used surveys conducted by education experts on facilities provided to both groups in the segregated school systems under litigation. He would use these experts to testify that the schools were in no way equal. Carter noted that winning this first point would only be a qualified victory—the court could merely order the state to equalize the facilities.[2] Carter's caution was justified, since in two of the trials the equality of the facilities was a moot point for the NAACP-LDEF. When *Briggs* came to trial, the first action by the state of South Carolina was to admit that the facilities of the two school systems were profoundly inequitable. The inequality, explained Robert Figg, the South Carolina attorney general, stemmed from rural schools lagging behind the city schools and not from any malicious racism on the part of the state. To rectify the situation, a new sales tax was being implemented to raise revenue that would quickly bring the facilities of the two systems to substantial equality.[3] Similarly, when preparing for the *Brown* trial, Jack Greenberg received a telegram from Hugh Speer, who had undertaken a survey of the educational facilities in Topeka and found no significant difference in teacher salaries or the facilities provided. The telegram advised "emphasis on social and psychological handicaps of segregation per se" in the upcoming trial.[4]

What South Carolina's admission in *Briggs* and the equality of the facilities in *Brown* did was underscore the importance of the social science testimony, since that testimony was the heart of the direct attack on segregation. From the beginning of the first trial, to get a genuine victory, Carter argued, the NAACP-LDEF would have to win his second point— that, even given equal facilities, "the requirement that plaintiffs attend racially segregated schools in and of itself . . . imposes upon plaintiffs burdens and disadvantages which deprive them of the equal protection of the laws required by the Fourteenth Amendment to the Constitution of the United States."[5] It was to prove this second point that Carter planned most of the social science testimony in the *Briggs* trial, with the other trials following the same pattern.

Previous chapters have shown that there were no studies that isolated legal segregated education as the specific variable that caused psychological damage in schoolchildren. As sophisticated users of social-scientific materials, the NAACP-LDEF attorneys were well aware of this limitation in the literature and had fashioned their argument to take it into account. In a 1952 public address, in the midst of the trial phase of the litigation, Thurgood Marshall explained that "the effects of segregation in education have not been isolated for a study by social scientists," but that "since this is a state-sponsored program, certainly the state, consistent with the requirements of the Fourteenth Amendment, should not be a party to system which does help produce these results [of insecurity and self-hate in Negroes]."[6]

In his instructions to the expert witnesses for the first trial, *Briggs v. Elliott* in South Carolina, NAACP-LDEF attorney Robert Carter wrote:

Unfortunately no study has been made . . . of the impact of segregated education itself on the development of the Negro's personality. Most studies have taken place in northern communities. In fact, both Eugene Hartley and Kenneth Clark have found little difference in the perception, assimilation, or impact of racial attitudes and resultant personality disturbances as among northern and southern Negro and white children.

Carter was not attempting to demonstrate that legally segregated education was isolated in the social sciences as a factor that caused psychological damage in African American children:

Although it would be wonderful to be able to demonstrate that *segregated education* imposes the disadvantages and hardships which we will try to establish, if we can demonstrate that segregation is the cause, we have succeeded in proving Point II, in my opinion. What is involved in this suit is state action and state responsibility. If, therefore, segregation causes harm, the state ought not be permitted to impose it in any area of public life, and it does not help the state to show that *segregated education* here is not solely responsible for harmful results or that the harm occurs in northern communities.

Carter's argument was predicated not on isolating *de jure* or *de facto* segregated schooling but rather on the general harms of segregation. Once he established that segregation was damaging, he felt the argument would be won, since the state could not constitutionally inflict such damage because such action would constitute discrimination. As he wrote, "If this be true, then it is unimportant where our studies come from as long as this thesis can be sustained." Hence, Carter hoped completely to sidestep the problem of isolating segregated education, or of isolating *legal* segregation, in the social science materials. He was well aware of the state of social science literature and cast his legal argument so that he was arguing only what could be proven with the data available.[7]

Even though social scientists could not meet the more stringent outlined requirements, their testimony, and much of the work on which their testimony was based, demonstrates that social scientists had much to say regarding legalized segregated education. I examine two facets of the arguments that the social scientists made to the courts. First, how did they deal with the problem of segregated education versus segregation in general? Second, how did they deal with the problem of legally imposed segregation versus *de facto* segregation?

Isolating Segregation in Education

To say that Carter did not ask the social scientists to isolate segregated education is not to say that the question did not arise during the trials. Whenever questioned about discrimination in other areas of life, however, social scientists consistently admitted that segregation existed in other places in society and that it was damaging in those areas as well. In the South Carolina trial, psychologist Helen Trager offered testimony based on projective tests, designed along the lines of the Clarks' doll tests, that she had conducted in Philadelphia.[8] The state attorney general pressed Trager about the source of the feelings of racial inferiority that Trager claimed to have discovered in her investigation. Noting that Trager had found feelings of racial inferiority in children as young as five years old, the attorney drove Trager to admit that these feelings could not have come from their school experiences, given that they had no school experiences at so young an age. Trager was quick to explain that "if anything our study demonstrated that it did not come out of schools." When pressed to name the source of such feelings, Trager explained:

> It was not always the home, although we know the home is an important factor in the learning of children. It was the playground. It was what they saw on the bus. It was what they knew about where father worked, or couldn't work. It was all of their learning in the total community in the society of their 5-year oldness, and they were aware of many things, and their sources included church and shop, and market place.

Trager also readily admitted that her study had been conducted in Philadelphia, which "does not have legally segregated schools."[9] Arguing that segregation and discrimination existed in areas of life outside education did little, however, to aid the state's defense of segregated education. After all, if segregation was damaging in general, then it should be eliminated—including segregated education.

In fact, far from hurting the case against segregated education, the existence of segregation and discrimination in other areas of life was crucial for proving that segregated education was damaging. The pre-existing "stamp of inferiority" that general discrimination represented was necessary to make the psychological damage argument work. The damage argument presupposed that one of the segregated groups had already been deemed inferior by the general society through widespread segregation and discrimination. Because the "inferior" group had been so labeled, the only way to view segregation of that group was as a means of keeping them inferior—to humiliate and discriminate against them. Far from attempting to isolate one specific variable in the social structure, the damage argument welcomed the Gordian knot that widespread discrimination represented, for it all served the same end—to keep African Americans in their place.

For example, in the Delaware school segregation trial, psychiatrist Frederic Wertham managed to take the typical objections of the defense and turn them on their heads. Wertham had made psychiatric examinations of the plaintiff's children (a form of empirical evidence beyond the doll tests, incidentally). During his testimony, he admitted that racism and discrimination in society were massive problems even absent school segregation. But, he argued, that was no defense of school segregation; rather, the existence of racism outside the school was what made school segregation particularly hurtful. Wertham put the matter this way:

> If there were no other manifestations of discrimination in a society, the school segregation would have a totally different significance emotionally for the child, but as it is these children are filled with all kinds of feelings about discrimination that they find in other places. . . . The children are indoctrinated with race hatred in other places, and that brings the school segregation, which is sanctioned by the State [in]to . . . focus with them.[10]

The point was that, in a highly discriminatory society, school segregation was inevitably viewed as something *imposed on* African American schoolchildren. Given this perception, it was reasonable to conclude that segregation would leave a sense of inferiority in the minds of African American children.

Even though social scientists were not required to isolate education as the key variable in causing psychological damage in schoolchildren, they *did* claim that they had good reasons to think that segregated schools were psychologically damaging. While the social scientists admitted they had no studies that isolated school segregation, that was not the end of their argument. For example, social scientists argued that school segregation was pervasive in a child's life, which meant that children would be constantly reminded of their inferior status. As sociologist John J. Kane of the University of Notre Dame testified in the *Brown* case in Topeka:

> The school, with the exception of the home, is the institution that makes the greatest impact on American youth. You see the school gets the child early in life, keeps him for a number of years, so that day after day, year after year it is transferring attitudes for him. . . . In a school system in which racial segregation is practiced, you have a day after day accumulation of attitudes that the Negro is inferior because segregation is differentiation and distinction.[11]

In addition to the inescapable nature of school life, social scientists argued that school segregation came at a particularly vulnerable time of life for children, when the sting of segregation would be especially severe. Psychologist Louisa Holt testified in the Kansas trial:

> A theory that would be accepted by virtually all students of personality development [is] that the earlier a significant event occurs in the life of an individual the more lasting, the more far-reaching and deeper the effects of that incident, that trauma will be. . . . Attending a segregated school, perhaps after the preschool years of free play with others of different skin color, is a trauma to the Negro child, that occurs early.[12]

Note here that Holt is basing her opinions on widely held psychological theories and inferring from them that segregation is damaging to personality development. When giving these reasons for the importance of school segregation in the life of a child, social scientists were usually careful to be clear that this was their *opinion* and not necessarily supported by any studies that specifically investigated these questions (though the opinion could be based on other sorts of scientific data or theories).

It is important to remember that the social scientists were brought to the stand to give their opinions rather than to present a scientific treatise on the subject of segregation. The standard function of expert witnesses was to give their expert opinions, and the NAACP-LDEF had briefed their witnesses to that effect.[13] In a 1954 letter, Isidor Chein, who had testified at one of the trials, remarked that "in the segregation cases . . . nobody asked us for the basis on which we reached our conclusions."[14] Indeed, during his testimony in the *Davis* case in Virginia, when Chein had attempted to explain the basis of his conclusions regarding the harms of segregation, the presiding judge cut him off and told him, "I think we have your position pretty clearly."[15]

Even if social scientists had good reasons to believe that education was responsible for damage, there remains the second issue—could they isolate *legal* segregation? Given the persistence of widespread *de facto* segregation in the United States, it seems an especially tricky burden to have isolated the effects of legally imposed segregation.

Isolating Legalized Segregation

To a large extent, the social scientists could respond in the same way they did with the arguments about isolating segregated education: if segregation is damaging, one should eliminate it wherever one can and certainly, the state should not sanction it. It is difficult to see how *de facto* segregation justified continuing *de jure* segregation. But, as was the case in the arguments above, the social scientists had reasons for believing that state-sponsored segregation was especially damaging.

Social scientists made arguments firmly grounded in the social-scientific literature that legally imposed segregation would be more injurious than *de facto* segregation. Certainly, there were good reasons to think that legally imposed segregation would have a different impact on the psyche from segregation that arose spontaneously or voluntarily. The law was pervasive, unambiguous, ongoing, and an official declaration of the status of African Americans. As Louisa Holt testified in Kansas:

> The fact that it is enforced, that it is legal, I think, has more importance than the mere fact of segregation by itself does because this gives legal and official sanction to a policy which inevitably is interpreted both by white

people and by Negroes as denoting the inferiority of the Negro group. Were it not for the sense that one group is inferior to the other, there would be no basis . . . for such segregation.[16]

Psychologically, it was significant that the law, which all Americans were taught to respect and obey, proclaimed that African Americans were not fit to associate with white Americans. Hence, prejudicial attitudes of the white population and feelings of inferiority in the African American population were inextricably tied to the law. During his cross-examination in Virginia, Chein was asked, "Just because of the law, you say the difference [in psychological harm to African Americans] is made?" Chein answered:

Yes, that is my opinion, that it is the official sanction which says to the child, "It is not only a matter of I, Joe Doaks, don't like you" but it says to the child that the government of the State of Virginia thinks that you are not fit to associate with white children. This is an authority source, and the effect of such authority is to inevitably make more impressive what is involved in the basic fact of segregation.[17]

A favorite tactic of state attorneys during the trial was to point out the pervasive *de facto* segregation in the northern hometowns of many of the expert witnesses. Social scientists often admitted that racial prejudice was a severe problem for the North as well. They made clear, however, that such racial prejudice did not lessen the impact of *de jure* segregation. M. Brewster Smith admitted:

It is perfectly clear that we [northerners] don't come with clean hands. There is prejudice in the North just as there is prejudice in the South, with this important difference, I think: that when segregation is supported with the full authority of the State, it is very difficult to make progress and do anything about it; whereas, the other situation is more fluid, more malleable. There is this further point that I mentioned in my testimony: that I think there is a difference between official insult and informal insult which people can't avoid.[18]

Social scientists did not invent arguments about the significance of the law for the trials but developed them within the postwar social-scientific literature. For example, in his testimony in the *Briggs* trial, David Krech, echoing the claims he made in his 1948 textbook (discussed in the previous chapter), argued that the psychological damage could indeed be traced back to legally imposed segregation:

No one can long maintain any attitude or belief unless there are some objective supports for that belief. We believe, for example, that there are trees. We would not long continue to believe that there are trees if we never saw a tree. Legal segregation, because it is legal, because it is obvious to everyone, gives what we call in our lingo, environmental support for the belief that Negroes are in some way different from and inferior to white people, and that in turn, of course, supports and strengthens beliefs of racial differences and racial inferiority.[19]

Given the nature of the NAACP's argument, social scientists in *Brown* were able to offer a series of arguments, grounded in widely accepted social science theories, that legally imposed school segregation was psychologically damaging to children.

Trial Testimony of M. Brewster Smith

A close examination of M. Brewster Smith's testimony in the Virginia trial shows how social scientists conducted themselves on the stand and how their arguments could be extended to argue that desegregation was a reasonable possibility.

On February 20, 1952, a week before the trial was scheduled to start, Annette Peyser, the sociologist on the staff of the NAACP-LDEF, sent Smith copies of expert testimony in the previous cases in order to familiarize him with the basic form his testimony should take.[20] Smith obviously studied the testimony well, for in his own testimony he reiterated the themes that the NAACP-LDEF had stressed in all their previous cases: that there was no difference in learning ability between African Americans and white Americans, that segregation imposed a feeling of inferiority on African Americans, and that official segregation set the stamp of inferiority much more firmly than unofficial segregation.

Smith, however, added a new argument to the mix: that segregation also had baleful effects on the majority group. He argued that "there are also parallel disadvantages to the white group in a system of segregation, particularly in the educational sphere in this matter of cutting down on the variety of experiences, the variety of personal relationships, to which the white child is exposed."[21] This was the first time that psychological damage to the majority group would be posited in the litigation. The social scientists began to emphasize psychological damage to white children when they wrote briefs for the appeal to the Supreme Court.

Smith's testimony also exemplified the second set of arguments offered by social scientists during their testimony, which posited that desegregation could be easily and quickly accomplished. It was during a vigorous cross-examination that Smith brought out these arguments. The lead attorney for Virginia was T. Justin Moore, a high-powered corporate lawyer and a fixture of the Richmond establishment. Moore was a product of old-fashioned southern traditions and had been practicing law six years longer than M. Brewster Smith had been alive. In the *Davis* trial, Moore set out to defend segregation to the death. As Spottswood Robinson, the local attorney for the NAACP-LDEF, noted at the time, Moore was out to "cut our throats."[22]

Many of Moore's questions had been raised by opposing attorneys ever since Robert Redfield's testimony in the *Sweatt* case in 1947. Moore got Smith to admit that he had spent almost no time in the South, for example. He questioned Smith about the speed of desegregation when he asked Smith to contrast the elimination of segregation "through a gradual process, what I will call a sort of evolutionary process, rather than through an effort to obtain some sort of court decree." Smith at first denied that a court decree could not be part of a larger, gradual process. When Moore pressed the issue, however, and insinuated that the white people of Virginia would never accept desegregation and that children learning of this attitude in the home would never accept desegregated schools, Smith referred to Gerhart Saenger's study of integrated sales personnel: "There is a lot of evidence that has been accumulated recently to show that people's behavior, what they actually do in real situations, frequently is by no means utterly consistent with these attitudes that they give verbal consideration to." He then explained the studies that had shown that people pursuing common goals very often got along very well, despite racial differences. Smith concluded, "The situation in a school, where you have together children pursuing a common educational goal, not studying race relations but studying arithmetic, is just the kind of situation where good relations can be had and where the home pattern can, perhaps be partially undone."[23]

Smith's testimony here foreshadowed the great amount of attention that social scientists would give to the possibility of desegregation in the South. Particularly between the 1954 and 1955 *Brown* decisions, social scientists would spend a great deal of time arguing that the weight of the law could, for all intents and purposes, force desegregation on white people of the South. This position became especially clear when Moore pressed the point even further, likening court-ordered desegregation to Prohibition. Since Prohibition had failed, Moore argued, it would seem logical that court-ordered desegregation would fail as well. Smith's reply obviously relied on the *Authoritarian Personality* study, which linked prejudice to a host of personality traits, such as deference to authority: those who suffered from the authoritarian personality were extremely deferential to authority, Smith argued, and were likely to follow the dictates of the law, "so that if, with the full authority of the court, with the full and sincere backing of the state authorities, segregation were ruled as being unconstitutional . . . the more highly prejudiced individual would be likely to fall in line and comply."[24]

During his cross-examination, Smith had succeeded in getting into the Court record many of the issues that the social scientists would write into their brief for the appeal to the Supreme Court.

In their testimony, the social scientists drew on arguments that had been circulating in the social science literature for a decade. In many cases, they made arguments that they had previously published in books or articles. Where they did not draw on their own works, they made arguments that had appeared in the social-scientific literature.

The most famous piece of expert testimony in the school segregation trials is that of Kenneth B. Clark, involving his use of children's dolls to measure psychological damage. In many ways the focus on Clark's doll tests is historically inaccurate. While he was a key organizer for the NAACP-LDEF and social scientists, Clark was only one of dozens of expert witnesses who testified during the litigation campaign. Clark himself testified at three of the four trials but used the doll tests in only two of those trials. Because Clark's testimony came to symbolize all the social-scientific testimony during the trials, however, it is necessary to examine it in some depth; for if there was a place where objective science began to appear as advocacy, it was in the testimony of Kenneth B. Clark.

Trial Testimony of Kenneth B. Clark

In 1950, just before Kenneth Clark began his work with the NAACP-LDEF, he and Mamie Phipps Clark were entering one of the most productive times of their careers. After the war, Kenneth joined the faculty at CCNY, and Mamie was the director of the Northside Testing and Consultation Center. The Clarks established the Northside Center in 1946 with their own funds in order to provide psychological services to troubled youth in the Harlem community, and to provide Mamie with a job commensurate with her skills as a doctor of psychology. During the war, Mamie worked as a research psychologist for the United States Armed Forces Institute. After the war, she found few job offers for an African American woman with a Ph.D. in psychology. The Clarks opened the Northside Center to fill what they saw as a genuine need in the Harlem community. The clinic offered services that ranged from pediatrics to psychological testing.[25] But the establishment of the Northside Center did not mean that the Clarks had abandoned empirical social psychology research altogether.

Throughout World War II and during the establishment of Northside, the Clarks had the data that Kenneth had collected in 1940, which they were intending to use in a series of follow-up studies to their papers on African American self-identification. In their postwar publications, the Clarks were expressly interested in racial self-preference—that is, did children wish to be white? As we have seen, prewar writers, notably those who published the ACE studies, stopped short of arguing that black children wished they were white. The Clarks would take this final step. Their postwar studies would be heavily influenced by Kurt Lewin's theories of Jewish self-hatred, which he had published on the eve of World War II. The Clarks would refashion Lewin's theory to apply to self-hatred in African Americans.[26] For example, Kenneth Clark used Lewin's approach in the study of Seaside that he undertook for CCI in 1945. Writing on "Negro-Jewish" relations in 1946, he used the concept of self-hatred to explain hostility between African Americans and Jewish Americans: "If the attitude of the dominant society is predominantly negative to one's own group the members of that group may be influenced even to the point of hating themselves as a group."[27] The Clarks would also use Lewin's concepts of group self-hatred when it came time to analyze their 1940 data set.

Because of the war, publication of any studies from this second data set was delayed until 1947. The first published results of the Clarks' second data set appeared in a volume edited by the SPSSI Committee on the Teaching of Social Psychology. For this study, the Clarks explicitly addressed what they had only tangentially explored in their earlier studies—did African American children want to be white?

In their 1947 paper, the Clarks presented the results of their "doll test," perhaps the most famous and controversial of the social-scientific work used in the *Brown* litigation. The subjects of the Clarks' study were 253 African American children, 134 of whom were in segregated southern schools while 119 were in integrated northern schools. The children were presented with two black dolls and two white dolls. Except for color, the dolls were identical in every way. The children were asked a series of eight questions concerning the dolls. The first four questions were designed to reveal racial preferences—"Give me the doll that you like the best" or "Give me the nice doll." The next three were designed to discover racial identification—"Give me the doll that looks like a white child," "Give me the doll that looks like a colored child," and "Give me the doll that looks like a Negro child." The final question, "Give me the doll that looks like you," was to reveal self-identification.[28] The Clarks controlled for age, sex, skin complexion, and geographical location. The racial identification portion of the tests substantiated the Clarks' and Ruth Horowitz's earlier studies. In the racial preference portion of the study, however, the Clarks' results "disturbed" them to such an extent that Kenneth later claimed that they delayed publication of the data.[29]

The Clarks wrote that "the majority of these Negro children prefer the *white* doll and reject the colored doll." Two-thirds of the children consistently wanted to play with the white doll and claimed that it was the "nice" doll. A concomitant percentage rejected the black doll. The Clarks wrote, "The importance of these results for an understanding of the origin and development of racial concepts and attitudes in Negro children cannot be minimized. Of equal significance are their implications, in the light of the results of racial identification already presented, to racial mental hygiene."[30] When the Clarks presented the results of the racial preference portion of the test and controlled for geographical location, they found, however, that

> northern and southern children . . . tend to be similar in the degree of their
> preference for the white doll—with the northern children tending to be
> somewhat more favorable to the white doll than are the southern children.
> The southern children, however, in spite of their equal favorableness to-
> ward the white doll, are significantly less likely to reject the brown doll
> (evaluate it negatively), as compared to the strong tendency for the major-
> ity of the northern children to do so.[31]

The Clarks reached a similar conclusion in the second and final study from this data set, published in 1950. In this test, the Clarks employed a "coloring test" wherein the children were asked to use crayons to color in drawings of a leaf, an apple, an orange, a mouse, a boy, and a girl. The child was asked to color in the objects to determine that the child had a "stable concept of the relation of color to object." If the child had a stable concept of color, then the child would be asked to color one of the children "the color that you are" and the other child "the color you like little boys (or girls) to be."[32]

The coloring test found that 48 percent of the children colored their preferences brown or black, 36 percent chose white or yellow, and 16 percent chose an "irrelevant color." But, once again, when the Clarks controlled for geographical location, they found that

> 44 percent of the Northern children color their preference white while only 25 percent of the Southern children do. . . . Additional evidence of greater emotional conflict in the Northern children is suggested by the fact that 20 percent of these children made an irrelevant response (colored their preference in a bizarre color). Only 5 percent of the Southern children colored their preference in a bizarre color.[33]

The fact that the northern children rejected the color brown to a greater degree than did the southern children would cause Kenneth Clark no end of trouble after the *Brown* decision. For the time being, it is enough to realize that the Clarks interpreted the rejection of the color brown as a "fundamental conflict at the very foundations of the ego structure" of the children tested. The Clarks closed their study by emphasizing "the need for a definite mental hygiene and educational program that would relieve children of the tremendous burden of feelings of inadequacy and inferiority which seem to become integrated into the very structure of personality as it is developing."[34] This finding of psychological damage harks back to the sociological work of E. Franklin Frazier and the other sociologists who conducted the ACE studies in the late 1930s (discussed in chapter 2).

When Kenneth Clark first took the witness stand in *Briggs v. Elliott* in South Carolina, he was armed not just with the studies he and Mamie had conducted on racial preference, nor just with his White House Conference paper, but with data from Clarendon County, where the South Carolina schools were located. Clark had come down the week before the trial with his dolls to run tests on the children of the area, in an attempt to make the academic work of his papers more relevant to the trial at hand. For Clark, being sent out to rural South Carolina was a terrifying experience. He had spent nearly his entire life in New York City and Washington, D.C., and for the first time he experienced the racism of the

Deep South. Accompanied by a few local African American men to act as bodyguards, Clark ran through his doll tests with local children at one of the schools named in the lawsuit.[35]

On the stand, Clark recounted the projective methods that he and his wife had developed and how they were used to gain insight into the minds of very young children. He also described the literature review he had prepared for the White House Conference. When Carter asked what conclusions Clark drew from this information, Clark testified that "discrimination, prejudice, and segregation have definitely detrimental effects on the personality development of the Negro child." Clark also noted that this conclusion was supported by 90 percent of the social scientists who had studied the area, citing Deutscher and Chein's survey of social science opinion.[36] Clark then presented the results of the tests on the local children, testifying that "in Clarendon County . . . we found eleven out of sixteen children picking the brown doll as looking 'bad.' . . . Over half of these children, in spite of their own feelings—negative feelings—about the brown doll, were eventually required on the last question to identify themselves with this doll. . . . Only one of these children . . . dared to choose the white doll as looking bad." Clark concluded that the children of "Clarendon County . . . have been definitely harmed in the development of their personalities."[37]

Because it would later become one of the more hotly contested claims of the entire trial procedure, it is important to note just what claim Clark made: that the identification of the brown doll as the bad doll indicated psychological damage. This claim was supported by the further finding that the children refused to identify the white doll as the bad doll. As we will see, in subsequent trials, Clark would find evidence of psychological damage in different sorts of identification.

On cross-examination, Attorney General Robert Figg asked Clark if these harms Clark listed stemmed from the school the children attended. Although Carter's pretrial strategy did not require that the schools be isolated as the only causal factor of the psychological damage, Clark felt he had some good reasons for blaming the schools. Clark answered that the school "definitely" was a causal factor. As proof, Clark cited a series of interviews he had conducted with ten older children in the school system. Clark claimed that these older children made "definite and categorical statements concerning their feelings and their attitudes about attending" the Clarendon County schools. From this information, Clark made his statement that the school system contributed to the harms he had cited.[38]

Because his techniques changed in later trials, it is important to note here that Clark used the projective test—the doll technique—with younger children and an interview to test older children. Clark's *Briggs* testimony, by and large, followed the logic of the papers he had published with Mamie. Children who consistently identified the brown doll as the bad doll were psychologically damaged. In subsequent developments, this logic would be abandoned by Clark, as he offered what were apparently inconsistent interpretations of his findings.

As he did in South Carolina, Kenneth Clark examined children from Delaware in an attempt to discover psychological damage for the next trial in which he participated, *Belton v. Gebhart*. His subsequent testimony about his examination underscored the difficulties he had in using the doll tests in a consistent manner.

Clark had arranged with the local attorney working with the NAACP-LDEF, Louis Redding, to examine forty-one children from the area, thirteen of whom were the plaintiff's children, a few weeks before the trial. At first, the NAACP-LDEF had hoped to arrange for Lois Barclay Murphy to analyze Clark's results, but that turned out not to be possible.[39] Clark gave the children the doll test and the coloring test and then interviewed them. On September 19, 1951, the month before the trial, he gave the results of the doll test to Louis Redding. Clark noted that "the results of the coloring test are just about what I had expected to find and the results from the interviews were most positive in showing that the youngsters were quite aware [of] and deeply resented the discrimination to which they were subjected." Clark did not, however, share the results of the coloring test or the interviews with Redding—only the results of the doll tests, because these were the "most significant findings and the ones which are most difficult to interpret."[40] As we will see, Clark's interpretation of his results in Delaware cut against his previous test interpretations.

In the Clarks' original 1947 study, a preference for the white doll was marked by "concomitant negative attitude toward the brown doll."[41] In his tests of the Delaware children, this relationship disappeared, as only three children said the white doll was the one they liked best, yet 75 percent of the children who identified a doll that would "act bad" chose the brown doll. In other words, the strong relationship that existed between acceptance of the white doll and rejection of the brown doll that Clark had found in his original study was not duplicated in the Delaware children. Clark noted that the verbalized preference for the brown doll "would seem to suggest that these children have not been damaged in their racial self-esteem" but added that "this assumption is contradicted by the fact that of those children who permit themselves to answer the question—which of those dolls would 'act bad,' 75% of them indicated that the brown doll would most likely be the one to 'act bad.'[42]

Beyond failing to duplicate the results of the 1947 study, Clark faced an additional problem with his Delaware results. The vast majority of the children refused to identify *any* doll as that which would "act bad." The 75 percent figure that Clark found applied only to *those expressing a preference*. The raw numbers consisted of twelve children who preferred the white doll and four children who preferred the brown doll. But, significantly, twenty-five children, or 60 percent of all the children, refused to make *any* identification of a bad doll. This figure was wildly out of line with Clark's 1947 results, where a paltry 3 percent refused to make an identification.

One possible explanation for the large majority of the Delaware children failing to make an identification of a bad doll may lie in the ages of the tested children. Projective tests had been developed as a method for the study of very young children. Ruth Horowitz and Lois Barclay Murphy, in describing the use of projective tests, referred to "nursery school" children being tested with the toys they would normally use for play.[43] In the Clarks' 1947 study, none of the children tested was over seven years old. Yet, in the Delaware sample, only two of the forty-one children were under seven years old. The other thirty-nine children were between the ages of twelve and seventeen, with a median age of fifteen. Hence, it could be argued—and in another context, Clark would himself argue—that the projective test using dolls would be inappropriate for use with this age group.

In his report to Redding, however, Clark dismissed the notion that the high percentage of children who refused to make a choice of a bad doll reflected "general sophistication [of the children] and methodological inadequacy [of the study]." Rather, Clark argued, the failure to identify *any* doll as a bad doll indicated that the children were "seeking to avoid coming to grips with the personally disturbing problem of racial status." This could have been a reasonable interpretation for results of tests with these older children, but on its face it seemed improbable. In contrast to the *Briggs* trial, where Clark argued that children picking the brown doll as bad indicated psychological damage, here he was arguing that *failing* to pick the brown doll as bad was "evidence of damage to the self-esteem, and the distortion of the self image."[44] Soon after the Delaware trial, Clark would argue that even if a child identified the *white* doll as the bad doll, that choice would also indicate psychological damage. In other words, no matter what choice a child made, Clark would interpret it as indicating psychological damage.

In his Delaware testimony, however, Clark did not argue that refusing to choose a bad doll indicated psychological damage. Instead, he took the same approach as in the *Briggs* trial. Clark testified that "the practice of segregation as perceived by these youngsters impaired their general functioning as revealed by the results of these tests and the results of my interviews with them." As evidence, Clark abandoned the idea that failing to identify a bad doll indicated damage and instead argued:

> The nature of the impairment seemed clearly indicated by the results in which it is seen that . . . three out of every four youngsters, who when asked the question "Which of these dolls is likely to act bad?" picked the brown doll. The brown doll to them was associated with all the negative stereotypes which are usually ascribed to Negroes in our culture. This indicated clearly the damage to the self esteem of these youngsters.

Clark then testified that the nature of the damage was heightened given that the children tested had a strong sense of self-identity. They had all correctly answered the final question of the projective test, "Give me the doll that looks like you." Clark testified:

> Now, when you see that 100% of these youngsters correctly identify themselves with the brown doll, and three out of four of them had made a choice of one of these dolls when asked "Which one is likely to act bad?" . . . we have clear-evidence of rather deep damage to self esteem of these youngsters, a feeling of inferiority, a feeling of inadequacy.[45]

That Clark found that all the children correctly self-identified should not have been surprising, given that he and his wife had found in their 1947 study that "there is a general and marked increase in the percent of subjects who identify with the colored doll with an increase in age," and that by age seven, 87 percent of the children correctly self-identified.[46] The median age of the Delaware children was twelve, the 100 percent figure should not have seemed out of line.

But beyond the issue of self-identification, Clark's testimony was not precisely what he had found in his examination. He had not, in fact, found that "three out of every four" children identified the brown doll as bad, rather that three out of four *who made a choice* made such an identification. Clark's rather strained interpretation about those children who refused to make any identification was not made public, and instead, Clark offered the straightforward point about the Delaware children equating the brown doll and the bad doll, even though it was not quite what he had found in his examination. These issues were not raised in the trial, at least partly because the state's attorney did not press them in a cross examination of Clark. He was not questioned about the sample size, the results of his tests, the percentages of each answer to his tests. In the next trial, in Virginia, Clark would be pressed much harder.

Kenneth Clark had examined the children in Virginia just as he had in South Carolina and Delaware. Like Delaware, the school at the center of the lawsuit was a high school. Perhaps recognizing that the projective tests he attempted to give the high school students in Delaware were, in fact, inappropriate to that age group, Clark settled on an interview with a group of the plaintiffs' children.

In his interviews, Clark asked fourteen children a series of questions designed to elicit their opinions about their school, the white school, and race relations generally. In notes made from those interviews, he observed that "not one ascribed any positive thing to the Negro school" and concluded that the "school is [a] symbol of the negative—symbol of stigma." By contrast, Clark noted that "not one assume any negative character of the white school." When asked what could be done about the state of the school, nine children responded that the state should build a new school for them. Two of the children thought it would require a court case to get the state to fix the schools. Clark remarked in his notes, "If [they] see any hope at all, [they] see it only in terms of their own efforts and the prestige of the law."[47]

On the stand, Clark related the general nature of his testing procedures, describing the various projective tests he had conducted in his scientific career. He also described the nature of the scientific literature that found feelings of inferiority in African Americans. Clark then testified to the results of his interviews with the children, relating his finding that the school was the "symbol of the negative" for the children and that they did not describe the white school negatively. In concluding his testimony, Clark noted that the children were "obsessed" with racial matters and that their opinion "toward their school, toward their family, toward their society, toward people who look like themselves, toward people who look differently, . . . the structure of practically everything they perceive, is racial."[48]

During Clark's cross-examination, Attorney General Justin Moore turned to the tests that Clark had conducted on the Virginia children.

Showing that he was familiar with at least some of the previous trials, Moore asked Clark why he did not use the doll test on the Virginia children, as he had in South Carolina. Clark replied, "Because the children with whom I had contact here were older children. The doll method has been found to be useful and sensitive almost exclusively for the use of children between the ages of four and eight."[49] Yet, instead of asking why, if Clark was not confident in the doll tests for high school students, he had used them in the Delaware case, Moore turned to the details of the interview in Virginia.

Clark's admission that the doll tests were not reliable indicators of psychological states in high school children made his Delaware testimony more problematic. Apart from basically misrepresenting the results of the doll tests in Delaware, Clark had now admitted that the entire test was an unreliable indicator of psychological damage the age group in question. That Moore did not pursue this line of questioning probably indicated that he had not paid enough attention to the Delaware trial, where the state had not defended segregation very vigorously.

Moore, however, had discovered an anomaly in Clark's studies. Referring to Clark's published work, Moore asked, "Isn't it true that you found the same reaction of colored children in the New England area in response to your doll tests that you did in South Carolina and these other places?" In fact, the Clarks' 1947 study had found that "southern children in segregated schools are less pronounced in their preference for the white doll, compared to northern children's definite preference for this doll."[50] Clark's response to this question was:

> I think that the reaction of children is never to just one aspect of their society. These children appeared to be sensitive to all aspects of their society. I think it was pointed out that there is segregation in parts of the country in which there is no legal, or legally-enforced, segregation. The child responds to the fact of segregation. He responds to the treatment of the Negro in our mass media—in our newspapers, on the radio—the dialect and menial role which is generally ascribed to Negroes—and, I presume, television. There are a myriad of factors in a society, North or South, which influence children's reactions.[51]

As we have seen in the testimony of the other social scientists, this was not, for Clark, a stunning admission about the limits of social science. Clark knew that the NAACP-LDEF was not arguing that psychological damage was caused only by legally mandated school segregation. Indeed, the basic social-scientific argument the NAACP-LDEF was presenting against segregation was little hurt by Clark's statement that psychological damage existed in northern school children. But Clark's response also underscores the shifting nature of his claims regarding the interpretations of his findings in the Delaware case.

Before Moore could question Clark further about what appeared to be his admission that the doll tests showed greater damage in the unsegregated North than in the segregated South, one of the trial judges interrupted the testimony to question Clark on an irrelevant tangent. When Moore finally gained control of the floor once again, the testimony had drifted away from the doll tests. But the testimony remained. One of Clark's main projects would soon be explaining away the seemingly incongruous results of his doll tests in northern areas. He was not called on to do so in any of the trials, partly because his conflicting interpretations emerged over the course of several trials and partly because the attorneys defending segregation did not question any of the expert witnesses to any great extent. In only one trial, *Davis* in Virginia, did the defense care to contest anything said by the expert witnesses.

Defense of Segregation: The States Respond

During the *Briggs* trial, the opposing attorney, Robert Figg, did not press Clark on his cross-examination, believing that Clark's testimony did little to damage the state's defense.[52] Figg simply thought that the expert witnesses were irrelevant to the case. He had made a half-hearted effort to enlist Howard Odum and Guy Johnson, two sociologists from the University of North Carolina, to testify for the state. When they refused, Figg was not too upset, since he thought the social science testimony was relatively unimportant.[53]

The situation was similar in Kansas and Delaware. The opposing attorneys made no real attack on the expert witnesses. One explanation is that, like Robert Figg, the opposing attorneys simply thought the social science testimony to be too weak to pose any real threat to segregation. Another explanation may be that the border states of Kansas and Delaware were not vigorous defenders of segregation generally. In Kansas and Delaware, the NAACP-LDEF was litigating in border states that were more moderate on racial issues than South Carolina or Virginia—the site of the last school segregation trial. For the attorneys representing Kansas and

Delaware defending segregated schools may have been a part of their job, but they had no strong emotional commitment to it. For the lead Virginia attorney, however, segregation was a way of life that was being attacked by the litigation of the NAACP-LDEF. Moreover, Virginia's attorneys had seen the NAACP-LDEF in previous trials and were well aware of the strategy the organization would employ. Consequently, when the NAACP-LDEF arrived in Virginia, they knew they were in for a fight. The lead attorney for Virginia, Justin Moore, would defend segregation with all the weapons at his disposal, including social science testimony.

The brunt of Moore's attack on the social science testimony was directed at the testimony of Isidor Chein, who was still with the American Jewish Congress in February 1952, the time of the trial. Chein had been brought down to testify on the survey of social science opinion that had been a mainstay of the NAACP-LDEF's use of social science since its publication in 1948.[54] On the witness stand, Chein testified to the methodology and results of the survey of social science opinion. He explained how the social science community overwhelmingly believed that legally enforced segregation harmed both the segregated and the segregating group. He also explained the lines of evidence he had listed in his 1948 article that supported the proposition of psychological damage.

On cross-examination, Moore, in an infamous display of bigotry, first determined that Chein was "one-hundred percent Jewish," worked for a Jewish organization, and was funded from money collected from Jewish charities. He also questioned Chein about the relationship between the American Jewish Congress and the NAACP and seemed disappointed when Chein answered that, while the Commission on Law and Social Action had worked with the NAACP, Chein himself had not.[55]

Moore then questioned Chein extensively on the methodology of the social science survey, especially on how many of those who responded to the survey were from southern states and on how many of the southern responses were from "Negro" social scientists. On the second point, Chein answered that he had no idea because "within the fraternity of science, we do not distinguish color. A colored person can be as competent a scientist as a non-colored one."[56] Moore also pushed Chein on self-hatred in Jews. Chein responded that the self-hatred in Jews was of a "much less marked degree than in the case of the Negro," and that this difference owed to the "weight of the government" telling African Americans they were inferior.[57] In the end, Moore, despite what the presiding judge described as a "grueling cross examination," failed to score many points against Chein's testimony.[58] Given that Chein had been arguing for the elimination of segregation since 1946, Moore's failure should not be too surprising. More was yet to come for Chein's survey, however, for Virginia was going to fight fire with fire. For the first time during the litigation campaign, the state was prepared to offer its own expert witnesses in defense of segregation.

The first two experts who testified for the state were William H. Kelly, a psychiatrist who was the director of the Memorial Guidance Clinic in Richmond, Virginia, and John N. Buck, a clinical psychologist from Whitestone, Virginia. Both of these men expressed a concern that the local white population in Virginia was not ready to accept unsegregated public schools, although under cross-examination both men admitted that segregation was psychologically damaging to segregated individuals.[59] It was the third and final expert witness for the state, however, who was the most significant.

The final witness for the state was Henry E. Garrett (1904–1973), the head of the Psychology Department at Columbia University. Garrett had been on Kenneth Clark's Ph.D. committee and had been Mamie Clark's Ph.D. adviser. He was a former president of the American Psychological Association and had received any number of honors from the profession for his work in psychological testing and psychometrics. He was, in short, a very senior member of the psychological community. He was also an unabashed segregationist who was convinced that African Americans were inherently inferior to white Americans. Soon after the *Davis* trial, he would leave Columbia to take a position at the University of Virginia, where he would become increasingly marginalized and extreme in his racial views.[60]

At the *Davis* trial, Moore first led his star witness through his extensive qualifications, not forgetting to emphasize that Garrett was a "Virginia boy that moved up to the big city."[61] Moore then asked Garrett if segregation was psychologically damaging to African Americans. Garrett answered:

> I do not think that one can possibly defend separation of one group from another, if the separated group is stigmatized or put into an inferior position. Separation can be of different sorts which does not involve, necessarily, any feeling of inferiority or any stigma. The principle of separation in education, for example, is long and well established in American life. . . . So long as the facilities are equal, the mere fact of separation does not seem to me to be, in itself discriminatory.[62]

Moore recalled for Garrett the testimony of M. Brewster Smith, who had claimed that segregation was "inherently an insult to the integrity of the individual." Garrett claimed that this was "fairly strong language" to describe segregation and that Smith was probably just an "idealistic person, who is likely to let his sympathies go beyond his judgment." Having thus dispensed with the "young Dr. Smith," the elder statesman of psychology, led by Moore, turned his attention to the survey of social science opinion conducted by Isidor Chein.[63]

Although he claimed he did "not like to comment on Dr. Chein's study," Garrett soon warmed to the task. An expert on the design of psychological tests, Garrett had two main criticisms of Chein's study. First, he argued, the questions were "blunderbuss" questions that conflated several issues into one. Garrett testified that Chein "asked whether enforced segregation—which has an implied threat, racial and religious, which is a double-barreled affair—is detrimental—without saying how it was detrimental; he did not specify whether he meant by segregation legally or segregation by custom, whether he meant it in buses, theaters, churches, schools, or what." Garrett claimed that Chein's questions, as posed, were unanswerable, and if he had been sent a questionnaire, he would have returned it unanswered.[64]

Garrett's second criticism was that Chein had selected a sample to skew the result of the study in the manner he desired. Garrett claimed that the American Psychological Association had more than 8,000 members, and yet Chein had polled only 416. Garrett professed that he was "surprised that he [Chein] did not select his sample well enough to have gotten a hundred per cent. . . . I would not like to make a bet, but I wager that I could send a questionnaire and phrase it rightly and get almost any answer I wanted." Regarding Clark's testimony, Garrett claimed that psychology had not developed any tests that could adequately measure a child's attitude toward segregation. He dismissed Clark's interviews with the local children because there had been general unrest in the community about segregation; indeed, the students had been on strike against the school just before Clark administered his tests. Under these circumstances, the students would naturally take the opportunity to criticize their schools.[65]

Garrett's testimony was designed to demonstrate how the idealistic young social scientists, some of whom he had trained, had let their good intentions get in the way of proper scientific procedure. As an expert in test design, Garrett had singled out the one social science study that had been designed specifically for use in the legal arena: Chein's survey of social science opinion. What Garrett had attempted to do was to show how Chein had become a pure advocate for the overthrow of segregation, using the facade of science to mask his true character. For the first time, but by no means the last, the social scientists had been accused of letting their feelings about segregation overcome proper scientific procedure.

At the Virginia trial, little was done to rehabilitate Chein's survey. Robert Carter had arranged for Kenneth Clark to sit at counsel's table with him during Garrett's cross-examination. Carter drew out more criticisms from Garrett on projective tests and how inadequate they were. Then Carter proceeded to quote from a recently published book by Garrett in which he spoke of the usefulness of projective tests and the interview method of testing to gain insight into people with personality problems. Carter then got Garrett to agree to the question: "In attempting to measure the impact of the discrimination, segregation, aren't these the very personal and intimate things for which the projected [*sic*] technique would be the most useful?"[66]

After Garrett admitted that the testing methods employed by Clark were well suited to the task, Carter further explored Garrett's position on segregation. He got Garrett to admit, "In general, whenever a person is cut off from the main body of society or a group, if he is put into a position that stigmatizes him and makes him feel inferior . . . it is detrimental and deleterious to him." Garrett, however, wanted to draw a distinction between segregation in general being harmful and segregation being so as it was practiced in Virginia, where "if the Negro child had equal facilities, his own teachers, his own friends, and a good feeling, he would be more likely to develop pride in himself as Negro. . . . They would develop their sense of dramatic art, and music, which they seem to have a talent for."[67] Carter ended his cross-examination with an admission from Garrett that the facilities in Virginia, as they presently stood, were unequal, and hence racial segregation caused a stigma of inferiority.

The repercussions of Garrett's testimony quickly traveled through the community of activist social scientists. The social scientists who had testified in Virginia were, in M. Brewster Smith's words, "completely and perennially shocked at the content of Garrett's testimony."[68] Carter worried that Garrett's testimony would give the appearance that there was a "wide diversion among social scientists on this particular issue."[69] For his part, Smith was outraged by Garrett's testimony and thought it was "something that no psychologist in his position should be allowed to get away with."[70] He suggested that Stuart Cook, then the president of SPSSI, attempt to get the APA to take some action regarding Garrett's testimony. Smith wrote to Carter that the reprimand had to come from the APA, rather than from SPSSI, because "members of SPSSI are already branded . . . as zealots in this area"; hence, "Garrett would not worry too much about what SPSSI had to say about him."[71] Nothing, however, seems to have come from Smith's call for official action against Garrett.

The most extensive criticism of Garrett's testimony was made by Isidor Chein. Stuart Cook once said of Chein that "when he analyzed a topic he, quite literally, exhausted its intellectual content."[72] Chein's penchant for exhausting analysis was certainly evident after he had read Garrett's testimony. Chein sent a five-page single-spaced letter to Robert Carter that attacked the logic of Garrett's testimony with scalpel-like precision. For example, he examined every instance where Garrett attempted to deny the "stigma which is attached to statutory segregation" and pointed out that Garrett never actually clearly claimed there was no stigma. And Garrett openly admitted that if a stigma was attached to segregation, it was necessarily discrimination. Chein noted that Garrett's very grammar betrayed the stigma: Garrett persisted in using the phrase "the separated group," which "admits that the separation is not equal for the two groups. He could have said, 'if one of the separated groups . . .' but he didn't. In other words, his perception of the status relationships involved is accurate." After closely examining Garrett's testimony, Chein concluded that "the sum total of Garrett's testimony on this point is not only that he does not challenge the existence of a stigma which is related to statutory segregation, but that he accepts it."

Chein also came to the defense of his survey of social-scientific opinion. He explained, as he did in his direct testimony at the trial, that he did not select particular social scientists for the survey but took all social scientists who were members of the relevant organizations for the subject matter. Moreover, on the wording of the questions, Chein wrote that "Garrett knows as well as I do that there are times when a shotgun question is perfectly justified." After defending his study, Chein remarked that Garrett's testimony had essentially attacked his "personal integrity" but that a close examination of the actual methods of the study demonstrated that the attack was without merit.[73] Much to Chein's chagrin, however, Garrett's criticisms of his study would be raised one more time. Unfortunately for Chein, it would be in front of the Supreme Court, and he would have little opportunity to defend himself.

Conclusion

One week after the trial in Virginia concluded, on March 7, 1952, the decision was handed down. To no one's surprise, the court found that segregated schools did not violate the U.S. Constitution. The expert witnesses, the court declared, canceled each other out—both sides offered equally cogent arguments.[74] The NAACP-LDEF immediately began the appeals process, hoping to have the case join *Briggs* and *Brown* before the U.S. Supreme Court. *Briggs* and *Brown* had already been decided against the NAACP-LDEF. In fact, by the time *Davis* was decided, the first two cases already had been appealed to the Supreme Court.

The decision in the Delaware trial finally came down in April 1952. The decision was a qualified victory for the NAACP-LDEF. The court had found a substantial denial of educational opportunities for African Americans in Delaware. While the court did not feel it had the power to overturn the separate-but-equal doctrine, it did order immediate desegregation of the Delaware schools. Moreover, the social-scientific testimony, especially because it was unopposed, seemed to be a deciding factor in the decision.[75] The state immediately began the appeals process that would eventually bring the case before the U.S. Supreme Court.

For the NAACP-LDEF, the social-scientific testimony appeared to be a gamble that had paid off—most significantly in the Kansas decision. While the court there had decided to uphold segregation, it had also issued a "finding of fact." Following closely on the testimony of Louisa Holt, one of the NAACP-LDEF expert witnesses, the court found:

> Segregation of white and colored children in public schools has a detrimental effect upon the colored children. The impact is greater when it has the sanction of the law; for the policy of separating the races is usually interpreted as denoting the inferiority of the Negro group. A sense of inferiority affects the motivation of a child to learn. Segregation with the sanction of law, therefore, has a tendency to retard the educational and mental development of Negro children and to deprive them of some of the benefits they would receive in a racially integrated school system.[76]

Judge Huxman later claimed that he was attempting to force the issue for the Supreme Court—to "wrap it up in a way that they could not duck it. They had whittled away at it long enough."[77] The finding of fact made by the district court in Kansas would play a large part in the shaping of the U.S. Supreme Court decision of 1954.

Social science testimony had also been quoted approvingly by the court in the Delaware decision. While it had failed to make any headway in South Carolina and Virginia, the NAACP-LDEF knew that they had no real chance of winning those decisions, regardless of the evidence presented. In short, social science had been successful enough for the NAACP-LDEF to work it into the appeals strategy. The next chapter examines just how the social scientists were enrolled in the appeals process.

For the social scientists, the trials were an opportunity to present their arguments against segregation. In particular, social scientists made a number of points that meshed well with the cases at hand. First, *legal* segregation was particularly damaging because the segregated individual could not possibly rationalize the status assigned to him or her. Second, segregation *in schools* was particularly damaging because the school's role in a child's life was so pervasive. Third, individuals would follow desegregation orders from the courts, because racial prejudice was particularly vulnerable to authoritative orders. All these points came out of the social-scientific literature that had emerged after World War II. Moreover, the defense attorneys had not really made any arguments that the social scientists had not anticipated long before the trials ever started. Too often the defense attorneys were reduced to asking the social scientists how much time they had spent in the South and, in the case of Justin Moore, dwelling on the racial or ethnic background of the witness. Such arguments were not likely to sway anyone's opinion, except among the local populace.

And yet there were signs of strain in the platform of the social scientists. The testing procedures of Kenneth Clark in particular seemed subject to his own interpretation, rather than based on firm, factual data. The Delaware case, in which Clark, either purposely or by accident, misrepresented the results of his doll tests, showed that the test was perhaps too flexible a device to prove the dangers of desegregation. As we see in subsequent chapters, the doll tests would become by far the most controversial aspect of social-scientific involvement in the *Brown* litigation. In fact, the first questions would appear publicly, even before the case was heard by the Supreme Court.

8

Supreme Court Hearings and Decision, *Brown I*

For two years, between October 1951 and December 1953, social scientists were working with the NAACP-LDEF on the appeal of the school segregation cases. Initially, the work done on the appeal was done within an official committee of SPSSI, but soon Kenneth Clark began to dominate the project, assisted by various friends and associates within SPSSI. While this activity was going on, Clark faced another problem—his doll studies were coming under increasing public scrutiny, and he was forced to explain just why it was that northern children seemed to suffer more damage than southern children. The end of this phase of the litigation was the Supreme Court decision that found segregated schools violate the Fourteenth Amendment. The prominent mention of Kenneth Clark's name in the opinion brought another round of criticism directed at the doll tests. The two rounds of criticism serve as bookends to the appeals process for the first *Brown* decision.

Defense of the Doll Tests

In February 1952, a law student at Yale, William Delano, was working on a Note for the *Yale Law Journal* that which focused on the school segregation trials. He had noted the discrepancy between Clark's testimony and the Clarks' data in their 1947 article. After meeting with Clark, Delano asked for an explanation of the seeming contradiction between Clark's claim that legal segregation caused psychological damage and the higher percentage of northern children who identified the brown doll as the bad doll.

A week before the Virginia trial, Clark wrote to Delano that "children in racially segregated schools are more seriously damaged in the area of self-esteem than are Negro children in a racially mixed school." Northern children, explained Clark, often refused to continue the experiment or broke down in tears when "confronted with the conflict of identifying with a brown doll which they had previously stereotyped negatively." In contrast, southern children had no such problems; they "either laughed or tried to appear casual about the whole question." The only children who remarked, "'Well it is a nigger and I am a nigger,' were southern children," Clark claimed.

Clark concluded that, although this appeared to demonstrate that southern children were better adjusted than northern children, in fact the opposite was the case: southern children had accepted their inferior position in society. He wrote, "The rigid patterns of segregation in all aspects of life, the fact of segregated schools characteristic of the South, may be responsible for the ability of the southern children to accept their inferiority status as a matter of fact." Clark warned that "apparent adjustment is an adjustment to a social pathology which in any fundamental approach to personality cannot be considered a basically healthy form of personality adjustment."[1]

This response skirted the initial issue raised by Delano (and by Virginia's attorney general Moore during cross-examination), which was that northern children identified the brown doll as the bad doll in greater numbers than did southern children. This basic fact was obscured when Clark moved the discussion away from a simple analysis of the quantitative data and into the realm of interpretation of the children's emotional reactions. Such an analysis made Clark's interpretation of his Delaware results especially troubling. In his note to Louis Redding in that case, Clark had argued that avoiding an identification was a sure sign of psychological damage. But in his analysis of his original data, Clark argued that avoiding such an identification was, in fact, a healthier response than making the identification. It would seem that the doll tests were very susceptible to Clark's own interpretations.

In any case, Clark's explanation for the behavior of the northern children was not terribly persuasive. In his analysis of the Clarks' 1947 article reporting the results of their doll tests, William Cross noted in 1991 that only 14 percent of the children made any "anti-Black statements" in any case, and only two southern children used the word *nigger*. He concluded, "The Clarks then assume that the negative remarks made by a handful of children in their study or clinical practice represent *pervasive* themes in the psychodynamics, not only of Negro children in general, but of the average Negro teenager and adult."[2]

In 1952, William Delano was similarly unconvinced of Clark's explanation. In his Note, published in May, Delano argued that because the tests indicated that damage started before the child reached school age, any such damage could not be traced to school segregation. Delano also pointed out the higher percentage of northern African American children who identified the brown doll as the bad doll. While noting Clark's explanation for the disparity, Delano concluded, "It is clear, however, that these tests do not isolate school segregation as the source of emotional disturbances in Negro children."[3] Of course, the damage argument did not necessitate the isolation that Delano demanded; however, the Note did seem to undercut Clark's claims for the doll tests' ability to measure personality damage.

Within the NAACP-LDEF, the appearance of Delano's Note increased the resistance to the use of social science materials in the briefs before the Supreme Court. Robert Carter would have to push hard to overcome the skepticism toward social science among some of the NAACP-LDEF staff. Carter's task may have been made easier by the fact that the doll tests faded into the background in the social science materials being assembled for the Supreme Court. By the time the Note appeared in May 1952, the social science brief was well underway. In fact, the brief had started half a year before.

The Social Science Statement

In October 1951, two of the school segregation trials, *Briggs* in South Carolina and *Brown* in Kansas, were complete. The Delaware trial, *Belton,* was underway, and the fourth and final trial, *Davis* in Virginia, was not scheduled to begin. Though the Supreme Court had not yet agreed to hear any appeal of any trial, the NAACP-LDEF was preparing for the Supreme Court. Immediately after the Delaware trial in October, Carter wrote to Clark and told him that "we deem it advisable to begin preparation of our brief on appeal at once." Carter listed two arguments that would need relevant social science materials: first, that racial classification was an unreasonable exercise of state power, "since there is no racial difference with respect to ability to learn and absorb knowledge"; second, that "segregation is detrimental and injurious to the mental and personality development of the Negro child and deprives him of educational opportunities and benefits which he would normally obtain in an unsegregated school system." Carter invited Clark to a meeting of the NAACP-LDEF staff to begin getting the brief assembled.[4]

Besides attending meetings with the lawyers of the NAACP-LDEF, Clark was a member of SPSSI's Committee on Intergroup Relations, one of a number of SPSSI committees dedicated to various aspects of social psychology. Immediately after World War II, the "race relations" committee was renamed the Committee on Intergroup Relations. Eugene Hartley was the chair, and Daniel Katz, who had conducted some of the first studies of racial prejudice at Princeton, managed to get the young Kenneth Clark on the committee as well.[5]

In October 1951, when Carter informed Clark that the preparation of the brief was to begin at once, SPSSI's Committee on Intergroup Relations decided to conduct an "evaluation of the work done on the field of minority personality and adjustment." The head of the project was Gerhart Saenger, the former CCI staffer who had conducted research on integrated sales personnel and had joined Stuart Cook at NYU after CCI's breakup. In a December 1951 letter to committee members, and in his report to the SPSSI council a month later, Saenger offered two justifications for undertaking the survey. First, such a study would be theoretically justified because it would serve to unite many disparate areas of research from different areas of psychology, sociology, and psychoanalysis. Second, on the "practical" side, Saenger explained that "this choice was dictated by the desire to be of assistance in the forthcoming court trials before state courts and the Supreme Court in which the southern formula of 'separate but equal' will be challenged."[6]

A subcommittee was formed to prepare a statement for the trials and to prepare a journal article for professional publication. The subcommittee included Kenneth Clark and Isidor Chein, as well as New York psychiatrist Viola Bernard; Samuel Flowerman and Marie Jahoda, both of the American Jewish Committee; and Marion Radke, another former CCI staffer. After conferring with CCI, Saenger informed his subcommittee that each of them would be responsible for one section of the social-scientific literature on a given topic. Saenger listed four possible topics for discussion: minority reactions toward frustration caused by discrimination, minority reactions to prejudice, the effect of prejudice and discrimination on adjustment in intra- and intergroup relations, and the effect of cultural conflict on minority adjustment and personality. Saenger suggested that the subcommittee meet once month to exchange ideas and prepare their results.[7]

The subcommittee had met only once before Robert Carter was asking to see a draft of their proposed statement. Carter had invited Clark to attend another NAACP-LDEF planning session, scheduled for the second week of January 1952, to discuss the NAACP-LDEF's use of social science materials.[8]

Carter would have to wait until May 1952 before the subcommittee had a working outline of their statement. Titled "The Social Scientific Argument against Segregation in the Schools," the outline appeared very much as the work of a committee, containing no fewer than ten major headings, not all of them distinct from one another. The SPSSI outline was essentially a reactive document: that is, it spent a great deal of time responding to "the case for segregation," arguing that the committee's expert, scientific opinion was superior to what most people, or at least most southerners, believed about race.

Among the arguments the SPSSI outline attempted to rebut were: that racial segregation alleviated racial tension, that racial segregation was necessary because of the inferiority of African Americans, and that segregation was necessary to prevent miscegenation. Typical of these arguments was the rebuttal that segregation was a "natural" response of people to congregate with those like themselves. "There is no such thing as natural segregation," declared the SPSSI outline, "If consciousness of kind makes for segregation, why wouldn't people then segregate according to height, weight, etc."[9]

The SPSSI committee was attempting to dispel the arguments that defense attorneys had raised against the expert witnesses during the trials. For example, several witnesses were explicitly asked about the application of the psychological damage argument to laws against intermarriage of African Americans with white Americans. Hence, the SPSSI outline contained three or four arguments rebutting the applicability of their argument to miscegenation statutes.

The SPSSI committee also indicated the wide range of arguments that social scientists believed they could address. The famous "damage argument" that segregation had "detrimental effects on the personality of minority group members" was only a small part of the original SPSSI outline and not necessarily given more weight than any other argument.

On June 9, 1952, the Supreme Court agreed to hear the first two of the School Segregation Cases. Saenger immediately wrote to the committee members with the news that "since the hearings are planned for the beginning of October we are forced to rush the writing of the memorandum to be used before the Court as representing the social scientists argument against segregation in the schools."[10] Despite the rush, the social scientists were still not sure exactly what would be done with the materials they were preparing. The NAACP-LDEF attorneys were deeply divided on the use of social-scientific materials before the Supreme Court.

Since the subcommittee could not be expected to get a statement together by the deadline, the task fell to Clark and Chein. Later, after they had written two drafts, they were joined by Stuart Cook. In 1967, Clark described Cook's involvement as "just wonderful because he brought the appearance of white, Anglo-Saxon dispassionateness to our task where I had a tendency to become a little strident."[11] Stridency and passion may have been important in a legal brief, but the Social Science Statement was not a typical legal brief. In drafting the statement, Clark, Chein, and Cook attempted to maintain the personas of "objective, scientific experts" while writing for the ultimate adversarial forum—a Supreme Court hearing.

The struggle between advocacy and objectivity was apparent in three different sections of the statement that changed during the drafting process: first, changes in style that eliminated any overt calls to democracy, morality, or other "extrascientific" dimensions of segregation; second, the elimination of attacks on the "defenses of segregation" that figured so prominently in the SPSSI outline; third, the elimination of careful nuances and qualifications that served to complicate the straightforward argument against segregation.

First, stylistically, the statement went from a broad screed against segregation to a narrow claim that social science was relevant and useful in the disposition of the case. For example, in the opening paragraph of the statement, Clark had originally written what sounded like a political speech against segregation, invoking problems of democracy and cold war concerns about world leadership:

> The problem of racial segregation, imposed by legal statutes or by the administrative practices of official agencies and supported or enforced by the use of police power and judicial processes, constitutes one of the major problems facing the American people today. It is a major problem because of the damaging effect that such segregation has on the leadership position of the United States in this critical period of world affairs. Even more important, it is a major problem because it has always constituted an unresolved or only partially resolved issue in the evolution of American democracy. It is an issue which is today coming to a head, as is evidenced by the many cases before the courts, by changes in some of the administrative

practices of the Federal government, and by the important place which the more inclusive issues of civil rights have occupied in the deliberations of the recent national conventions of the major political parties.[12]

Virtually all of this paragraph was struck from the final version, most probably by Cook, leaving only a portion of the first sentence:

> The problem of the segregation of racial and ethnic groups constitutes one of the major problems facing the American people today. It seems desirable, therefore, to summarize the contributions which contemporary social science can make toward its resolution. There are, of course, moral and legal issues involved with respect to which the signers of the present statement cannot speak with any special authority and which must be taken into account in the solution of the problem. There are, however, also factual issues involved with respect to which certain conclusions seem to be justified on the basis of the available scientific evidence. It is with these issues only that this paper is concerned.[13]

Perhaps the final version would not stir the blood as the original version did; however, it was more in keeping with the objective tone of a scientific paper. Presumably, any authority the Social Science Statement had would be as a dispassionate and objective statement about the nature of segregation and the possibilities for desegregation. Any invocation of value-laden concepts such as freedom and democracy would be inappropriate for a strictly "scientific" examination of the facts.

Also eliminated from the final document was much of the material attacking popular justifications for segregation that had been raised by defense attorneys during the trials. An early draft of the Social Science Statement argued, "Those favoring segregation argue that segregation is desirable because (1) of the existence of a natural, instinctive aversion against close contact between races; (2) because of the innate inferiority of the darker races; (3) because it prevents or alleviates racial tension."[14] The response to the first of these arguments was eliminated completely from the final form of the statement. The second argument was mentioned only in passing, when the Social Science Statement denied the innate inferiority of African Americans by referencing Klineberg's work and observed that, at any rate, the argument was an "argument for homogenous groupings of children by intelligence rather than race." The third of these arguments was transformed into a positive statement, rather than a reactive one, by positing that *de*segregation would alleviate racial tensions, citing much of the contact literature funded by CCI and Lee and Humphrey's book on the Detroit race riot.[15]

Eliminating this material made sense in a legal brief, in which, unlike a scientific paper, one would not want to raise possible points against one's own argument. Conceivably, the brief could have been raising arguments the other side would not bring up during the appeal, which would have been very poor legal strategy.

The third kind of argument to be eliminated consisted of careful qualifications and nuances of the basic argument against segregation. For example, in an early draft of the statement, the general argument that segregation causes low levels of aspiration was much more complicated than in the final form. Probably reflecting Chein's interest in Jewish identity, the draft statement developed a carefully nuanced argument that contrasted "socioeconomic" and "cultural" discrimination against Jews, especially in the "East European shtetl," and against African Americans living in the South.[16] Such fine points probably were not necessary to make the general point about the psychological damage caused by segregation and could have been more confusing than helpful. In the end, the statement had to be a simple, nontechnical document aimed at the Supreme Court justices rather than the social-scientific community.

The final Social Science Statement made only two arguments: first, that segregation was psychologically damaging to both minority and majority group children; and second, that desegregation could proceed smoothly and without trouble if done quickly and firmly.

For the first argument, the Social Science Statement followed the assertions that were laid out in Clark's White House paper, prepared two years before. For support, it relied on the Clarks' studies using projective tests, as well as on other projective tests such as those conducted by Helen Trager (who had testified at the Kansas case) and Marion Radke (who was on the SPSSI committee that drafted the original outline). The statement also relied on the theoretical perspectives offered by David Krech and Theodore Newcomb in their textbooks on social psychology. Beyond the social psychological literature, the Social Science Statement cited the sociological works of E. Franklin Frazier and Gunnar Myrdal, on the pathology of African American culture, and Alfred McClung Lee's book on race riots, on the breakdown of the social order caused by segregation. The section on psychological damage concluded with the citation of Chein's social science survey, affirming that the view presented was shared by a large majority of the social science community. Finally,

Chein's four lines of evidence were cited for the support of the social science opinion.[17]

The second argument made by the Social Science Statement was that segregation could be accomplished easily if it were so ordered by the Court. First, relying on Klineberg, the statement dismissed the notion that African Americans were intellectually inferior to white Americans. Second, the statement put forth the evidence that contact between the races could lessen racial friction. Relying heavily on CCI's studies of contact in housing and employment, as well as on studies of the desegregation of the military, the statement argued that while outbreaks of violence were often predicted, in fact, few actually ever occurred. It concluded that the Court should order desegregation quickly, firmly, and unequivocally if racial tension was to be avoided.[18]

The entire brief was only eighteen pages long, with a four-page bibliography appended. By the middle of September, the Social Science Statement was finished. But a question remained: how was it to be used? Carter had not yet convinced all the members of the NAACP-LDEF staff of the usefulness of the social science material. Eventually, the warring factions within the NAACP-LDEF came to a compromise and appended the entire statement to the main brief.[19]

To give the statement more weight with the Court, the NAACP-LDEF wanted it signed by as many social scientists as possible. On September 15, 1952, Clark and Chein sent the statement out to a group of social scientists, asking for signatures.

The Campaign for Signatures

The question of whether the Social Science Statement was a scientific document or a legal document arose again in the campaign for signatures. Questions about the proper role of the social scientist in the larger society would be asked time and again as Clark and Chein attempted to garner support for the document.

One way to give a scientific imprimatur to the Social Science Statement would have been to release the statement under the name of the Society for the Psychological Study of Social Issues. As a matter of policy, however, SPSSI would not release the Social Science Statement under official organizational auspices. Stuart Cook, acting in his role as SPSSI president, explained to Gerhart Saenger in February 1952 that SPSSI preferred the role of "arranger and stimulator. When a statement seems needed, the Society would help get a group of experts to issue a statement in their own names. This recommendation would apply to the current request of the Intergroup Committee for a statement on the effects of segregation."[20] Cook's comments, of course, left as an open question who would sign the document to give it the force of "expert opinion." To address this problem, Clark and Chein used the advice of Cook's friend and SPSSI founding member Alfred McClung Lee.

Lee had served as an expert witness in Virginia. In late 1951, at about the same time that the SPSSI committee began drafting the statement on segregation, Lee was founding the sociological equivalent of SPSSI, the Society for the Study of Social Problems (SSSP).[21] In September 1952, when asked by Clark for suggestions, Lee responded with a list of fifty-three people who, he explained, were "all people who are especially active (not just members) and in some instances officers of SSSP."[22] Examining whom Clark chose to solicit from Lee's list gives some indication of what was considered important for a signer of the Social Science Statement.

The first person Clark and Chein chose was Arnold Rose, who had been courted by the NAACP to serve as an expert witness in the *Brown* case in Topeka but had declined to do so. As the only American listed as Gunnar Myrdal's co-author on *An American Dilemma,* Rose was a very prestigious race relations researcher, and adding his name to the document would give it some professional weight. One criterion, then, would be the professional standing of the individual. Another criterion would be geography.

Clark and Chein also asked Bingham Dai of Duke University Medical School, Noel P. Gist of the University of Missouri, and Harry Estill Moore of the University of Texas. While these researchers did not have Rose's prestige, they had something equally important: southern affiliations. Since the first question asked by the defense attorneys was always the length of time the expert witness had spent in the South, Clark and Chein were happy to take any southern offerings from Lee.

Dai and Gist readily agreed to sign the statement. "I was wholly in agreement with your analysis," Gist wrote, "and was quite willing to have my name used in presenting it to whatever agencies might be interested." By contrast, Harry Estill Moore of the University of Texas was a rare failure for Clark. In refusing to sign the statement, Moore wrote that he did not want to be put in "the position of accepting *in toto* a statement which I had no part in compiling." Moore further questioned the wisdom of having the statement signed at all. He argued that if he signed, he "might be considered to be posing as one of the originators of that statement. An admission that I had signed under such circumstances would destroy any value which my signature might conceivably have; and would put me in an embarrassing position would the point be pressed."[23]

Moore's concerns underscored a fundamental question: what did it mean for a social scientist to sign this statement? Moore did not want to appear as having written the document. But if signing the document meant something other than authorship, then what exactly did the signature mean? In the form letter Clark and Chein sent out with the Social Science Statement, they were ambiguous about what a signature might mean, noting only that "in order that this should not appear to be the private notion of the few of us who prepared the statement, we felt it should bear the signatures of those who are in substantial agreement with its content."[24] Moore obviously felt that he was being asked to pose as an originator of the statement.

Psychiatrist Charlotte G. Babcock of Chicago expressed a different concern. While agreeing to sign the statement, Babcock wrote to Clark that she objected to the word *endorse.* For Babcock, "if this is a scientific statement, we should simply sign it as a statement of the state of our knowledge." Babcock was concerned that "the word 'endorse' is full of political and other implications and lays open the report to being unread or interpreted on the basis of the word rather than on the content of the report." Here, as in the drafting of the statement, the concern was that politics and science be kept distinct. In his reply, Clark attempted to allay Babcock's fears about the word *endorse;* he wrote that "no where in the statement as submitted, is that word used. The names of the thirty-two individuals who signed the statement are merely listed at the end of section 4."[25]

What Clark and Chein clearly recognized by this time was that the strength of the Social Science Statement flowed from its objective and dispassionate nature. To make it a political tract would be to subtract from its force as a scientific document. In other words, to fulfill their wishes to change society, the social scientists had to refrain from overtly campaigning for or against the very changes they wished. This is the fundamental paradox of activist social science, and a lesson that Clark and the others would have difficulty remembering through the course of the litigation.

Most of those asked were eager and happy to sign. Jerome Bruner noted that the statement was "thoughtful and moderate."[26] Robert

Redfield was "glad to have" his name on the "excellent statement on the effects of segregation."[27] Psychiatrist Helen McLean and sociologist E. Franklin Frazier were asked to sign but were out of the country and failed to respond in time. Two other individuals (one of whom was Harry Estill Moore) refused to sign. On those refusing, Clark wrote to Jerome Bruner, "Both of those are on the faculties of Southern universities and indicated that their refusal to sign was not a reflection of disagreement with the contents of the statement; but was due to other factors."[28]

In the final analysis, thirty-two social scientists, including fourteen past or future presidents of SPSSI, signed the statement. Included among the signatories were most of those who had been studying race prejudice since the 1930s: Floyd Allport, Gordon Allport, Isidor Chein, Kenneth Clark, Mamie Clark, Stuart Cook, Allison Davis, Else Frenkel-Brunswik, Daniel Katz, Otto Klineberg, David Krech, Alfred McClung Lee, Gardner Murphy, Theodore Newcomb, Robert Redfield, Ira De Augustine Reid, Arnold Rose, Gerhart Saenger, R. Nevitt Sanford, and M. Brewster Smith.

The Social Science Statement was filed with the Supreme Court in December 1952, when the Court heard the oral arguments on all four of the state school segregation cases and one school segregation case from the District of Columbia. During the oral arguments, the Court would be hearing about the social science evidence that the NAACP-LDEF had carefully prepared.

Oral Arguments: Round One

There were two points during the oral argument where social science became a point of contention before the Supreme Court. Not surprisingly, they were from the South Carolina case and the Virginia case, in which segregation had been defended most vehemently during the trials. In both instances the same charge was leveled at the social scientists: they were merely advocates dressing up their arguments in scientific guise.

Arguing for South Carolina in the *Briggs* case was John W. Davis, who had argued more cases before the Supreme Court than any other person. Davis had run for president in 1924 and was a senior partner at one of the largest law firms in New York City. Born in the Deep South, Davis had offered his services to South Carolina without a fee, and the state eagerly accepted the offer.

Davis had nothing but contempt for the social science evidence that NAACP-LDEF had assembled. In September, he wrote to the attorney general of South Carolina that "it is perfectly clear from interior evidences that the witness Clark drafted the appendix which is signed by the worthy social scientists. I can only say that if that sort of 'guff' can move any court, 'God save the state!'"[29]

During his oral argument Davis contrasted Clark's South Carolina doll test results with those in his published 1947 study. For the first time in the litigation, the supporters of segregation clearly got on the record the fact that northern African American children identified the brown doll as the bad doll with a greater frequency than did the southern children. After pointing out the discrepancy to the Court, Davis asked rhetorically, "Now, these latter scientific tests were conducted in unsegregated states, and with those results compared, what becomes of the blasting influence of segregation to which Dr. Clark so eloquently testifies?"[30] After the 1954 *Brown* decision, Davis's rhetorical question would be put to Clark in earnest. For now, however, Clark's explanation of his data was not public knowledge. Given the nature of the Social Science Statement, however, any points scored against Clark's doll tests had to be rather minor. The Clarks' 1947 article was merely one of nearly sixty sources cited in the statement, and it was only one bit of evidence arguing for the damage argument generally.

The second point where social science testimony became a point of contention was in the Virginia case, which was being argued by the indefatigable T. Justin Moore—who had also tried the case. Moore made a great deal of the fact that "we knew there was this great body of expert opinion which was in conflict with that which had been presented without conflict in Kansas and South Carolina, and we presented it." Moore argued that the defense's expert witnesses, unlike those of the plaintiffs, had experience in Virginia, and all had held that segregation was less damaging than desegregation for the psyches of African American children.

As in the trial, Moore attacked Chein's testimony most strongly. He noted that Chein had sent his survey out to only "some 850 social scientists," and "we showed on cross-examination that there were some six or eight thousand persons who were eligible to have that questionnaire sent to them." Moore's implication was clear and followed Garrett's testimony in the Virginia case: not only was the survey not a representative sample of social-scientific opinion, but Chein had chosen his sample in order to maximize the desired outcome.

Considering that he thought this charge was akin to calling him dishonest, having it leveled in front of the Supreme Court must have been galling to Chein. The social science survey, however, was to fade in importance as the litigation continued past this stage. And at the time, the social scientists and the lawyers thought that the litigation was over. The cases had been heard by the Supreme Court; once the oral arguments were done, there was nothing to do but wait for the Supreme Court to decide.

After the Supreme Court

The NAACP-LDEF attorneys and the social scientists moved on to other matters. Kenneth Clark continued to meet occasionally with the NAACP-LDEF, however. For example, in January 1953, he received a form letter from Thurgood Marshall inviting him to a conference of "a select group of lawyers." Clark accepted the invitation and added:

> Your sudden decision to elevate me from the lowly status of a Ph.D. in psychology to that Olympian peak of a member of the legal profession leaves me stunned with happiness. . . . With one grand gesture Mr. Marshall, you have restored my self-esteem . . . you have undone, with one memorandum what these many years of racial segregation and discrimination have done to my personality. . . . You have performed the miracle of changing me overnight from a psychologist to a lawyer. Is it too presumptuous to hope that someday I might do the same for you and transform you from a lawyer to a psychologist?[31]

That Clark continued to meet with Marshall and the NAACP-LDEF indicates his belief that the *Brown* litigation was only the beginning of social scientist–attorney collaboration. In a February 1953 address to a joint meeting of the Society for the Psychological Study of Social Issues and the Society for the Study of Social Problems, he proclaimed that "the present school cases may be viewed as merely the beginning of this type of social science–legal collaboration. . . . The social science testimony in the public school segregation cases has opened the door of the courts to the social sciences." Clark was both enthusiastic and cautious about the future of such collaboration. The testimony of the opposing social scientists in the Virginia trial, particularly Garrett's, was an unexpected shock for him and had demonstrated that social science could be used to block democratic change as well as advance it. Clark believed that social scientists who became involved in social science–legal collaboration had a burden to "exercise the maximum degree of care and objectivity in the collection and interpretation of the relevant data." Because social scientists could always have honest disagreements over the interpretation of data, the professional societies—here he presumably meant SPSSI and SSSP—should "develop safeguards against possible ethical abuses; e.g. flagrant manifestations of prejudice, distortion of data and deliberately misleading interpretations." Clark did not spell out the form these safeguards would take other than a general call for "some kind of machinery" to prevent such abuses.[32]

Whether or not Clark believed that Garrett's testimony had overstepped the boundary between an "honest interpretation" and an "ethical abuse" is not clear. Some social scientists believed that the charge leveled against them—that they allowed their political beliefs to taint their science—was more appropriately leveled at Garrett. Smith found Garrett's analysis of Isidor Chein's social science survey "particularly dishonest" and had called for some sort of official action against Garrett by the APA.[33] Chein had also described Garrett's representation of his own survey's methodology "flagrantly dishonest."[34]

In his public address, however, Clark stopped short of making such a charge against Garrett. He had applied some of Chein's logic to Garrett's testimony, showing that Garrett had essentially agreed with the plaintiffs.

Clark's address demonstrates the stance that he and the other social scientists would take toward criticisms of their role in the school segregation cases. Their activities in the case were becoming increasingly well known, and therefore they were facing increased scrutiny. For example, as a brief submitted to the Supreme Court, the Social Science Statement would be read only by a select circle of legal experts. Arnold Rose, however, had arranged for it to be published in the *Minnesota Law Review* in May 1953, which brought it to the attention of a much wider circle of people.[35] After the 1954 decision, the social scientists would be facing questions regarding their objectivity. Clark's 1953 address foreshadowed their response to this criticism—to claim that they had remained objective scientists despite their association with the NAACP-LDEF. At the time of his address, however, unbeknownst to Clark, the work of the social scientists was not yet complete in the case at hand.

Oral Arguments: Round Two

The Supreme Court justices were deeply divided on the school segregation cases. No clear consensus had emerged from the deliberations in the course of six months. Rather than issue an opinion that undoubtedly would have had vigorous dissents, Justice Felix Frankfurter convinced his colleagues that the Court should call for a reargument of the issues. Therefore, on June 8, 1953, the Supreme Court finally acted on the arguments the NAACP-LDEF had made six months before.[36] But rather than issue a decision, the justices asked each side to prepare a new argument on the basis of five questions the Court handed down. Three of the questions had to do with the historical meaning of the Fourteenth Amendment. The fourth and fifth questions had to do with the nature of the remedy: assuming that segregation was found to violate the Fourteenth Amendment, what sort of decree should the Court issue? For the next year and a half, the social scientists would be seeking an answer to "Question IV," namely:

> Assuming it is decided that segregation in public schools violated the Fourteenth Amendment:
> (a) would a decree necessarily follow providing that, within the limits set by normal geographic school districting, Negro children should forthwith be admitted to schools of their choice, or
> (b) may this Court, in the exercise of its equity powers, permit an effective gradual adjustment to be brought about from existing segregated systems to a system not based on color distinctions?[37]

The immediate effect on the NAACP-LDEF was to draw their attention away from social science materials. The attorneys thought that the first three questions that focused on the history of the Fourteenth Amendment were much more germane to the legal issues at hand, for two reasons. First, constitutional litigation is often decided on the "intent of the framers" of the Constitution, or in this case, of one of its amendments. Second, at first glance at least, the history seemed to be against the NAACP-LDEF position. For example, the same Congress that had passed the Fourteenth Amendment had established segregated schools in the District of Columbia; hence the argument that they wished to abolish segregated education with the amendment seemed difficult to sustain. For these reasons, convincing answers to the historical questions were seen as of first importance if the NAACP-LDEF wanted to prevail in the reargument that was scheduled for October—a mere four months away.

Beyond the apparent urgency of the historical questions, another factor made the NAACP-LDEF de-emphasize the importance of a social-scientific answer to Question IV. Question IV seemed to assume that a constitutional violation had been found, and the idea that the Court could order a "gradual" decree—that is, a decree that ordered any sort of delay in remedy—cut against firmly established constitutional principles. The NAACP-LDEF attorneys took the position that, "in view of the fact that the rights which plaintiffs here assert are personal rights and constitutional rights, this Court has no power to enter a gradual decree."[38] For once, the NAACP-LDEF believed the law was on their side and the need for "nonlegal" material was not pressing to answer question IV. Like any good legal team, however, they wanted to make sure they touched all the bases. The social scientists, therefore, would be brought on board once again.

Apart from the strictly legal research that the lawyers would undertake, the NAACP-LDEF quickly assembled a staff of specialists to assemble "nonlegal" answers to the Court's questions. The nonlegal research was of two kinds. First, a staff of historians would attempt to determine the intent of the framers of the Fourteenth Amendment in order to answer the first three questions. Second, the NAACP-LDEF wanted to assemble whatever social science material was available on the process of desegregation, in order to answer Question IV. This task was put in the hands of Clark and a young NAACP-LDEF staffer, June Shagaloff, who had replaced Annette Peyser as the resident "sociologist." On June 22, Robert Carter assigned Clark "to collect and analyze all the extrinsic evidence available, particularly in the South, on how a change from a segregated to a non-segregated situation can be smoothly accomplished."[39]

Though Clark had been collecting information relating to desegregation since he began with the NAACP-LDEF, he now set out to undertake a truly exhaustive literature review of all the published and, if possible, unpublished research that had been carried out in the area of desegregation. He wanted to supplement this literature review with a series of field studies. Because they never came to fruition, it is useful to examine the planned field studies first.

In the field studies, Clark proposed that he and Shagaloff travel to seven towns in six states to make "field observations" of recently desegregated schools and labor unions, in order to "determine the mechanics and operation of this transition in those places where it has actually occurred rather than indulge in theories or speculations about such changes." Clark feared that his presence in the community under the auspices of the NAACP-LDEF would jeopardize his chances of getting reliable data. He wrote that "in order to assure objectivity, it will be necessary to minimize the study's immediate practical purposes. Thus, it will be necessary to play down in the field the relationship between the NAACP Legal Defense and Education Fund, Inc., and the activities of the research workers."[40] This overt recognition that, to be useful to the NAACP-LDEF, his research had to be distanced from them was a further development in Clark's views on social scientist–attorney collaboration. From this moment onward, Clark began to stress that his scientific research and reports owed their first allegiance to scientific objectivity and only secondary allegiance to practicality.

The fieldwork was never undertaken. The press of time made the ambitious program nearly impossible. Clark's original schedule had called for twenty-two days of fieldwork by Shagaloff and thirty for himself. Given that the NAACP-LDEF had only four months to gather all the materials together, it would have been miraculous for the fieldwork to be completed and written up before October's oral arguments. Moreover, Clark had asked for a budget of over $2,000 just for travel and expenses. The NAACP-LDEF had estimated that the entire process of reargument would be $39,000.[41] Money was tight, and undoubtedly, the NAACP-LDEF would not want to spend over $2,000 on a project of dubious utility to their immediate cause. Finally, the Ford Foundation was funding a series of field studies, and Clark felt that if he could get access to those studies, his own efforts would be duplicative.

The Ford study was troubling for Clark. One reason was that one of its leaders was a southern journalist, Harry Ashmore. While Ashmore was a liberal southerner, Clark described him as "on record as being identified with the gradualist position" regarding desegregation. Clark, who would soon call for immediate, unequivocal desegregation, was suspicious of any form of gradual desegregation. In addition to Ashmore's presence, there were plenty of rumors flying around about the Ford study: that it was started at the request of some justices of the Supreme Court, or, alternately, that it was started at the request of the U.S. attorney general's office. Clark arranged for a meeting with Philip Coombs, the director of the Ford Foundation's Fund for the Advancement of Education.

In the meeting, Coombs managed to assuage many of Clark's fears. The study was undertaken at the behest of a group of southern African

American educators to aid them in the desegregation process they believed was coming. During Clark's interview in October 1953, the study was still in preliminary stages, with no organized reports available. With relief, Clark reported back to the NAACP-LDEF that while the study would not be of use to them, neither would it be available to their opponents. Given Ashmore's presence on the staff, Clark predicted that "the actual study might bend over backwards in its presentation of results in order to present the southerners' position in a more favorable light than the objective facts might warrant."[42] Again, Clark had no way of knowing it, but the Ford Foundation study would come to haunt the NAACP-LDEF before the end of the litigation campaign. In 1953, however, even if it could not help, it did not seem to pose any problem.

With the fieldwork portion of the study canceled, Clark spent the summer of 1953 assembling as much material as possible on the process of desegregation. Combing the published literature was not enough; Clark carried out a voluminous correspondence with dozens of people in the social science community in order to discover any study that he might have missed and to find the results of unpublished studies.

Most responses that Clark received emphasized that desegregation was best accomplished quickly and forcefully. This, of course, fit perfectly with the NAACP-LDEF's purely legal arguments that the remedy found by the Court should be immediate. Gordon Allport, for example, sent Clark a chapter from his upcoming book, *The Nature of Prejudice,* and told Clark, "All experience, FEPC, Army, National Maritime Union, public housing, industrial changes, show that a policy pronouncement, in line with conscience, is accepted. The threatened violence seems never to result in social upheaval. . . . Let the line of public morality be set by authoritative pronouncements, and all the latent good in individuals and communities will be strengthened."[43] Gordon Allport's older brother, Floyd, agreed and wrote to Clark, "When people understand that the legal structure has changed and there is no hesitancy about putting the rule into effect, I think they are more likely to go along with it than in a step-by-step procedure."[44] Daniel Wilner, who had conducted some of the housing studies at CCI, claimed that "integration can be 'imposed' in a variety of settings with no *trouble* ensuing."[45] Isidor Chein, in typical fashion, sent Clark a detailed five-page plan for desegregation, stressing, "The *fait accompli* minimizes resistance to change."[46]

One of the few dissenting voices on forced desegregation came from Theodore Newcomb at the University of Michigan. Although he had arrived too late to testify at the *Briggs* trial as he had planned, Newcomb had been following the litigation with interest. He suggested to Clark that Clark examine more general studies of attitude change, because Newcomb believed "there is very little evidence regarding race-relation changes, as such." Newcomb felt that forcing a sudden change on an unwilling populace would result in a backlash, polarizing the issue and entrenching attitudes against desegregation. Newcomb cautioned Clark that "attempts to enforce a sudden and complete change not only might have very serious results but might be deleterious to good race relations in the long run."[47]

All the material assembled by Clark resulted in something his previous work for the NAACP-LDEF never had: a professional publication. Clark published the results of his study in an article titled "Desegregation: An Appraisal of the Evidence," which took up the entire fourth number of volume 9 of the *Journal of Social Issues* in 1953.

Clark opened the article with an account of his involvement with the *Brown* campaign. He noted that the lawyers and the social scientists worked very closely: "In fact, there were times when the lawyers could speak as social psychologists and the social psychologists began to sound like lawyers." Clark was quick assure his readers, however, that they had maintained their scientific authority. He concluded, "In spite of this mutual accommodation, however, a clear distinction of roles and responsibilities had to be maintained for effective collaboration."[48]

Clark's article surveyed the desegregation process in twelve different areas of life, ranging from labor unions and industrial employment to elementary and secondary public schools. He also arranged the data according to the specific factor responsible for desegregation. For example, did desegregation occur because of population changes, a referendum of electorate, moral arguments, or court action?[49] After examining the collected data according to area of life and the motivating force, Clark compared "immediate versus gradual" forms of desegregation to see which was more effective. He concluded that immediate desegregation was the more effective alternative and met with the less resistance, provided certain conditions were met. The five conditions that Clark believed would ensure effective desegregation were:

A. A clear and unequivocal statement of policy by leaders with prestige and other authorities;
B. Firm enforcement of the changed policy by authorities and persistence in the execution of this policy in the face of initial resistance;

C. A willingness to deal with violations, attempted violations, and incitement to violations by a resort to the law and strong enforcement action;

D. A refusal of the authorities to resort to, engage in, or tolerate subterfuges, gerrymandering or other devices for evading the principles and the fact of desegregation;

E. An appeal to the individuals concerned in terms of their religious principles of brotherhood and their acceptance of the American traditions of fair play and equal justice.[50]

Clark concluded that desegregation did not have to be preceded by an attitude change of the population in question, but rather that the attitude change could follow the desegregation process. These conditions suggested that effective desegregation would be imposed swiftly and with firm authority from above.

Clark's findings meshed well with the NAACP-LDEF's purely legal stand that once a violation of rights had been found, the remedy had to be immediate. This conception of swift and forceful segregation would soon become the focal point for the social science community involved in the litigation. It would also be one more argument that the legal team could use in its argument before the Supreme Court. Marshall and the other attorneys for the NAACP-LDEF could argue that not only did the Constitution require an immediate remedy, but there was no practical reason why the Court should not issue such a decree.

Even given the meshing of social-scientific data with the legal argument, however, the NAACP-LDEF preferred to make a clear legal case for immediate desegregation. In the brief they submitted for the cases, social science was not mentioned. Thinking that the legal case for immediate segregation was strong, NAACP-LDEF attorney Jack Greenberg said they "hung tough and in a handful of pages set forth the straight legal proposition that the children should be admitted to integrated schools, forthwith."[51]

The second round of arguments took place in December 1953, almost exactly a year after the first. The one change in the Court was that a new chief justice was in charge. A few weeks before the presentation of rearguments, Chief Justice Fred Vinson died of a heart attack. President Dwight D. Eisenhower replaced him with the governor of California, Earl Warren.[52]

During the oral argument, each side presented its view of the intent of the framers of the Fourteenth Amendment, complete with copious historical documentation. But to the frustration of the NAACP-LDEF, the justices did not seem the least bit interested in the historical arguments, preferring to dwell on other matters. Jack Greenberg recollected, "It all seemed rather curious. . . . Did they, perhaps, not care about the history? Or were the questions at oral argument just a game the justices play?"[53]

Supreme Court Decision

The oral argument may have left the NAACP-LDEF wondering just what it was the justices were thinking, but they did not have to wait too long before they found out. On May 17, 1954, the U.S. Supreme Court handed down its decision in the School Segregation Cases, finding that segregation was a violation of the Fourteenth Amendment. Not only had the Supreme Court decided the case for the NAACP-LDEF, but social science received a prominent mention in the process.

Chief Justice Earl Warren, in his first opinion on the Supreme Court, wrote the unanimous opinion. It was impossible to "turn the clock back" to discover the original intent of the framers of the Fourteenth Amendment, wrote Warren. Rather, "we must consider public education in the light of its full development and its present place in American life throughout the Nation. Only in this way can it be determined if segregation in public schools deprives these plaintiffs of the equal protection of the laws." Then, referring to the Kansas court's finding of psychological damage, Warren concluded, "Whatever may have been the extent of psychological knowledge at the time of *Plessy v. Ferguson,* this finding is amply supported by modern authority." The "modern authority" was Warren's eleventh footnote on the case, citing Clark's White House paper and the book chapter that he had written summarizing that paper, Isidor Chein's two papers presenting his survey of social science opinion, a book chapter by Theodore Brameld, E. Franklin Frazier's *The Negro in the United States,* and, "generally," Gunnar Myrdal's *An American Dilemma.*[54] With the exception of the book chapter by Clark, which was merely a summary of his White House paper, all these works were cited in the Social Science Statement.

The prominent mention of social science in the opinion seemed to indicate that the NAACP-LDEF's strategy had paid off. At a victory celebration two days later, Thurgood Marshall requested that Bill Coleman and Robert Ming, two lawyers who doubted the worth of the social science testimony, bow down to Kenneth Clark and admit they were wrong.[55] But the war was not quite over. In its opinion, the Supreme Court had found a constitutional violation but had not devised any remedy. The justices called for yet another round of arguments, focusing on their previously issued questions IV and V.

The call for the third round of arguments would suddenly push all the work Clark had done during the summer of 1953 to the top of the NAACP-LDEF agenda. But the prominent mention of Clark's name in Warren's footnote 11 had pushed Clark into the national spotlight. *Brown* was, needless to say, a controversial opinion, and Kenneth Clark was, quite unexpectedly, in the center of the controversy.

Clark's Defense of Brown

Clark had begun the litigation campaign as a fairly junior psychologist in New York, but his work with the NAACP-LDEF established him as an expert on desegregation. In social science circles, his monograph on desegregation brought him a certain amount of fame. SPSSI soon sold the issue out and, in an unprecedented move, ordered another printing of two thousand more copies. Both SPSSI and the NAACP printed the issue separately and distributed it to various community agencies around the country to aid in desegregation.[56] The prominent mention of his name in the *Brown* opinion brought Clark to the attention of those outside the social science community.

At least in New York City, Clark was becoming a public figure, asked to appear at celebrations and make speeches explaining "the meaning of the Supreme Court decision." In a radio broadcast on May 28, eleven days after the decision was handed down, Clark spoke of the decision as a "victory for all mankind." African Americans, Clark said, "need no longer bear the burden of state imposed stigma and the obvious inferiority implicit in involuntary segregation."[57]

On the national front, there was little immediate attention paid to the inclusion of social science in footnote 11. James Reston, the day after the decision, noted that the decision was "sociological" rather than legal, but he was the exception. Most press coverage paid very little attention to the social science in the decision.[58]

In the South, *Brown* would have been despised regardless of any reference to social science. The inclusion of footnote 11 gave Georgia senator Richard B. Russell the chance to excoriate the justices as "amateur psychologists," but it is doubtful Russell would have been any happier had the *Brown* opinion been based firmly on case precedent. Senator James Eastland of Mississippi called for an investigation of Gunnar Myrdal as part of a worldwide Communist conspiracy, signaling the first volley in the South's war on Myrdal and other social scientists.[59]

Much more serious to Clark than the expected attacks from the white South were the embarrassed explanations from *Brown's* supporters that the decision did not really rely on psychology and sociology. For example, in early June 1954, the *Saturday Evening Post* editorialized that the "current doctrine could certainly be sustained on the basis of plain, ordinary constitutional law, without the benefit of sociology or psychology." This was a good thing, the editorial continued, given the "socialistic" thinking of many social scientists.[60] The executive director of the NAACP, Roy Wilkins, sent the editorial to Clark, noting that "it's a glory of sorts to be mentioned in the *Saturday Evening Post,* especially in an editorial, and glory, indeed, when you arouse extended editorial opposition." Clark, perhaps not welcoming the sort of glory offered by the *Post,* fired off a letter that explained that social scientists were not "socialists": "As a psychologist who is concerned with a scientific approach to the problems of man and society, I believe that it is essential to objective social science that the students in this field be as objective as human intelligence permits."[61]

A much more serious attack was made by Edmond Cahn, a professor of jurisprudence at New York University. Cahn published an annual review of jurisprudence in the *New York University Law Review.* His review of the events of 1954 was dedicated to an analysis of the *Brown* decision. Cahn wrote that the decision reached by Warren was a good one, but that the inclusion of the social science evidence was a serious mistake: "I would not have the constitutional rights of Negroes—or of other Americans," he declared, "rest on any such flimsy foundation as some of the scientific demonstrations in these records." Fortunately, Cahn argued, the Court merely quoted the social scientists as a "courtesy" and based its decision on firm constitutional principles. As proof of this, Cahn noted that Warren's opinion did "not mention either the testimony of the expert witnesses or the submitted statement of the thirty-two scientists."[62]

Cahn argued that the proposition that segregation was harmful was "obvious and evident": "Hardly anyone has been hypocritical enough to contend that no stigma or loss of status attaches to these forms of physical separation." The justices could "see it and act on it even after reading the labored attempts by plaintiff's experts to demonstrate it 'scientifically.'" Hence, claimed Cahn, the ideal that the decision was somehow based on social science was obviously in error.[63]

Cahn focused on Clark's doll tests as an example of the social scientists' flimsy claims. He recounted Clark's testing of sixteen children in the South Carolina case, where eleven of the children had identified the brown doll as the bad doll. Cahn argued that this sample size was far too small to have any validity and that, at any rate, the test did not demonstrate the effects of *school* segregation. He also suggested that asking the children to pick a "bad" doll was a trick, for if they had already identified the white doll as the "nice" doll, then they would naturally choose the other doll as bad by process of elimination. Cahn faulted the opposing attorneys for not preparing an adequate cross-examination of Clark and singled out Justin Moore of the Virginia trial for particular criticism. Calling Moore a "bigot," Cahn suggested that his cross-examination demonstrated "how very sick" segregation could make a person.[64]

Cahn concluded that, given the undeveloped state of social psychology, it was dangerous for the law to commingle with it. It was imperative, he argued, for judges to "learn where objective science ends and advocacy begins. At present, it is still possible for the social psychologist to 'hoodwink' a judge who is not over wise." Recalling Clark's comment in his "Desegregation" article on the importance of maintaining effective collaboration between lawyers and social scientists, Cahn concluded, "It seems possible that the distinction of roles would be maintained more satisfactorily if the social psychologist's primary motive in maintaining it were strict fidelity to objective truth rather than 'effective collaboration.'"[65]

Edmond Cahn was a friend of Will Maslow at the American Jewish Congress, and Maslow passed a copy of the article on to Clark and Chein.[66] Clark was incensed. He immediately wrote a lengthy reply to send to the *NYU Law Review.* Before sending it off, however, he sent a copy to M. Brewster Smith, whose skills as an editor Clark had learned to appreciate while writing his desegregation article. Smith liked the article but recommended to Clark that he "utterly avoid any, irony, innuendo, rhetorical devices, or loaded adjectives, on your own part. Put your emotions aside. It will be *much* more effective this way, I am *positive.*"[67] Clark dutifully purged from his text phrases that, for instance, noted when Cahn had a "rare glimmer of humility" and that "one would have to be gifted with . . . the wisdom and foresight of Professor Cahn in order to prepare himself for the role of advocate in these specific trials 10 years in advance."[68]

Clark began his response with an extended quotation from Alexander Pekelis to the effect that a knowledge of social science was essential to the operation of the law. He and Pekelis had known each other, albeit distantly, when Clark had worked for the American Jewish Congress, and Clark obviously admired him.[69]

To Clark, who had spent the past five years of his life arguing against southern attorneys general, Cahn's assertion that the harms of segregation were "obvious and evident" was absurd. The white South obviously denied such harms vigorously. What was self-evident for white southerners was that African Americans were happy under segregation, that African Americans weren't as smart or trustworthy as whites, and that integration would be the death of the "southern way of life." This was all common sense to southern whites.

Asked Clark, "How could the social scientists be so unreliable yet nonetheless come out with a picture of social reality which Professor Cahn and everyone else 'already knew'?" Moreover, he argued, Cahn's insistence that damage from segregation was obvious to all was belied by the opinions of the trial judges in the segregation cases, who held that no such damage occurred. How would Professor Cahn distinguish "common knowledge" from the "personal biases of judges"? According to Clark, Cahn fundamentally misunderstood the value of science, which was to "provide a scientific, objective method for measuring and comparing . . . 'common knowledge.'" He asserted that Cahn's conception of science would render biochemistry, nutrition, and genetics useless, for it was "common knowledge that a living organism needs food and oxygen in order to survive and that members of the same species when they mate reproduce offspring with similar physical characteristics."[70]

Clark also ridiculed Cahn's criticism of the doll tests methodology, which was "discussed in standard textbooks in social psychology," as that of someone who has left "the field of his competence" and was communicating his "biases, confusions, and misconceptions as if they were fact." He pointed out that the original research had been conducted a decade before the first of the trials, and he concluded, "Professor Cahn's allegation that the writer served in the role of the advocate rather than that of an objective scientist seems difficult to sustain in the face of the testimony given on the basis of research conducted 10 years before these cases were heard." As to the size of the sample in the South Carolina case, Clark argued, Cahn completely misunderstood the intent of the tests conducted there. It was not meant to be a scientific sampling, Clark explained, merely a method to "give the general scientific findings . . . more weight in a courtroom by demonstrating that they also applied in the specific cases . . . before the court."[71]

Clark found Cahn's charge that the social scientists did not have "strict fidelity to objective truth" to be "serious, grave, and shocking." He stated that the social scientists who were involved in the case were "men of integrity" who were incapable of "testifying to a fact or stating an opinion which they did not believe to be consistent with the scientific evidence as they knew it." Clark pointed out that the NAACP-LDEF had asked for the social scientists to supply exactly what Cahn had claimed was necessary: scientific studies that isolated legally segregated public school education as the sole factor responsible for psychological damage. But the social scientists, Clark claimed, told the lawyers they could not supply such studies, for none existed. An examination of the testimony, Clark wrote, would verify that the social scientists "made not a single concession to expediency, to the practical and legal demands of these cases, or even to the moral and human issues involved." As further evidence of his objectivity, Clark argued, the attorneys had asked Clark himself to include a study with a methodology that was "scientifically questionable," and he had refused.[72]

The key, Clark argued, was that all the decisions on trial strategy and whether or not to use social psychological research were made by the attorneys, not by the social scientists. The social scientists' only role was to inform the attorneys of relevant scientific studies that might be of use to them. Moreover, no studies were conducted specifically for the trial at hand; the social scientists merely drew on the existing literature to make their arguments. The final decision on whether or not the social science material was relevant rested not with the scientists but with the trial judges, who could have ruled the testimony out of order, or the Supreme Court, which could have refused to accept the Social Science Statement. Hence, the role of the social scientist was simply that of a supplier of facts; any decision on how to use those facts rested elsewhere.[73] In this way, Clark combined a strong sense of social activism with a claim for objective knowledge. Far from being polar opposites, Clark argued, the two were perfectly compatible. By maintaining a very strict standard of objectivity and neutrality, the social scientist could be the most useful for social change.

Clark sent his manuscript off to the *NYU Law Review,* but the journal refused to publish it. He had to wait five years before being granted a forum in which to reply to Cahn. Cahn, however, devoted his next review of jurisprudence to further analysis of the use of social science in constitutional litigation. It was not Clark who drew his opprobrium this time, but Isidor Chein.

Will Maslow had also shared a copy of Cahn's paper with Chein, who, as was his wont, quickly typed up a six-page, single-spaced letter in reply, sending the original to Maslow and the carbon to Cahn. Chein made many of the same points Clark did (indeed, Clark's reply to Cahn owed much Chein sharing his letter with Clark). Chein commented that as he was speaking more "of matters of law than of science, my *khutzpah* no more than rivals his [Cahn's] in setting himself up as a judge of science." Fundamental to Chein's letter was the point that "a great deal of 'common knowledge' just ain't so," and that in any case scientists, if they happen to agree with common knowledge, do so "on the basis of a more critical examination of the relevant concepts and facts." Besides, Chein argued, if it were only common sense being offered by the expert witnesses, there was really no other way to get such common sense as part of the Court's record. Finally, regarding Clark's doll tests, Chein argued that Cahn made some good points but mistakenly assumed that Clark could not answer them. In reality, Chein explained, it was simply the case that no one had asked such questions during cross-examination. This was hardly the fault of the social scientist, Chein explained, but rather of the defense attorneys for not preparing an adequate cross-examination.[74]

In a reply article, Cahn maintained that legal doctrine allowed for judicial notice to be taken of "the facts, circumstances, and value patterns obtaining in the social order," or what Cahn described as the "given." Hence, Cahn maintained that there simply was no need for expert witness testimony on the dangers of segregation.[75] But, as Clark had argued in his reply, given that the courts consistently upheld segregation between 1896 and 1938, and that even in the *Sweatt* and *McLaurin* decisions in 1950 the Supreme Court had failed to notice the harms of segregation, Cahn's insistence that expert testimony was not needed seemed rather naive.

Cahn ended up agreeing with Chein that the weakness of cross-examination was responsible for letting Clark's doll tests go unchallenged, and he closed his article with a call for each lawyer to "make himself thoroughly familiar with the methods and literature of the subject" under examination. Where Chein and Cahn differed, of course, was over whether or not Clark would have been able to answer the questions put to him.

Cahn's articles were the first serious questioning of the use of social science in the school segregation cases, but they would not be the last. Further criticisms would be forthcoming in the years after the 1954 decision. The doll tests would be the synecdoche for those wishing to criticize the use of social science in the *Brown* litigation. Because of Clark's fluid interpretations of his results, the doll tests became the favorite target of *Brown*'s critics. As noted previously, no matter what was answered by a child, Clark could make it a sign of damage. This fluidity would be a red flag for those who would argue that the social science in *Brown* was merely a political argument dressed in scientific garb.

All this, however, was in the future. In 1954, Clark was basking in the glow of the first *Brown* decision. Soon, however, he would be back at work preparing for the third round of arguments, for once again, social science would take a central role in the preparation for the Supreme Court.

9

Supreme Court Hearings and Decision, *Brown II*

In its 1954 decision, the Supreme Court had delayed any course of action and called for yet another round of arguments to determine what sort of order best ensured a transition from segregated to unsegregated facilities. The key issue was the speed of desegregation. Referring back to question IV, which it had issued in 1953, the Court wanted a round of hearings on whether it should order desegregation "forthwith" or allow for "gradual adjustment." To all appearances, the preparation of a brief on the speed of segregation would be an easier task than the 1952 brief on the harms of segregation. Clark's "Desegregation" article provided a ready-made synthesis of the available literature—but it was not the only available summary of the literature on desegregation. The Ford Foundation study, which had so worried Clark the previous year, had been released in book form. In fact, the book had been published May 16, 1954, the day before the Supreme Court issued *Brown* I.[1]

As Clark had feared, the book contained recommendations that the South would use to argue for gradual desegregation. Clark's notes, which he made for the NAACP-LDEF on Ashmore's book, indicated that it gave the "usual reasons for gradual approach":

1. Fear of adverse public reaction.
2. Uncertainty as to ability of Negro students to hold their own in mixed schools because of generally inferior educational and cultural background.
3. Problems of teacher tenure, hesitancy to assign Negro teachers to white students.

With the exception of teacher tenure, which Clark believed to be an administrative problem outside the purview of social science, Clark had addressed these issues in his 1953 article. In short, the Ford Foundation study contained little that surprised Clark. Additionally, it contained enough case-study material for Clark to argue that the best program of action would be forceful action carried out by all sectors of the community.[2] This would soon become the core of the second brief drafted by the social scientists for the Supreme Court.

In addition to these two ready-made summaries of the available evidence, a formal conference would be held for the express purpose of establishing a firm social science consensus on the issues surrounding desegregation. The framing of an argument for the Supreme Court would, however, be more, not less, contentious for the social scientific community. Some of Clark's closest confidants would begin to question his objectivity regarding desegregation.

Conference of Social Sciences

After the May 17 ruling, the law was on the side of the NAACP-LDEF: a constitutional violation of rights had been found, and they believed the only remedy legally available was to rectify the situation immediately. In the previous two hearings, the NAACP-LDEF had maintained that the Supreme Court had to order immediate desegregation, and the call for the third round of arguments on the point put them, in Thurgood Marshall's phrase, "back on the veritable 'merry-go-round' concerning" immediate desegregation.[3]

Despite the strength of their purely legal case for immediate desegregation, the NAACP-LDEF decided that they would use some social-scientific evidence to build a complete case. In a memorandum to the legal staff, Robert Carter reported Kenneth Clark's opinion that the social-scientific evidence indicated "the transition from a system of segregation to one of non-segregation takes place best and most effectively when an order for immediate desegregation is issued and immediately implemented by responsible authorities." Carter noted that Clark was arranging a meeting of social scientists to "get a group interpretation of what this data proves so that we can be sure that the interpretation just indicated reflects the consensus of sociologists in the United States."[4]

The meeting took place in New York City on July 23, 1954. Those invited included Mamie and Kenneth Clark, Stuart Cook, Isidor Chein, Alfred McClung Lee, Columbia sociologist Robert Merton, Arnold Rose, Gordon Allport, Theodore Newcomb, Goodwin Watson, and a handful of others. Merton could not attend, nor could Allport. Allport, however, sent along a letter that was distributed to those who did attend.[5]

Clark announced that the goal of the conference was "to arrive at a consensus on the most effective answer to Question IV based upon the available social science data."[6] The social scientists compared various plans for "gradual" versus "immediate" desegregation. One form of gradual desegregation was, for example, allowing a period of time "for the purpose of public education and general preparation for desegregation." Another form of gradual desegregation was "segmentalized or piecemeal desegregation," which included desegregating different geographical units within the state; desegregating different institutional units or grades; or desegregating through a given numerical quota. Various forms of immediate desegregation included eliminating the segregated "Negro facilities and admitting Negroes to the previous white units or opening all facilities to everyone regardless of race."[7]

The tone of the conference participants toward gradual desegregation was set by Gordon Allport, who did not even attend because of a prior commitment. In his letter, which Clark distributed to conference participants, Allport made it quite clear that "a firm stand should be taken, so as to brook no pussy-footing, unnecessary delays, or skullduggery. What we know favors the strong administrative stand, the 'fait accompli.'"[8] The conference participants quickly took up Allport's argument and expanded on the dangers of any sort of "gradualism." Gradual options that allowed for a given period of time to elapse were rejected because they were "predicated on the assumption that attitudinal changes must precede social changes. . . . There is no evidence to support the contention that public education and attitudinal preparation for acceptance of desegregation in themselves increased the chances of effective desegregation." Piecemeal approaches were rejected because "an examination of the actual instances of desegregation approached in this manner revealed that this type of segmentalized desegregation, rather than allaying anxieties and doubts, appeared to be associated with an increase in resentment when the individuals . . . are actually faced with desegregation."[9]

The conclusion of the conference was that desegregation should be done as swiftly as possible, allowing time only for redrawing of new school districts that were not based on race:

> In making the transition from the present system of segregated to non-seg-regated education, all school facilities can be opened to children without regard to race within that time required only for specified and necessary administrative adjustments. There is no available evidence which suggests that this time need be any longer than a school year. There was no evidence which suggested that any modification of these conclusions was required by any known and relevant peculiar local conditions.[10]

The "peculiar local conditions" referred to obliquely in the conclusion meant, of course, the South. The conference participants spent some time attempting to discover "the degree to which the tradition of the Southern states in regard to the treatment of Negroes would in effect make impossible effective desegregation of public schools in these states."

The problem about the South was this: the very authorities who would be responsible for enforcing strict desegregation were the most vocally opposed to desegregation. The conference participants had agreed that desegregation was best accomplished if it met the five conditions that Clark had outlined in his "Desegregation" article. The conditions centered on a firm authoritative stand that did not allow any deviation from the desegregation demands. These conditions applied with extra force to the South, since "the southern tradition in the area of race relations might require a greater decisiveness and clarity and a more overt use of authority" to achieve effective desegregation.[11] But, as Gordon Allport phrased it in his letter, the authorities "constitute[d] the rub, especially in Georgia, So. Carolina, etc."[12]

The conference participants had three solutions to this conundrum. The first was a vague call for the Supreme Court to "make itself felt by the decisiveness of its decree." The conference participants concluded defiance of the decree would be "essentially a legal and police power question with which social scientists are not particularly competent to deal."

The second response the social scientists had to the "peculiar" nature of the South was to minimize the importance of the problem. Many southern communities had already declared their "willingness to abide by the [*Brown I*] decision and follow the implementation decree when it is given by the court." Moreover, even in those areas where resistance and violence had been predicted, experience had demonstrated that such predictions seldom came to fruition. Clark made a note to himself to "collect all lists of dire predictions; NAACP cases in equalization of graduate and professional schools; white primary, etc." He noted that a "heavy burden rests on the other side to demonstrate high probability of dissension or violence with 'forthwith decree.'"[13]

The third and final solution to the problem of southern authority was offered by Gordon Allport in his letter. Allport proposed the establishment of special statewide committees charged with overseeing the implementation order. The committees would have "some official standing: and would consider the local situation, recommend necessary legislation, hear complaints, and generally oversee the progress." Allport even suggested some individuals in the southern states who could possibly serve on such a committee.[14]

In the end, the conference had come out strongly for quick and forceful desegregation. Even those participants who had initially doubted the wisdom of "forced" desegregation had been converted. Perhaps no one exemplified the new consensus better than Theodore Newcomb, who had written to Clark with his doubts about quick desegregation the previous year. In a handwritten note to Clark, Newcomb remarked, "Will you tell [NAACP-LDEF attorney] Bob Carter this has been a good meeting—obviously since I've rather markedly changed my mind about 'gradualism.'"[15] Indeed he had—gone were Newcomb's concerns about a reactionary backlash and polarization of the issues surrounding desegregation. Three days after the conference, he wrote to Clark that "groups and whole populations, like individuals, change their attitudes *as soon as* it is clear that events have changed the nature of things. . . . In the case of attitudes toward desegregation in the southern states, I can think of no more convincing evidence that events have changed than to implement the legal consequences of those changes." The only delay, Newcomb argued, "should be justified in terms of administrative necessity, not in terms of what I believe to be a false psychology of inherently slow attitude change."[16]

This conference, and the strong consensus that arose from it, formed the basis of a second brief that Clark prepared for the Supreme Court, which he called "the Social Science Memo," in contrast to the Social Science Statement of 1952. Despite the fact that the Social Science Memo had its origins in a conference where even the doubting Newcomb was convinced of the issues, the document was to cause more dissension within the social science community than the Social Science Statement had. At the heart of the dissension were those issues surrounding objectivity and neutrality that Clark had been concerned with since his 1953 address to SPSSI and SSSP.

The Social Science Memo

The Social Science Memo began as Clark's summary of the conclusions of the July conference. It included the call for a strict one-year time limit, downplayed possible southern resistance to a firm decree, and recommended establishing Allport's committees to oversee the implementation of desegregation. The Social Science Memo ended with this list of specific recommendations:

> The Court should grant a decree which specifies that "within the limits set by normal," non-racially determined, "geographic school districting" all children, Negro and white, should be permitted to attend existing public schools

> In making the transition from the present system of segregated to non-segregated education, all children should be assigned to the available school facilities, without regard to race.

> The only delay permitted should be that time required by specified and necessary administrative adjustments.

> There is no available evidence which suggests that this time need be any longer than a school year.

> Also, there was no evidence which indicated that any modification of these conclusions was required by any known or relevant local conditions.[17]

On August 10, 1954, Clark mailed out this draft to the participants of the conference for "suggestions, comments, and modification." He explained that while the attorneys had not yet decided if the social science materials would be used as a separate appendix or as "an integral part of their legal brief," he had been asked to "document our memorandum by detailed reference citation as if it were going to be used as a separate brief."[18] The briefs were due at the Supreme Court by October and time was of the essence, as evidenced by Clark's handwritten note to Mamie's form letter: "I love you honey—but get your comments and suggestions in soon."[19]

Clark received many favorable comments on the Social Science Memo. Columbia sociologist Robert Merton, who missed the July conference because of an attack of appendicitis, was recovering at home when Clark, who lived in the same neighborhood, came over and read the memo to him. Merton found it a "topflight document."[20] Although the responses were generally favorable, Clark soon faced a number of criticisms—some of them that cut to particularly vital issues in the brief. The general conclusions of the Social Science Memo were those of the July conference, but the forceful way in which Clark presented the conclusions troubled some of his respondents.

Gardner Murphy, who had been invited but did not attend the July conference, believed the argument that the South's views on segregation would be easily changed was "wishful thinking" and unsupported by evidence. Murphy wrote, "There is a magical ease with which the profoundly organized attitude patterns are to be swept away, as they are more easily in Northern cities where minority groups work together through the political instruments which all share." In the end, Murphy recommended that the whole approach to the South be scrapped for lack of evidence. He concluded:

> There is certainly no serious research evidence *either for* or *against* such a wide generalization as that Southerners (or any other group) are "less capable of changing their patterns of behavior. . . ." I believe this whole line of argument got into the draft because no really good evidence about how to cope with the South is at hand, especially its political structure, that makes the problem so massive. Let's face it![21]

Gordon Allport thought Clark's demand of a one-year time limit was "the real punch-line." He put the matter to Clark with his typical tact while suggesting that Clark had more work to do on the point. "The date," Allport claimed, "will be most carefully scrutinized and debated. What the Memo contains on this issue is not entirely convincing. I know you have some documentation on the point; but I would urge making it really 'good' and convincing."[22]

Arnold Rose also objected to Clark's claim that all the administrative changes could be accomplished in one year. Rose further expressed doubt about the creation of commissions to oversee implementation of segregation, "even if it was Gordon Allport who suggested it." On a more general level, he thought that the entire argument had to be made more provisional—that to make strong claims that could not be substantiated would weaken the entire brief. Rose wrote, "In general, I believe that the more cautious and closely-reasoned our statements, the more effective they are likely to be. Opponents will look for loopholes and thus seek to discredit our whole statement."[23] Rose's concern for the general tone of the document was echoed by Theodore Newcomb. Although generally favorable, Newcomb wished that the draft "could be made to sound more like the product of social scientists and less apparently like a document prepared by lawyers and/or people eager to prove something."[24]

Clark received a thorough criticism from a most unexpected source. He had appended a handwritten note on the statement's cover letter when he mailed it off to Stuart Cook, who was vacationing in Ontario. Clark wrote, "I know you will be as 'ruthless' as if we were working over this first draft together."[25] And ruthless Cook was. His objections to the draft were so wide-ranging that he could not bring himself to write to Clark with his critique. In a note to himself he wrote, "Convinced that to produce anything acceptable to me, would have to start over. Hesitate to write to Ken. Believe only solution is to wait until after APA."

Cook objected to the fact that the draft was "an undisguised argument for immediate desegregation." His concern was that in making such an argument, Clark had failed to distinguish between what "evidence" there might have been for immediate desegregation and his own "interpretation" of that evidence to mean that desegregation should proceed in a one-year time limit. For Cook, the only solution was to "discard the present form" of the draft, which he believed was nothing more than a "legal brief" that urged a "certain course of action." Instead, Cook argued that the statement should be reworked as a simple presentation of "relevant data and conclusions [that] are available to social scientists which the Court might find helpful in making its decision on decrees implementing its decision." According to Cook, the brief should state "if a decree to admit [Negro schoolchildren] forthwith, what consequences might be anticipated. If a decree permitting gradual adj[ustment], what consequences might be anticipated."[26]

In fall 1954, Clark began the process of redrafting the document, but there was still no firm policy from the NAACP-LDEF as to how these materials would be used. As usual, Robert Carter urged his colleagues that "there is no question but that the approach of the social scientists is one which we favor and want to use."[27] Others were less sure. Clark's militant demand for immediate desegregation was becoming too extreme for some of the more pragmatic members of the NAACP-LDEF staff.

Marshall, still weighing the options, had not yet decided on a final strategy in fall 1954.[28] In the meantime, the task of the social scientists would
undergo some changes in response to changing circumstances. The opposition briefs had begun to be filed at the Supreme Court in October
1954. The states had discovered how to use social science as well.

Florida's Amicus *Brief*

The Supreme Court had invited all states that had segregated education
to write *amicus curiae* briefs for the 1955 argument. In Florida, Attorney
General Richard W. Ervin decided that since social science had seemed to
influence the Court's 1954 decision, that social science might possibly influence the Court to issue a moderate desegregation decree in their 1955
decision. The state of Florida appropriated $10,000 for the effort, and
Ervin enlisted Florida State University sociologist Lewis M. Killian to
head a project that would use social science to support the position of the
states, rather than that of the NAACP-LDEF.

Born and raised in the Deep South, Killian received his Ph.D. under
the direction of Louis Wirth at the University of Chicago after World War
II. Wirth had convinced him to concentrate on race relations, and Killian
soon became a self-described racial liberal. For the project on desegregation, Ervin had suggested to Killian that he make a poll of the Florida
population to demonstrate the widespread resistance to desegregation
that Ervin was convinced existed. Killian rejected this option, feeling that
the Supreme Court would rightly reject the results as having no bearing
on the enforcement of constitutional rights.

The approach Killian chose was suggested to him by Kenneth Clark's
"Desegregation" article. Since Clark had argued that firm enforcement
was necessary from community leaders, Killian decided to poll community leaders to determine if they would enforce desegregation. Under
pressure from the attorney general's office, Killian was forced to skip any
pretesting of his questions and to rush them to various community
groups. He polled the police forces, school principals, Parent-Teacher Association (PTA) presidents, school boards, judges, newspaper editors,
radio station managers, state legislators, and a sample of religious leaders.
Because the attorney general's office thought that the citizenry of Florida
would be impressed with large numbers, all these people were polled,
rather than representative samples.

The results of the study were much as Killian expected: white community leaders disagreed with *Brown* while African American leaders did not. About 30 percent of the white leaders said they would actively oppose any movement to end segregation. Killian's own conclusions were attached as "Appendix A" to the main brief from Florida.[29]

When the Florida brief appeared at the NAACP-LDEF offices, the attorneys turned to the social scientists to help devise a response. Bob Johnson of the American Friends Service Committee had been at the University of Chicago with Killian and described him as "a dogged, plodding, and earnest sociologist." Johnson found it "incredible" that "a state would choose to make an opinion survey the core of its legal argument, particularly in the light of what we now know about the relationship of expressed opinion to actual behavior." He noted that the brief itself was marked by a tendency to use quotations that "would be negated if they had been quoted *in toto* rather than in part," observing that Robert Merton, Harry Ashmore, and Kenneth Clark were quoted as supporting positions that were diametrically opposed to the ones they actually held. Johnson concluded his letter by recommending that the NAACP-LDEF "invoke the skills of a number of social scientists and educators to evaluate how much of the information in the Florida brief is a) true, and b) relevant."[30]

The NAACP-LDEF enlisted two experts in polling procedures, Norman Rosenberg and Lou Harris, to examine the Florida brief. In April, Jack Greenberg relayed their conclusions to the rest of the NAACP-LDEF staff: "The public opinion poll," wrote Greenberg, "conducted by Dr. Killian cannot possibly prove how people will feel or what they will do when they are faced with an actual instance of desegregation in process." Rosenberg's analysis concluded that the poll was an example of Robert Merton's "self-fulfilling prophecy." Because of constraints of time and staff, Killian had been forced to eliminate any open-ended questions—respondents had to choose among options that the poll offered them. Given the wording of the questions on expected violence, for example, Rosenberg argued that the opinions reported by the poll were

> brought into being by the instrument that measures them. . . . To accept these positive responses as representing in any meaningful sense real considered judgments or opinions . . . of a future state of fact requires the complete surrender to the pollster's variation of the "intelligence test fallacy" . . . as Herbert Blumer puts it, "that public opinion consists of what public opinion polls poll."

Lou Harris conducted an extensive methodological critique of the Florida poll and concluded, "From the results of this survey, it might be entirely within the limits of legitimate analysis to conclude that 'There is no uniform opposition to the Court's decision among the white leadership groups of Florida as represented in this survey. . . . A majority of all groups—white and Negro—expect neither mob violence nor 'serious violence.'" In fact, Harris argued, the poll could be turned back on the state because "the people most likely to have informed opinions on the subject, school principals and supervisors clearly think these problems are not insurmountable, since a majority agree with the decision and the vast majority say they would comply with it."[31] The NAACP-LDEF believed they had the answers to the state of Florida's attempt to enroll social science in the cause of segregation, and the Florida brief caused no serious problems during the reargument.

A more interesting effect of the Florida brief lay in the repercussions for Lewis Killian, who had designed the study used in the brief. Killian had believed he was doing a service to the cause of desegregation by offering a realistic and sober analysis of the public attitudes of community leaders. But his data had been used by the state of Florida to argue for a desegregation plan that would have clearly kept African Americans in segregated schools for decades. The lesson Killian learned from his experience with the attorney general's office was "Social science is to a politician as a lamppost to a drunk: it is supposed to provide support, not light." Killian was dismayed at the use his data were put to in the body of the brief. He later recounted, "Some of the harshest criticism I received after the brief was published was based on statements I had never seen."[32]

And he did receive heavy criticism. Alfred McClung Lee attempted to have Killian censured by the Eastern Sociological Society for his role in the preparation of the Florida brief. The attempt failed, but Killian was deeply hurt by the move.[33] Finally, out of self-defense, if for no other reason, Killian presented his case to the 1955 meeting of the Society for the Study of Social Problems. Killian argued that for a social scientist to work with a lawyer was dangerous because "the lawyer is first and foremost the advocate; the social scientist constantly guards against becoming an advocate." The problem was further complicated for those social scientists working in the South, for while "the sociologist [was] expected to take a position in opposition to 'gradualism,'" gradualism was "considered radical by many southern politicians." What his audience must understand, said Killian, was that the very act of calling for the survey was a bold and daring step for the attorney general in Florida: "In the South, it seems to be a widespread assumption that the politically safe course at this time was to ignore or defy the Supreme Court. When the Attorney General accepted the Court's premise [that] the propositions state[d] in [Question] IV . . . were the only available alternatives . . . he closed this door." Hence, Killian's role in the entire affair should be understood not as blocking desegregation but as pushing for it.[34]

Of course, the fact that Killian was pushing for desegregation, however gradual, meant that he was criticized roundly in Tallahassee by those white citizens who considered any form of desegregation to be a betrayal of the South. Beset on all sides, Killian could only stand by while the governor and attorney general for whom he had worked on the study, and whom Killian had believed to be racial moderates, lost their re-election bids to a pair of racists who rallied public support with cries of "Segregation forever!"[35]

The Second Social Science Memo

While the NAACP-LDEF was working on its response to the Florida brief, and to the other briefs that started appearing, Clark was busy redrafting the Social Science Memo. The second draft was very similar to the first. Clark was stubborn on the point of the one-year time limit, and it remained. The recommendation for locally created commissions to implement desegregation also remained. In deference to Cook's complaints that the Social Science Memo did not distinguish "fact from interpretation," Clark added the following footnote on the first page: "When an opinion—as distinct from a conclusion based upon evidence—is stated, it is generally introduced by a statement such as, 'It may be postulated,' or 'the evidence suggests,' or some other phrase indicating that what follows is an opinion or an interpretation of available evidence."[36]

In terms of the arguments made, the only significant change between the first and the second draft was the amount of space and material dedicated to arguing that the Court did not have to wait for an attitude change on segregation before they ordered desegregation. This was the argument that had been put so clearly by CCI at its founding a decade before. Clark now enrolled both the argument and the studies that CCI had conducted to prove the point in the Social Science Memo. All calls for gradual desegregation, Clark argued, were "predicated upon the assumption that attitudinal changes must precede social changes." But, he continued, an examination of the available studies on "the relationship between racial attitudes and situationally determined behavior" showed that "there was no substantial support for the contention that public education and attitudinal preparation for acceptance of desegregation in themselves increase the chances of effective desegregation." Here Clark called up the studies of Lapiere and all who had followed his lead at CCI—Bernard Kutner, Gerhart Saenger, Morton Deutsch—and the rest of the research that had shown that racial attitudes did not influence behavior. "There is a considerable body of evidence," Clark concluded, "indicating that where the situation demands that an individual act as if he were not prejudiced, he will do so in spite of his continued prejudice."[37]

In response to Gardner Murphy's criticism on southern folkways, Clark considerably beefed up that part of the brief as well. Although he kept the argument that the South might need an especially firm hand to guide it, Clark made three arguments in favor of his position that southern schools could desegregate as easily as any others. First, they already had desegregated other areas of life. Clark pointed to other victories by the NAACP-LDEF and the armed services: "Significant changes in race relations involving southern whites and Negroes have taken place in the Armed Services, army camps and schools on army bases, first class accommodations on railroads, graduate and professional schools, politics and government." Second, there were a host of institutions in the South that "have indicated at least a willingness to deal with the problem of desegregation of the schools within the framework of law and order." Clark appended a list of southern leaders who had indicated they would abide by the Court's 1954 ruling. Third, Clark argued that the South was, in any case, "undergoing dynamic and extensive changes. One might postulate that under these conditions individuals are in a position of 'indefinite equilibrium' and are as susceptible to those influences which reinforce past anti-democratic tendencies." Perhaps understandably, this last argument drew a large question mark in the margin from M. Brewster Smith when he read the draft.[38]

The second draft proved to be the final draft. Perhaps because they believed the law to be clear on the point of immediate relief from deprivation of constitutional rights, the lawyers of the NAACP-LDEF chose not to submit a separate social science appendix to their main brief. The NAACP-LDEF did incorporate parts of Clark's work into the main brief, however.[39] Moreover, the NAACP-LDEF demanded that the schools be immediately desegregated, allowing no more than a year.

Despite this stand, however, the NAACP-LDEF was not sanguine about the possibility of immediate segregation. While it was important to demand immediate desegregation, the NAACP-LDEF knew that, whatever the Court decided, the desegregation of Southern public schools would be a long and drawn out process. As Mark Tushnet has noted, "immediate" desegregation was more rhetorical than real.[40]

The footnotes of the NAACP-LDEF brief may have contained some social science material, but the NAACP-LDEF no longer had an urgent need for it. Finally, the law was on their side. They had always believed that theirs was the moral position, the *right* position; finally, theirs was also the *legal* position. In his masterful analysis of the career of Thurgood Marshall, Mark Tushnet noted that the overarching goal of the NAACP-LDEF desegregation campaign was the transformation of unfavorable case precedent into favorable case precedent, "through a careful litigation strategy pointing out anomalies in doctrine and identifying the inevitable failure of society's efforts to explain why unjust doctrines nonetheless were acceptable." For this task, the social scientists were perfectly suited. Once the victories were won and favorable case precedent assured, however, the rule of law became an advantage for the NAACP-LDEF. Tushnet concludes, "The same theme pervaded Marshall's arguments about the proper remedy in *Brown.* As Marshall repeatedly told the Court, implementing desegregation put the rule of law itself at stake. Delay based on 'attitudes' meant that the Court would be implicitly accommodating resistance to its statement of what the Constitution meant."[41]

No one put the rule of law more eloquently than Marshall himself in the last oral arguments on *Brown.* Marshall told the Court, "I don't believe any argument has ever been made to this Court to postpone the enforcement of a constitutional right. The argument is never made until Negroes are involved." Finally, Marshall claimed, we have the law on *our* side: "The other side has not produced anything except attitudes, opinion polls, et cetera."[42]

The Supreme Court closed this particular case on May 31, 1955, when it remanded the cases back to the federal district courts, who were ordered to desegregate the public schools "with all deliberate speed."[43] Although the litigation campaign was over, it would be another decade before any real progress was made in the desegregation of southern schools. The NAACP-LDEF had been right: the difference between "immediate" and "gradual" was more rhetorical than real.

PART IV

Dissolution

10

Committee of Social Science
Consultants

The Supreme Court decision in *Brown II* may have ended one phase of the NAACP-LDEF's struggle against segregated education, but it did not end the association of the NAACP-LDEF with the social-scientific community. Throughout 1954, the NAACP-LDEF was struggling to form a Committee of Social Science Consultants (CSSC) within the NAACP-LDEF. The CSSC was to be a formal body of social scientists that would aid communities that were starting the desegregation process.

The CSSC, by nearly any measure imaginable, was a failure. Indeed, it was very nearly a committee that did not ever exist. To understand *why* this was the case is to understand the very real nature of the tension between the role of the neutral and detached social scientist and that of the involved attorney-advocates. By the mid-1950s, the social scientists had recognized that in the new political climate created by the *Brown* litigation, they could not afford too close an association with the attorneys of the NAACP-LDEF. Kenneth Clark, in particular, was aware of the tension in his association with the attorneys, and this chapter concludes with his final defense of his role in *Brown*.

Origins of the CSSC

The CSSC originated before the first *Brown* decision. In January 1954, after the argument and reargument for the first Supreme Court decision, Kenneth Clark and Anna Caples Frank began planning for the creation of a "project on community education." The first draft of the project argued for widespread adult education in those communities that were facing desegregation. While the draft assumed that the Court would soon overrule segregation throughout the nation, even absent a Supreme Court victory, many communities in border states were already desegregating. These communities "face[d] the prospect of adjusting their mores and preconceptions to newly-defined applications of the law" and needed "systematic local efforts of a participative adult education nature" in order to overcome "long-standing prejudices, misconceptions, fears and superstitions."[1]

An example of what Clark had in mind was the NAACP-LDEF experience in Cairo, Illinois, in December 1951. Cairo was one of a number of communities in southern Illinois that was attempting to desegregate its public schools. June Shagaloff went to Cairo and conducted a "program of popular education," including public and neighborhood meetings; addresses to church, social, and school groups; and the distribution of printed educational material.

During this time, four crosses were burned, one home was bombed, and other intimidation was attempted by "irresponsible elements" of the community. Despite this effort at intimidation, the community proceeded with desegregation, and in March 1951, twenty-one African American students transferred to the previously all-white school; in September 1952, an additional sixty-four transferred. The desegregation proceeded smoothly, and the threats of widespread violence in the community never materialized.[2]

At first glance, it might seem paradoxical for Clark to have been arguing for the importance of education to prepare a community for desegregation. After all, he would soon argue forcefully that desegregation had to be firm and immediate, and that education would not, in and of itself, help smooth the process. In his briefs written for the Supreme Court, however, Clark was always careful to note that education *alone* would not help desegregation. The situation in Cairo was exactly what Clark had been arguing for—desegregation proceeded in the face of threats of violence and protests from a very vocal minority of the community. The fact that desegregation was coming, regardless of attempts at intimidation, was what made community education successful. In other words, the education was not designed to make desegregation possible; it was designed to explain how the community could best cope with what was an inevitable situation.

Although the events of Cairo gave hope that community education could aid desegregation, the proposal noted that the NAACP-LDEF was not willing to do further fieldwork unless it was supervised by an experienced social scientist who could adequately evaluate the fieldworker's efforts. Clark noted that the involvement of social scientists could help determine the most effective methods for preparing a community for desegregation. Rather than approach the problem on an *ad hoc* basis, Clark proposed that the social scientists develop "techniques which can be applied by the citizens as a result of good demonstration."

The proposal concluded with the thought "As always, a key problem will be to secure enough money to meet an adequate budget." Since the NAACP-LDEF had been unwilling to fund Clark's much more modest set of field studies in 1953, when preparing for the first reargument of *Brown* before the Supreme Court, Clark recognized that they would not be willing to fund the much more extensive community education project. He noted, "The best solution would be to ask a small working committee of social scientists to serve as consultants in planning the program in accordance with standards which would merit grants from dispersing foundations."[3] Securing foundation money would be the sticking point for the CSSC. The first order of business, however, was to enlist the social scientists who would serve on the new committee.

Clark declined the opportunity to chair the new committee. Instead, he recommended that the committee be chaired by sociologist Alfred McClung Lee of Brooklyn College. In many ways, Lee was a logical choice to chair the new group. He was the sociologist who had worked the closest with the NAACP-LDEF during the *Brown* litigation, testifying at the trial level of one of the cases, helping Clark assemble materials for the briefs the social scientists wrote, and suggesting names of scientists who would sign the briefs. Lee also had administrative experience: he was a charter member of the SPSSI in 1936 and one of the moving forces in founding the Society for the Study of Social Problems in 1952. Moreover, Lee had chaired two academic sociology departments: that of Wayne State and, after his move in 1949, that of Brooklyn College.[4]

In April 1954, Lee began recruiting social scientists for the new committee. In his recruitment letter, he related the successes of the NAACP-LDEF field agents in Cairo and in a few other areas, such as communities in southern Delaware. Lee noted that the LDEF wanted to "ensure the translation of NAACP court victories into social realities" by building on these experiences within a "carefully structured program carried out in consultation with a Committee of Consultants, including social scientists, legal authorities, and individuals experienced in community relations."[5]

Lee's description of the actual work to be carried out by the social scientists was vague, leading Gordon Allport to ask, "The accomplishments in Southern Illinois and Delaware are impressive, and must be due to a field staff of unusual common sense and personal ability. Can social science improve this approach? What, in short, have eggheads like myself to offer?"[6] Lee replied that Allport was being "much too modest." He explained that the fieldwork by the NAACP-LDEF agents was only half of the job: "The other half of the job . . . will be an effort to study the processes which are going on as a result of the impact of court decisions and as a result of the facilitating efforts by community relations workers." This study, Lee told Allport, was why the CSSC needed social scientists.[7]

Lee also included a more detailed proposal, to explain clearly what it was the CSSC would do. In this proposal, two communities would be singled out, the first in a "border state where segregation has been abolished by law, but persists in practice. The second would be in a Southern state where school segregation was previously established by state law." The role of the CSSC, explained Lee, would be to "assist in planning the projects, in selecting project staff. The members would be available for consultation with project staff members, would receive periodic reports from the field, and would give advice on the conduct of community programs and on collection and evaluation of data."[8]

Robert Redfield's concerns were different from Allport's. "Insofar as new and additional money may be needed," he wrote to Lee, "is there any difficulty in persuading foundations to give it to the NAACP? I have a very high regard for that organization; it has done the work in this business. But I have a feeling that some donors don't like it—more's the pity."[9] Lee agreed that "the raising of funds for such an active organization as the NAACP is not an easy matter. However, the organization has had more success in the past two years."[10]

Despite any uncertainties they may have felt about the project, Allport and Redfield consented to join the new committee, as did forty-four other social scientists recruited by Lee. The list of members read like a virtual "who's who" of important names in race relations for 1950s social science—Herbert Blumer, Isidor Chein, Stuart Cook, E. Franklin Frazier, Else Frenkel-Brunswik, Charles S. Johnson, Robert M. MacIver, Gardner Murphy, Theodore Newcomb, Robert Redfield, Ira De Augustine Reid, Arnold Rose, and Robert C. Weaver among them.

Lee promised the new committee members that detailed plans would be fleshed at the committee's first meeting, scheduled in New York City for May 18, 1954. Although at the time it was scheduled Lee could have no way of knowing it, this would be the day after the Supreme Court handed down *Brown I*. The fortunate timing gave new impetus to the fledgling committee. Since the Supreme Court had delayed any order regarding the method of desegregation, there was a possibility that the CSSC could influence the decree that was due the next year. In June 1954, Lee wrote to Allport that while Allport's "thought . . . concerning having NAACP lawyers attempt to 'build in' the organization's advice into the Supreme Court decree is a very good one," it might not be possible to get the CSSC off the ground in time. Lee confided to Allport, "At this stage of the effort, we are naturally devoting a lot of our time to negotiating financial support for the project."[11]

The Funding Problem

The NAACP-LDEF was unwilling to support the CSSC financially in any significant way. The LDEF was under constant budget shortages, and although its financial situation was improving, it was constantly seeking ways to gain additional foundation support.[12] It believed that its money was for legal battles, not community action work. Any money spent on community action work had to be secured from outside foundations and be earmarked for such a purpose.[13] Moreover, the foundations that Lee was allowed to approach could not have previously supported the NAACP-LDEF, as the LDEF felt that "under no circumstances should funds be diverted from support of the general work of the organization to projects advocated by the Committee."[14]

Lee and Clark soon prepared a proposal calling for pilot studies of the desegregation process. The initial proposal was for a grant of $146,000 and was made to the Carnegie Foundation, the Ford Foundation, and the Rockefeller Foundation. Lee and Clark also put together a second proposal, very similar to the first, in the amount of $30,640, to be submitted to foundations with more modest resources. Both proposals were submitted during the summer of 1954.

In these proposals, Lee emphasized the role of social science in the May 17 *Brown* decision and observed that, as a result of that decision, many communities would need assistance in desegregating. The proposal noted, "Haphazard trial and error can be regrettably costly in exaggerated hatreds, exacerbation of prejudice, and violence." To avoid such problems, Lee suggested the creation of "action research teams," each of which would work in a single community in a border state. Like Lewin's plans at the AJCongress, Lee proposed that each team consist of two parts: "a community organization specialist" or an LDEF fieldworker and a "research associate and his assistant," the latter two being social scientists. The person working in the community would do all those things that had made the NAACP-LDEF so successful in the past, and the social scientist would study the effects of that work. The two roles were distinct, with the "action research worker" implementing policies and programs but not "concerned with measurement or analytic factors seeking applicability to situations elsewhere." The "evaluating personnel," by contrast, would not have "any functional responsibility for implementation of the action program."[15]

Redfield wrote to Lee about the second proposal, wondering why it was so limited. "I should think," wrote Redfield, "one would want to study several cases in which it [desegregation] is occurring, attempting to discover the elements of the situation which favor or disfavor a peaceful outcome." As it was, Redfield argued, the study would be far too limited to accomplish what it purported to discover—the effectiveness of desegregation education. Redfield asked, "Why not enlarge the project and ask for more money?"

Lee explained to Redfield that there was a larger project being suggested to the larger foundations.[16] But the truth of the matter was that whether or not the project was of a grand enough scale was quickly becoming irrelevant, for the foundations were not interested in funding the project at any level. By November 1954, both proposals had been rejected by every foundation to which they had been submitted.

Lee submitted an entirely new proposal, with a budget of $17,440, to a third group of small foundations. Just as Kenneth Clark's original plans in his 1953 research had called for original fieldwork but were scaled back to a literature review, the third proposal had no provision for carrying out original research. Lee proposed that the CSSC serve as a "coordinating center" to make existing research available. Lee was quick to distinguish this clearinghouse from the Southern Educational Reporting Service, which had just begun the *Southern School News*, which merely "undertakes to report news events relevant to the desegregation process throughout the country." The CSSC, by contrast, "seeks to publicize and place in use the type of social scientific research that has been so useful in briefs submitted to the Supreme Court, leading to the recent decision outlawing segregation." The new project resembled Clark's 1953 study on school desegregation and Lee's own research into discrimination at college fraternities.[17] The CSSC would send letters to community leaders and social scientists, requesting "copies of materials already prepared in this field [of desegregation], and information on studies currently underway." The material would be analyzed and "turned over to communication specialists working on a free-lance basis to prepare for publication in periodicals, in pamphlet form or in bulletins especially designed for persons working in the field.[18]

Like the previous two proposals, this third and final effort failed to secure support from any of the foundations approached. All told, sixteen foundations were approached and rejected by the CSSC. These foundations ranged in size from the large Carnegie and Ford Foundations to the smaller Old Dominion Foundation and F. A. Bean foundation. Anna Caples Frank reported back to Thurgood Marshall that while the response to the CSSC in the social-scientific community had been "extraordinary, . . . we have received no foundation grants."[19]

One explanation for the lack of foundation support for the CSSC was that *An American Dilemma* was viewed as the definitive word on race relations, and foundations became very hesitant to fund any new studies in race relations or intergroup relations.[20] Stuart Cook, who was a member of CSSC, complained in 1957, "Within the last few years research on intergroup relations has practically come to a stop. Foundations which formerly supported race relations research no longer do so."[21]

In this atmosphere of scarce foundation money, the CSSC faced additional problems. As a committee within the NAACP-LDEF, the CSSC had trouble presenting itself as a purely scientific organization. To many foundations, it appeared as if the LDEF were attempting to secure money not for pure scientific research but for its legal activities. After all the grant applications had been rejected, Anna Caples Frank reviewed the reasons foundations did not make the grants available to the CSSC and reported to Thurgood Marshall that she thought the social scientists "could at the present, secure grants from some of these same foundations for similar social science projects to be carried on under their own direction or in connection with a university." The problem was that the foundations were unwilling to give money to "an action organization of the character of the NAACP Legal Defense and Education Fund even if the funds were to be expended for a social scientific project whose general merits some of the foundations recognize and in conjunction with social scientists whose prestige they acknowledge."[22] In other words, the fears that Robert Red-field had expressed at the beginning of the project were realized. The foundations did not recognize that the NAACP-LDEF, an organization composed almost completely of lawyers, could be capable of carrying out objective scientific research. Frank wrote to Marshall, "The problem now is how the rather remarkable structure already created in the Committee . . . can be utilized to further the interests of the NAACP Legal Defense and Educational Fund during the critical period of desegregation."[23]

Marshall managed to find some money to support at least a token presence of social science within the NAACP-LDEF. In January 1955, with a grant of $8,000 from the Prince Hall Masons, the CSSC would "make social science findings and materials available to educators, school officials, and civic organizations."[24] Essentially, the CSSC would function as the clearinghouse envisioned by Lee's third foundation proposal, although on a much smaller scale.

For the next two years the CSSC limped along, continually under-funded, although the indefatigable Lee continued to seek funding to keep the Committee going. The CSSC would have its official meetings at the annual meetings of the SSSP or SPSSI.[25] The functions of the committee were described by Lee as limited to "the preparation from time to time of joint public statements on matters concerned with desegregation where authoritative professional opinion will have needed influence."[26] Lee continued to act as a one-man clearinghouse, carrying on correspondence with any number of individuals for any research on desegregation "to bring their findings to the attention of individuals and organizations directly concerned with the problems of desegregation."[27] But with no funding forthcoming, the effort was largely a symbolic one and produced no significant results.

The End of the CSSC

For the NAACP-LDEF, the dissolution of the CSSC was a mere formality. Just as the AJCongress was able to dispense with CCI with no qualms in 1952, so, too, the NAACP-LDEF dispensed with the CSSC in 1957. The NAACP-LDEF had needed social science for one specific reason in the 1950s: to turn bad case precedent into good case precedent. As noted in the previous chapter, the law was now on the side of desegregation, and the NAACP-LDEF thought that the courtroom, armed with the Supreme

Court decisions of *Brown*, would be the place where the battle would be fought. The CSSC had become superfluous to the battle that was at hand, one that would bring Marshall and the NAACP-LDEF back into courtrooms all around the nation. In April 1957, Thurgood Marshall wrote to all committee members to ask "(1) whether or not it is advisable to continue the Committee, and (2) if the Committee is continued, how it may function most effectively."[28]

On June 3, 1957, Isidor Chein, Otto Klineberg, M. Brewster Smith, Kenneth Clark, June Shagaloff, and a handful of others met to discuss the future of the CSSC. June Shagaloff put forth the issues that the NAACP-LDEF thought the social scientists could help them with: How fast was "gradual segregation?" How could the NAACP-LDEF aid communities that wanted to desegregate but did not know the most effective way to do so? What could be done about communities that were in open defiance of the Court's decree? How could the NAACP-LDEF fight subterfuges such as "classification of children in terms of academic achievement," which was merely a way to group African American children in segregated classrooms?

The social scientists attempted to answer the NAACP-LDEF's questions. On gradual desegregation, the social scientists thought they would have to know the exact circumstances of the communities in question. For communities who wished to desegregate, doing so was not a problem that social scientists could address—it was a "public relations and community organization problem." Open defiance was a matter of "legal and political power" rather than social science. The social scientists thought they could help with the development of "a simple, clear, and authoritative guide on the meaning of test results" that could prevent abuses of intelligence tests.

There was, however, an overriding issue presented by the social scientists, which was that they could be the most useful if they ceased their official link with the NAACP-LDEF. Clark's report to Thurgood Marshall stated in part, "It was the unanimous opinion of those present at this meeting and the communicated opinion of Robert Merton that the social scientists could be most effective in their help to the Legal Division of the NAACP if they were *not* organized in a formal committee structure." The social scientists had finally come to understand that "formal association with the Legal Staff of the NAACP would raise the question of the freedom and independent status of social scientists and would leave them open to the criticism of being 'advocates' rather than objective students of the social process."[29]

The social scientists' feeling that they should maintain their distance from the NAACP-LDEF was a marked contrast with the sentiments expressed in the previous decade by the same individuals. In 1948, Isidor Chein wrote of the urge for social scientists to be social engineers. In 1952, Smith participated in the *Davis* case "with greatest satisfaction."[30] In 1953, Clark spoke of *Brown* being only the first step in a long and fruitful collaboration between social scientists and lawyers. Nor did this fear of "being advocates" appear in 1954, when the social scientists eagerly signed on to be part of the CSSC.

In some ways, the CSSC was the victim of the success of the collaboration between social science and lawyers in the *Brown* decision. *Brown* was a pinnacle of activist social science in the United States, and it brought with it a new level of scrutiny into the nature and motivations of activist social science. Edmond Cahn's questioning of Clark's objectivity in his *New York University Law Review* articles exemplified the new level of scrutiny. Clark's defense of his objectivity in the face of Cahn's criticism was that the relationship between the social scientists and the lawyers was a clearly defined one of fact provider to advocate. But by being part and parcel of the same organization, as the CSSC was in relation to the NAACP-LDEF, the relationship could be perceived as too close. If their bills and salaries were being paid by the NAACP-LDEF, the social scientists no longer could claim to be disinterested providers of factual knowledge; they would be too intertwined with the lawyers.

Of course, the decision to disband the CSSC was in some sense already made; it was woefully underfunded and had no significant accomplishments and no promise of a productive future. Still, the perception of the close association mattered to the social scientists, who were anxious to preserve their authority as objective observers of society. With the South calling for "massive resistance," it was clear that the battle against segregated education was far from over. If they wanted to have any authority in the post-*Brown* United States, it was essential for the social scientists to maintain an air of objectivity in the face of a polarized debate over desegregation.

Kenneth Clark: Life after Brown

No other social scientist felt the need to protect his objectivity more than Kenneth Clark. The *Brown* decisions had transformed Clark from an unknown social psychologist into a nationally known figure. The effect of the *Brown* case can be seen in the fate of the manuscript he prepared for the Mid-Century White House Conference in 1950.

Clark had prepared his White House Conference manuscript while he was under contract to the American Jewish Committee, which was planning to publish it as part of their "Studies in Prejudice" series. The AJ-Committee, however, could not find a publisher for it. In 1953, Clark wrote to Bernard Kutner that his manuscript had "been in the hands of at least four publishers" but still had not been accepted.[31] Four days before the *Brown* decision, May 13, 1954, Clark wrote to Bigham Dai that he had "reworked the original manuscript for possible publication in book form. So far, no publisher seems particularly enthusiastic about this material."[32]

Immediately after the *Brown* decision, with the prominent mention of Clark's name, all that changed. In June 1954, Clark wrote to a friend that "Harpers is seriously considering having it revised in light of new developments."[33] Eventually, Clark's book was published in 1955 as *Prejudice and Your Child*.[34] In the press release announcing the book, the publisher made sure to mention that "the psychological studies behind the book were cited by the Supreme Court to show that 'separate-but-equal' schools are not 'adequate.'"[35]

While *Prejudice and Your Child* was not a particularly successful book for Clark, its publication demonstrates how Clark was becoming identified with the *Brown* litigation, and how that identification brought him increasing attention—not all of it welcome.[36] For example, in the wake of Edmond Cahn's criticisms came those of Ernest van den Haag.

Van den Haag was a psychoanalyst who also taught at the New School for Social Research at New York University. For van den Haag, the solution to inequality in educational opportunity was not to eliminate segregation, for "when opportunity to be educated is equal, segregation should not be illegal. Surely no group should want a law compelling people to congregate. Legal and political efforts, therefore, should be directed toward equalizing opportunity regardless of segregation." To assure freedom, argued van den Haag, one had to respect the "right of disassociation." The solution he offered was to replace the two segregated school systems not with a single school system but with a tripartite system in order to avoid "compulsory congregation." "The desire for the maximization of liberty," wrote van den Haag, "leads to the contention that there should be schools for white, schools for Negroes, and schools which both can attend, just as there are colleges for males, females, and coeducational ones." Van den Haag waved away the argument that communities could not possibly afford three completely equal school systems. The expense involved was to be decided democratically, for "in a democracy, a community has the right to decide whether it wants less education *per capita* and lower taxes, or more education and higher taxes, and also whether it desires good (but equal) facilities, for the sake of the desired separation."[37]

Van den Haag also had no patience for the argument that segregation inflicted psychological damage on minority children. The doll tests in particular drew his fire. In his critique, van den Haag merely repeated the criticisms put forth by Cahn, offering very little that was new—Clark's South Carolina sample was too small; no control group was tested; the children's identifications could be explained away on other grounds; and so on. Van den Haag also pointed out, however, that Clark's 1947 paper showed that northern children rejected the dolls at a greater rate than southern children, proving that "Professor Clark's findings then can be explained without any reference to injury by segregation or by prejudice."[38]

By the time van den Haag's criticisms appeared in 1957, Clark was weary of explaining his positions on segregation. For the past six years he had dedicated nearly all of his professional time to desegregation. In 1955, he confided to Alfred McClung Lee that he was tired of talking about segregation and "would much prefer to escape into my first love of studying the effects of attitudes on memory," which had been the topic of his Ph.D. dissertation in 1940. Clark told Lee, "Every now and then I am obsessed with the idea that it is a tragic waste of time . . . we have to spend so much [time] discussing a problem that should be so clear to reasonable men."[39] Nonetheless, he responded to van den Haag when invited to participate in a 1960 symposium, sponsored by the *Villanova Law Review*, on the relationship between law and social science. The symposium also offered Clark an opportunity, at long last, to publish his response to Edmond Cahn, which he edited and combined with his response to van den Haag.

Clark spent little time defending the doll tests. He did not offer his interpretation that southern children had grown to accept the stigma, which indicated a greater degree of psychological damage. The doll tests, he argued, were only a tiny portion of the evidence presented to the Supreme Court. It was hard to take van den Haag seriously, Clark protested, for he had obviously not "examined carefully the nearly sixty references which were used as the basis of the social science brief which was submitted to the Supreme Court. If this were too arduous a task, then he could have examined the seven references cited by the United States Supreme Court in footnote 11 of the *Brown* decision."[40] To focus on the doll tests was to mistake the nature of the case put to the Court. In the criticism leveled by van den Haag, and by Cahn before him, Clark could find no evidence that the writer showed the slightest familiarity with the social science literature that had developed since World War II, arguing against segregation. In the end, Clark believed, that literature spoke for itself; all one had to do was go out and read it.

Moreover, van den Haag's argument that Clark's tests did not isolate segregated education as the sole variable responsible for psychological damage was simply irrelevant, Clark argued. No one had ever made such a claim. The elimination of segregation was seen by Clark and the other social scientists as a *necessary* rather than a *sufficient* condition to the elimination of the disease of racism. All the arguments that the opponents kept raising about the inability to isolate "legally segregated education" as the precise variable responsible for the psychological damage missed the main point of the social scientists' testimony. The social scientists agreed—it could have been discrimination in employment, it could have been discrimination in housing, it could have been social discrimination that African Americans encountered in stores or theaters or on the sidewalk. In fact, argued the social scientists, it probably was *all* those things, together with discrimination in education, that caused psychological damage among African Americans. But the fact that discrimination existed elsewhere in society did not justify it in education. If discrimination caused psychological damage—and no one seriously argued that it did not—then it was wrong to discriminate in education. That it was also wrong in housing, voting, or employment did not make it right in education. Eliminate it where you can, argued the social scientists, and you can in education.

Van den Haag responded to Clark's article with a vituperative piece that essentially accused Clark of being either incompetent or guilty of perjury regarding the inconsistency between his trial testimony and his 1947 article.[41] Clark did not respond to van den Haag a second time. Perhaps Clark had recognized that van den Haag was that rarest of creatures—a postwar social scientist who firmly believed in segregation and the separation of races. Soon after the exchange, van den Haag would testify in U.S. federal court that segregation was healthy for children, and before the World Court that apartheid in South Africa was justified. He would be a leading light in the International Association for the Advancement of Ethnology and Eugenics, one of the last bastions of scientific racism. As such, van den Haag represented a fringe element in contemporary social science, and Clark may not have wanted to dignify him by engaging him further on the issue of the doll tests.[42]

The marginalization of someone like van den Haag demonstrated that the issue of whether or not school segregation was psychologically damaging was no longer a live one. The attention of the country had moved on, and Clark had moved with it. Clark became an important figure in the 1960s War on Poverty and turned his attention to an analysis of the ghetto. In fact, Clark may be as well known for his book *Dark Ghetto* as he is for his role in the *Brown* litigation.[43]

Clark's activities in the 1960s can be seen as a direct outgrowth of his work in *Brown*. The key argument that the social scientists made in *Brown* was that the elimination of segregation was a necessary first step toward the elimination of racism. Clark and his fellow social scientists, not to mention the NAACP-LDEF, had no illusions that all that needed to be done was to repeal the segregation laws. But only by repealing segregation laws, they believed, could any progress be made. Clark's work in the 1960s can be viewed as taking the further steps that he thought necessary to eliminate racism.

It was during the 1960s that Clark began to despair of winning the fight against the disease of racism. In 1968, he told an interviewer that he felt that "the involvement in social action and social change that have dominated my life add up to one big failure. I fear the disease has metastasized."[44] While Clark continued with his work for social justice, his despair, if anything, grew even more palpable. In 1989, he could "look back and shudder at how naive we all were in our belief in the steady progress racial minorities would make through programs of litigation and education. . . . I am forced to recognize that my life has, in fact, been a series of glorious defeats."[45]

11

Conclusion

The key to understanding social scientists' involvement with the *Brown* litigation is their view of the social power of the law. If the social scientists had not believed in the power of the law to impose social stigmata or to create a new social climate, the NAACP-LDEF never would or could have enlisted their help.

In the five years after the end of World War II, the NAACP-LDEF developed their legal arguments against segregation. They whittled away at the *Plessy* precedent by attacking graduate school education. The 1950 graduate school victories of *Sweatt* and *McLaurin* had proclaimed that form of segregation unconstitutional on the basis of "intangible factors." The next year, the NAACP-LDEF turned to social scientists to prove the existence of these intangible factors in elementary and secondary education. For the social scientists, the court cases provided just the avenue they needed to use their expertise in the fight against segregation. There was a body of literature that fit their needs and a group of social scientists to present that literature, because social scientists had also been building a case against segregation in the years after World War II.

Clark and his colleagues were interested in using their expertise as social scientists to engineer society to become more racially just. They had developed a body of research that argued that legal segregation was damaging and could be eliminated. Moreover, the research was conducted by a close-knit group who shared a commitment to social justice and a willingness to act on their commitments. Their interests converged with those of the NAACP-LDEF in the *Brown* campaign and were an outgrowth of the "retreat of scientific racism" of the 1930s.

In the interwar period, psychologists became interested in discovering ways to measure seemingly ineffable attitudes such as racial prejudice and the origins of racial identity. One reason for the growth of this activity was the development of new forms of measurement techniques that allowed psychologists to quantify the previously unquantifiable psychological phenomenon of "attitude." The choice of *racial* attitudes for a topic of scientific investigation was governed by a combination of scientific challenge and social awareness of a "race problem."

Social scientists rejected explanations for racial differences based on intrinsic characteristics of a "race" and preferred those based on "culture." In the older, race-based scientific explanation, white people were innately superior to black people. Hence racial attitudes were real and rational responses to real differences between groups of people. In the new way of thinking, however, all differences between groups of people were "cultural," meaning the differences were not fixed but fluid. For example, if white people scored better on intelligence tests than African Americans, the explanation did not lie in the white people's innate superiority to African Americans but in the culture-bound nature of the tests. Researchers concluded that if an African American person could possibly be raised as a white person, his or her performance on an IQ test would be the same as that of a white person.

The cultural explanation for differences between groups did not provide a ready explanation for why there seemed to be antagonism between groups. If the differences between the races were cultural, that is, a product of societal interaction, how did the aversions between groups arise? To answer this question, psychologists began to study "race prejudice," which posited the individual reacting to cultural "stereotypes" and to "unfortunate contact" with individual members of a racial group. Such thinking, argued psychologists, was inherently irrational, since it made no sense to posit that merely because one member of a group had a trait, all members of that group shared that trait.

Research in race prejudice seemed to indicate that prejudice arose in response to cultural stereotypes, but it did not address exactly how the society transmitted these stereotypes. To begin to discover how society's racial stereotypes were transmitted, researchers in racial identify attempted to discover when concepts of race entered a child's worldview. When did children begin to realize that they were members of a particular race? What circumstances made for a strong sense of racial identity and what circumstances made for a weak sense? In answering these questions, researchers posited that racial attitudes were taught by society, rather than being something instinctual and ingrained into children at birth.

One explanation for the rise of the study of race prejudice is that new areas of scientific exploration were opening up with the adoption of the scientific concept of "culture." But to gain a full understanding of this rise, I have argued, a further explanation is required. It is not just that new studies were conducted but that the studies were conducted by a particular group of researchers. The leaders in studies into racial attitudes during the interwar period were a close-knit group aware of the existence of race prejudice and discrimination. Some, such as Otto Klineberg, Ruth and Eugene Horowitz, and Daniel Katz, were Jewish and sensitive to social discrimination on a firsthand basis. Kenneth and Mamie Clark were African Americans, who, even more than their Jewish counterparts, had to struggle with overt discrimination on a day-to-day basis. Other members of this group were white, Anglo-Saxon Protestants—Gardner and Lois Murphy, Goodwin Watson, Theodore Newcomb, and Gordon Allport. These individuals ranged from the politically liberal (the Murphys, Allport) to socialistic (Watson, Newcomb). Many of the white Protestant social scientists were informed by a religious belief in the "social gospel," which demanded that to achieve the reign of God on earth, one had to strive to make the world a more just and equitable place.

The Society for the Psychological Study of Social Issues provided lines of communication between the New York group of social scientists and others throughout the country, such as Isadore Krechevsky (David Krech) and Alfred McClung Lee, who believed in an egalitarian social science. During World War II, the SPSSI psychologists transformed their concern with racial prejudice into a national concern. For social scientists, fighting the war became synonymous with fighting racial prejudice. They were motivated not just by the fact that the Nazi regime championed racial hatred (although that figured largely into the equation) but by an overriding concern for national unity in the United States. Social scientists such as Allport, Lee, Clark, and Klineberg pushed racial prejudice to the forefront of social-scientific concerns during the war.

Social scientists emerged from the war with two things: first, an overriding concern with racial prejudice, and second, the confidence that they could do something about it. During the war, social scientists attempted not just to understand social phenomena such as prejudice and race riots but to seek ways to control and eliminate these. After the war, they looked for ways to transform their scientific conclusions into concrete social results through organizations such as the American Jewish Congress and its Commission on Community Interrelations.

After World War II, social scientists transformed themselves into social engineers by reversing the relationship between attitudes and behaviors.

Although this reversal was put most clearly by the social engineers in the CCI, it was also put forth by others such as David Krech, Theodore Newcomb, and Arnold Rose.

Social scientists had two arguments for reversing the relationship between attitude and behavior. First, they argued, the law itself was a powerful tool to inculcate attitudes. The law was pervasive; it touched every aspect of people's lives. Moreover, it was official—a declaration of society's views. In the status quo, attempts to teach the equality of all people would fail because the law, which was pervasive and official, would always be teaching the opposite. By contrast, if the law did not discriminate, it would be teaching that all people were equal. In fact, attempts to eliminate prejudice through education would be much more effective, given that the teaching would be supported by the laws of society

The second approach postwar social engineers used to reverse the traditional relationship between laws and attitudes was to abandon any attempt to change attitudes at all. According to this argument, prejudice was not, in itself, harmful to others. The outward manifestations of that prejudice, in the form of discrimination, were what was harmful. Hence, if the law could change people's discriminatory *behaviors,* whether or not it could actually change their prejudiced *attitudes* was irrelevant. Social engineers amassed evidence, such as Bernard Kutner's restaurant studies and Gerhart Saenger's department store studies, that prejudiced individuals would *act* in nondiscriminatory ways, even while maintaining their prejudiced attitudes.

Using these arguments, social engineers began to write about the need to eliminate segregation in American society, even before the NAACP-LDEF decided to use social science in their litigation campaign. Social engineers argued that segregation could be eliminated without waiting for the attitudes of the people to "be ready for the change." If people claimed they would never accept the elimination of segregation, such claims were not to be taken seriously. Prejudiced people would obey the law, even if they remained prejudiced.

What social engineers gained by reversing the relationship between attitude change and legal change was a way to push for their view of a just social order. By letting the law do the work of re-education, social engineers could advance the cause of equality without facing the grueling task of changing the inner psychological attitudes of hundreds of thousands of people.

It was this stance toward legal change that made social scientists so attractive to the lawyers of the NAACP-LDEF who wanted to argue that the prejudiced attitudes held by the majority did not constitute a good reason to deny the minority its constitutional rights. If desegregation were pushed with enough vigor, the social scientists assured the NAACP-LDEF, the population would accept it, despite claims to the contrary.

Toward a Reappraisal

In recent historical literature, *Brown* has undergone a re-examination. Twenty years ago, the case was viewed as one of the great moments in American history. Richard Kluger, in his masterful examination of the case, cast *Brown* as an unqualified triumph for African Americans and for American society. More recent writers have seen *Brown* as more problematic. Mark Tushnet has portrayed the case as more qualified victory. Gerald Rosenberg and Mark Klarman have both questioned *Brown*'s place in civil rights history, arguing that the case was insignificant or nearly irrelevant for guaranteeing rights to African Americans.[1]

Part of the problem, as Isidor Chein noted in his 1979 address, is that "the sequellae of that decision have not been nearly as magnificent as we might have wished." In the shadow of decades of racial violence and turmoil since *Brown*, many ask how social scientists could be so foolish as to believe that legal change could eliminate racial tension and bring about harmonious race relations. "But," as Chein concluded, "we never promised anyone a rose garden."[2] Indeed, one searches in vain through their testimony or their briefs for the Supreme Court for social-scientific claims that racial change could be accomplished by legal fiat. While social scientists came to court with definite ideas about the power of the law, they did not believe that the court case would be the magic bullet that eliminated racial turmoil in the United States.

Essentially, the basic social-scientific viewpoint toward the law was reversed from its prewar viewpoint. The commonly accepted wisdom before the war, and the wisdom that many in the intercultural education movement clung to after the war, was that the law was nothing more than an expression of individuals' attitudes. If the law was discriminatory, it was because people were prejudiced; it was the attitude of people (prejudice) that caused the law (discrimination). Hence, to ensure a just and equitable society, it was necessary to educate prejudiced people to overcome their prejudices. Once the basic attitude of people changed, discrimination in the law, and in other social institutions, would also change.

It is, of course, this seeming failure of other institutions to change that brings forth the charges of naiveté against the social scientists of *Brown*. The fundamental argument that the social scientists made, however, was that legal change was *necessary* to better race relations, not *sufficient*. No one during *Brown* argued that the Supreme Court provided a magic bullet that would eliminate race prejudice and discrimination. Indeed, in their struggles with the Social Science Memo, described in chapter 9, it is apparent that Clark and his colleagues were all too aware of the deeply entrenched racial attitudes of the South. But the fundamental question was: should legal change wait for those attitudes to change? It is too easy to forget that *Brown* was about the *law*.

In their work on the contact hypothesis, social scientists in the early 1950s had identified a number of conditions that had to be fulfilled before interracial contact could reduce prejudice. These conditions revolved around the two groups having mutual interests and coming together on terms of equal status. It is difficult to see how these conditions could possibly have been met in climate of legalized segregation. As long as the law proclaimed that the two races had to be separate, it would be impossible for contact between the races to reduce prejudice, for the law would forbid the two races from sharing common goals or from possibly having equal status. Hence, the social scientists were quite correct when they argued that a necessary step to better race relations would be to eliminate legalized segregation.

A similar point arose in social scientists' criticisms of the intercultural education movement. As long as legalized segregation existed, any education that attempted to decrease racial tension was doomed to failure. If education was teaching that "all men were brothers," the law would be teaching that the two races should not live together. Given the power that the law has for inculcating values, it is doubtful that education alone could overcome its message. If the law forbade segregation, however, education would be much more effective.

Finally, social scientists argued, as Frederic Wertham did after the first *Brown* decision, that the call for attitude change to precede legal change was "anarchy speaking."[3] One did not, for example, eliminate laws against murder simply because homicide laws did not deter the hard-core killer. Similarly, the law should keep segregation legal simply because the law could not be effective against the hard-core racist. To believe otherwise would be to question the very function of law in society. For example, in the criticisms of Lewis Killian's survey, social scientists argued that despite the fact that people *said* they would never accept desegregation, they would not so easily flout the law once the change was proclaimed.

The power of the law was also reflected in Clark's 1953 "Desegregation" article. There, Clark argued that the evidence indicated a firm, authoritative stand was the best chance for smooth desegregation. In the 1955 Social Science Memo, Clark struggled to find a way to take this scientific finding and turn it into a practical plan for desegregation. In *Brown II*, the Court failed to follow the NAACP-LDEF's call for immediate desegregation, thus failing to provide the firm authority that Clark believed necessary for successful desegregation.

Objective Experts or Advocates?

The charges that social scientists in *Brown* were naïve and that they made claims unsupported by the scientific literature are specific manifestations of a more general issue in the history of the social sciences in the United States. The larger issue is that of scientific objectivity in the face of social activism on the part of social scientists. According to the received view, these two forces, advocacy and objectivity, are in opposition. Either social scientists attempt to model their discipline on the natural sciences, constantly struggling to maintain objectivity or they are concerned with ameliorating social problems and are therefore struggling to become advocates for social policy. The conclusions of my study show that this is a false dilemma between advocacy and objectivity. In short, the social scientists of *Brown* believed they were functioning as both objective scientists and effective advocates.

If there was one aspect of the involvement of social scientists in the *Brown* litigation that remained controversial long after the trial, it was the charge that they acted as advocates rather than as objective scientists. Long after the details of their involvement in the cases were forgotten, their role was questioned. Twenty years after *Brown* was decided, Clark's use of the data from his doll tests during the trials was still called "the problem of Kenneth Clark."[4] Beginning in the 1970s, members of the social-scientific community began to look back at the *Brown* case and note that the social scientists involved had let their good intentions get the better of them during the trials and appeals.[5]

The charge that social scientists were merely advocates was, of course, nothing new. Throughout the trial, the objectivity of the social scientists was constantly being questioned—not only by the defense attorneys but also, in less obvious ways, by the social scientists themselves. For example, Stuart Cook felt it necessary to check Kenneth Clark's "stridency" when preparing briefs for the Supreme Court. The social scientists, then and more recently, claimed never to have surrendered their scientific objectivity for the sake of winning the case. And yet, they were deeply interested in winning the case. The question then arises as to what mechanisms they used to cope with acting as scientists in this adversarial system.

The answer can be found in the recognition that the social scientists attempted to be effective advocates through a strict allegiance to their scientific principles. They attempted to maintain objectivity through four different strategies, all of which enabled them to serve in the capacity of objective experts while being social activists. Each of these strategies was designed to ensure that the social scientists followed proper scientific procedures in their activities conducted for the NAACP-LDEF. Yet the motivation for being objective and scientific was to enable the social scientist to be effective in the fight against segregation.

First, the social scientists made very limited claims. For example, if one charge was consistently leveled against the social science of the *Brown* litigation, it was that it did not isolate legally segregated school segregation as the cause of the psychological damage the social scientists discovered among the segregated children in question. Yet the NAACP-LDEF did not require the social scientists to testify that they had isolated such a variable, nor did they ever claim they had isolated it. Nor did the social scientists ever claim that eliminating legal segregation would eliminate psychological damage. They were always careful to note that the problem of damage arising from discrimination was exceedingly complex, and that it undoubtedly was intertwined with countless other aspects of society. In fact, far from despairing of the fact that all of society discriminated, many witnesses turned it into a strength of their testimony, noting that legal segregation served to *reinforce* the discrimination that other parts of society inflicted on African Americans.

The second strategy adopted by the social scientists was to carefully separate their opinions and interpretations from the "facts" of their data. The most obvious example of this was Cook's criticism of Clark's first draft of the Social Science Memo. The defense attorneys were usually satisfied with the social scientist's admission that this was opinion evidence. Other critics, such as Edmond Cahn and Ernest van den Haag, took another tactic: they merely ignored the offered opinions and did not ever attempt to refute them. The case of the doll tests, however, was a different story. Both defense attorneys such as John W. Davis and critics such as William Delano and Ernest van den Haag pointed to the extreme flexibility in Clark's interpretations of his doll test results. These criticisms of Clark were not informed by Clark's results in the Delaware trial, where he had offered yet a third interpretation of the results. Clark had not made the results of his testimony public.

Clark's performance in the Delaware trial is an example where the urge to be an effective witness outstripped his loyalty to the objectivity of science. His results indicated that the vast majority of the children did not make an identification of the "bad" doll, but his testimony did not make those results clear. A possible explanation for this is that Clark simply misspoke when he claimed that "three out of four" children identified the brown doll as the bad doll. A similar slip of the tongue in the South Carolina trial, when Clark discussed "drawings of dolls," led both Cahn and van den Haag to believe that Clark had presented drawings to the children, not actual dolls.[6] But even granting that explanation for a moment, it would seem that Clark could interpret the doll tests to indicate psychological damage, no matter what the children chose. As such, the doll tests became the lightning rod for criticism of the social scientists' role and were perhaps the weakest part of the social science evidence in the *Brown* litigation.

Because the doll tests have seemed so vulnerable, it is there that critics of the use of social science in *Brown* have focused their attacks. Those wishing to argue that social science could not or should not have been used in the case trot out the standard criticisms of the doll tests and rest their case. Indeed, the critics often claim that the doll tests were referred by the Supreme Court in footnote 11.[7] Yet the doll test was only one sort of evidence offered, and the Supreme Court did not refer to it. The doll tests figure so prominently in critiques of *Brown* because they are the one instance where a social scientist, Clark, stepped over the bounds of proper scientific procedure and into the realm of advocacy.

Clark himself may have recognized the weakness of the doll tests, for in his defenses of the social scientist's role in the *Brown* litigation, he did not attempt to defend the doll tests with any particular vigor. He did detail his rather strained interpretation of how northern children's' identification of the brown doll as bad indicated better mental health than their southern counterparts, but on the whole, he shifted the argument to other parts of the social science data that could be found in the Social Science

Statement he had prepared for the first Supreme Court hearing. The social scientists had built "one long argument" against desegregation that required a deep reading of many different sources. The doll tests did not make or break the case the social scientists made against desegregation.

The third strategy adopted by the social scientists to defend their objectivity was to prepare no evidence directly for the trial. Social scientists had been arguing against segregation in their published works for many years before being approached by the NAACP-LDEF. As I argued earlier, this stand against segregation arose because social scientists had come to believe that legal change was an important element in the fight for social change. Hence, their works were already informed by a stance toward the law that was shared by the NAACP-LDEF. Clark could then defend the social science used in the *Brown* litigation as predating the social scientists' involvement in the litigation, proof that their presentation was not prepared merely to win a court case—thus making it more likely that the social science would, indeed, help win the court case. Hence, the drive to disassociate the evidence from the needs of the NAACP-LDEF was what made the evidence so useful for the NAACP-LDEF.

There were, of course, two social-scientific studies, that were prepared to help win a court case: Chein's 1948 survey of social science opinion and Clark's 1953 "Desegregation" article. Both pieces, however, were published in the professional literature, rather than merely for the private use of the lawyers. A more interesting dilemma would have arisen if the NAACP-LDEF had sponsored fieldwork by social scientists, either in 1953, when Clark wanted to undertake fieldwork to examine desegregation, or later, through the CSSC. In 1953, Clark expressed concern that the NAACP-LDEF would be behind the research and noted that it would be necessary to hide that fact from those in the communities he visited. If the NAACP-LDEF had funded this research, how would Clark have justified it as objective social science? Given the fact that the NAACP-LDEF refused to sponsor the fieldwork, such questions cannot be answered.

The fourth strategy for claiming objectivity was social scientists' presentation of themselves "we are only the fact providers." Time and again, Clark denied that the social scientists had any power in making the important decisions during the litigation. In a 1960 address to SPSSI, Clark claimed that whatever power social scientists have "is secondary and ancillary, derived through the sufferance or request of those who control power in our society. Social scientists do not establish policy or make definitive decisions on crucial social issues."[8]

The role of the social scientists in the *Brown* litigation was simply to provide whatever information they could to the NAACP-LDEF, who supplied it to the Court, the real decision maker. If asked to testify to something that was unsupported by evidence, such as ability to claim that psychological damage in schoolchildren was caused by legally segregated education, the social scientist had to refuse. The responsible social scientist, Clark argued, owed his or her first allegiance to science and only secondary allegiance to a particular social policy. But in making such a move toward science, of course, Clark also ensured that his scientific credibility could be used by the NAACP-LDEF to fight for the very social policy Clark desired.

The social scientists learned the limitations of being "fact providers" in the *Brown II* decision. The social scientists always claimed that the problem with the Supreme Court was not that they listened to the social scientists in the first decision but that they apparently stopped listening in the second. *Brown II*, with its "all deliberate speed" order, failed to supply the strong authority that was necessary for effective desegregation. By allowing the local authorities to drag their feet, the Court was responsible for "massive resistance" in the South and the decades of turmoil that followed.

All four of the strategies outlined above served to keep social scientists from becoming "advocates." While Clark may have stepped into the realm of advocate with the use of his doll test, he never admitted it. He maintained that he could explain his results within a strictly scientific framework. Nothing drew Clark's fire like Cahn's accusation that Clark had functioned as an "advocate" rather than a scientist. One must ponder, then, how to explain Clark's claim that during his "involvement with the lawyers of the NAACP in the desegregation cases that led to the *Brown* decision, I was functioning primarily, if not exclusively, as a social technician. Even in my role as a social science consultant to the NAACP lawyers, my perspective of myself was an agent of social change, as an advocate."[9] At first glance, it would appear that Clark is finally confessing that Edmond Cahn was right after all—Clark was, in fact, acting like an attorney rather than a scientist. But I think that is a serious misreading. For Clark, the dichotomy between "advocacy and objectivity" was a false one. The best way for a social scientist to change society was to be a good, careful, and objective social scientist.

For example, Clark often recounted that the NAACP-LDEF frequently requested him to make use of a certain study that the lawyers thought would be useful.[10] Despite the fact that the study in question directly addressed the issues at hand, Clark refused to include it because he thought it poor social science. By rejecting the study in question, Clark was behaving as he thought a good social scientist should but also as a good advocate should. Enrolling poor social science to the cause, Clark knew, would hurt, not help, the case. The opposition would seize on the weaknesses of the questionable article as surely as Clark would; hence the case would be made weaker, not stronger, by the material's inclusion.

The same principle held across the board: by adopting the hallmarks of good science—limiting claims, issuing caveats, distinguishing interpretations from results, and so forth—the social scientists would also be effective advocates. By contrast, if the social scientists presented a weak scientific case for their claims, they weakened the case for the NAACP-LDEF, for the opposition would surely attack whatever overarching claims were made by the social scientists. The criticisms directed at Clark's interpretations of the doll studies offer the best proof of this general point.

Social scientists were vital and active players in the early civil rights struggle that *Brown* represented; but as social scientists, they faced unique problems in that struggle. For most civil rights activists, such as Thurgood Marshall, passion and a strong moral sensibility were seen as the source of the strength that they brought to the movement. The same cannot be said for social scientists. In fact, the opposite was true: the social scientist drew credibility not from passion but from *detachment* from passion—the essence of "scientific objectivity." Only by collapsing the artificial distinction between objective inquiry and social activism could social scientists become effective advocates.

Conclusion

Perhaps if the Court had issued a firmer order than to desegregate with "all deliberate speed," the ensuing racial turmoil would have been avoided. Perhaps the opposite is the case, and a more gradual approach would have been better. Counterfactuals are dangerous in historical works. The best we can do is ask: given what social scientists knew *at the time*, were they justified in making the claims they did and acting in the manner in which they did?

The conclusion that arises out of the present study is that they *were* justified. Four decades after the decision, it is easy to forget how the inferiority of African Americans was proclaimed by the very laws of the land. The social scientists of the *Brown* case lived in a world where it was inconceivable that southern schoolchildren of different races could ever sit next to each other in the public classroom. Certainly, racism and discrimination are continuing and ongoing problems in this society, but it is almost impossible to argue that our present problems of racism would be less severe if legal segregation still existed. Clark and his colleagues clearly recognized what we in the twenty-first century appear to have forgotten: the elimination of legal segregation was a necessary step on the road toward racial equality. That the road is a long and difficult one should not blind us to the necessity and value of that very important step.

Notes

NOTES TO CHAPTER 1

1. 347 U.S. 483 (1954) and 349 U.S. 294 (1955).

2. M. Brewster Smith, "The Social Scientists Role in *Brown vs. Board of Education*: A Non-Revisionist Appraisal" (paper presented at the Eighty-seventh Annual Convention of the American Psychological Association, September 1, 1979), in Stuart W. Cook Papers, Box M2363, Folder 12, Archive for the History of American Psychology, Akron, Ohio (hereafter SWC Papers).

3. Isidor Chein, "*Brown vs. Bakke*" (paper presented at the Eighty-seventh Annual Convention of the American Psychological Association, September 1, 1979), in SWC Papers, Box M2363, Folder 12.

4. James T. Patterson, *Grand Expectations: The United States, 1945–1974* (New York: Oxford University Press, 1996), p. 391.

5. Ellen Herman, *The Romance of American Psychology: Political Culture in the Age of Experts* (Berkeley: University of California Press, 1995), p. 199.

6. William H. Tucker, *Science and Politics of Racial Research* (Urbana: University of Illinois Press, 1994), p. 144.

7. Harold Cruse, *Plural but Equal: A Critical Study of Blacks and Minorities and America's Plural Society* (New York: William Morrow, 1987), p. 73.

8. Daryl Michael Scott, *Contempt and Pity: Social Policy and the Image of the Damaged Black Psyche, 1880–1996* (Chapel Hill: University of North Carolina Press, 1997), p. 238.

9. David Hollinger, *Postethnic America: Beyond Multiculturalism* (New York: Basic Books, 1995), pp. 54, 55.

10. Kenneth Stampp, *The Peculiar Institution: Slavery in the Ante-Bellum South* (New York: Vintage Books, 1956), p. vii.

11. On this point, see Philip Gleason, *Speaking of Diversity: Language and Ethnicity in Twentieth Century America* (Baltimore: Johns Hopkins University Press, 1992), pp. 47–90.

12. On the collapse of the "liberal orthodoxy" regarding race relations, see

Walter A. Jackson, *Gunnar Myrdal and America's Conscience* (Chapel Hill: University of North Carolina Press, 1990), pp. 272–311.

13. Stephen Steinberg, *Turning Back: The Retreat from Racial Justice in American Thought and Policy* (Boston: Beacon Press, 1995), p. 89.

14. A concise treatment of this shift is Gary Peller, "Race against Integration," *Tikkun* 6 (1991): 54–70.

15. Harold Cruse, *The Crisis of the Negro Intellectual* (New York: William Morrow, 1967), p. 9.

16. On the central place of the pathology of African American culture in *Brown* and in integrationist thought generally, see Lee D. Baker, *From Savage to Negro: Anthropology and the Construction of Race, 1896–1954* (Berkeley: University of California Press, 1998).

17. Albert Murray, "White Norms, Black Deviance," in *The Death of White Sociology*, ed. Joyce A. Ladner (New York: Vintage, 1973), p. 98.

18. Robert Mann, *Walls of Jericho* (New York: Harcourt Brace, 1996).

19. Walter G. Stephan, "School Desegregation: An Evaluation of Predictions Made in *Brown v. Board of Education*," *Psychological Bulletin* 85 (1978): 234.

20. Kenneth B. Clark, "Desegregation: An Appraisal of the Evidence," *Journal of Social Issues* 9 (1953): 1–77.

21. Harold B. Gerard, "School Desegregation: The Social Science Role," *American Psychologist* 38 (1983): 869–77.

22. Earl Lewis, "To Turn as on a Pivot: Writing African Americans into a History of Overlapping Diasporas," *American Historical Review* 100 (1995): 781. For a general treatment of this shift in African American scholarship, see John Hope Franklin, "On the Evolution of Scholarship in Afro-American History," in *The State of Afro-American History*, ed. Darlene Clark Hine (Baton Rouge: Louisiana State University Press, 1986), pp. 13–22.

23. For example, see Steven Goldberg, *Culture Clash: Law and Science in America*, (New York: New York University Press, 1994).

24. Mitchell G. Ash, "Historicizing Mind Science: Discourse, Practice, Subjectivity," *Science in Context* 5 (1992): 196. Although sociologists were well represented, as well as a handful of psychiatrists and anthropologists, the core group of social scientists involved with the *Brown* case were social psychologists. Consequently, many of my remarks in this chapter are concerned with the history of psychology rather than with the other social-scientific disciplines.

25. Graham Richards, "Of What Is History of Psychology a History?" *British Journal for the History of Science* 20 (1987): 207.

26. Franz Samelson, "From 'Race Psychology' to 'Studies in Prejudice,'" *Journal of the History of the Behavioral Sciences* 14 (July 1978): 270. Similar claims are made in, Carl N. Degler, *In Search of Human Nature* (New York: Oxford University Press, 1991), pp. 187–211; and Elazar Barkan, *The Retreat of Scientific Racism* (Cambridge: Cambridge University Press, 1992), pp. 343–46.

27. Jill G. Morawski and Gail A. Hornstein, "Quandary of the Quacks: The Struggle for Expert Knowledge in American Psychology, 1890–1940," in *The Estate of Social Knowledge*, ed. JoAnne Brown and David K. van Keuren (Baltimore: Johns Hopkins University Press, 1991), p. 106.

28. Mary O. Furner, *Advocacy and Objectivity: A Crisis in the Professionalization of American Social Science, 1865–1905* (Lexington: University of Kentucky Press, 1975); Mark Smith, *Social Science in the Crucible: The American Debate over Objectivity and Purpose, 1918–1941* (Durham, NC: Duke University Press, 1994).

29. Hamilton Cravens, "History of the Social Sciences," in *Historical Writing on American Science: Perspectives and Prospects*, ed. Sally Gregory Kohlstedt and Margaret W. Rossiter (Baltimore: Johns Hopkins University Press, 1986), p. 185.

30. Major monographs on this point include: JoAnne Brown, *The Definition of a Profession: The Authority of Metaphor in the History of Intelligence Testing, 1890–1930* (Princeton: Princeton University Press, 1992); Kurt Danzinger, *Constructing the Subject: Historical Origins of Psychological Research* (Cambridge and New York: Cambridge University Press, 1990); John M. O'Donnell, *The Origins of Behaviorism* (New York: New York University Press, 1985).

31. Jackson, *Gunnar Myrdal and America's Conscience*, p. 292.

NOTES TO CHAPTER 2

1. Franz Samelson, "From 'Race Psychology' to 'Studies in Prejudice': Some Observations on the Thematic Reversal in Social Psychology," *Journal of the History of the Behavioral Sciences* 14 (1978): 265–78; Will B. Provine, "Geneticists and the Biology of Race Crossing," *Science* 182 (1973): 790–96. Elazar Barkan advocates a similar position *The Retreat of Scientific Racism: Changing Concepts of Race in Britain and the United States between the World Wars* (Cambridge: Cambridge University Press, 1992). For the response, see Bentley Glass, "Geneticists Embattled: Their Stand against Rampant Eugenics and Racism in America during the 1920s and 1930s," *Proceedings of the American Philosophical Society* 130 (1986): 130–54.

2. Graham Richards, *"Race," Racism and Psychology: Towards a Reflexive History* (London: Routledge, 1997), pp. 65–159. A similar position was articulated by Hamilton Cravens, *The Triumph of Evolution: The Heredity-Environment Controversy, 1900–1941* (1978; reprint, Baltimore: Johns Hopkins University Press, 1988), pp. 157–90.

3. Richards argues that the research generated to answer these questions did not develop specifically because of the rejection of scientific racism but grew out of a new interest in the measurement of attitudes on the part of psychologists. See Richards, *"Race," Racism and Psychology*, pp. 133–39. I argue that, while he is

correct that the study of attitudes was growing during this time period, the application of these ideas to race prejudice did owe something to the new questions posed by the rejection of scientific racism.

4. The literature of Boas and his influence are immense. Two book-length biographies exist: Melville Herskovits, *Franz Boas: The Science of Man in the Making* (New York: Charles Scribner's Sons, 1953), and Marshall Hyatt, *Franz Boas, Social Activist: The Dynamics of Ethnicity* (New York: Greenwood Press, 1990). On the importance of women and people of color among Boas's students, see Leonard Lieberman, "Gender and the Deconstruction of the Race Concept," *American Anthropologist* 99 (1997): 545–58.

5. George W. Stocking Jr., *Race, Culture, and Evolution: Essays in the History of Anthropology* (Chicago: University of Chicago Press, 1968), pp. 133–60.

6. Audrey Smedley, *Race in North America: Origin and Evolution of a Worldview* (Boulder, CO: Westview Press, 1999), p. 297. Also see Barkan, *Retreat of Scientific Racism*, pp. 76–90.

7. John S. Gilkerson, "Domestication of 'Culture' in Interwar America," in *The Estate of Social Knowledge*, ed. JoAnne Brown and David K. van Keuren (Baltimore: Johns Hopkins University Press, 1991), pp. 153–74; Richard Handler, "Boasian Anthropology and the Critique of American Culture," *American Quarterly* 42 (1990): 252–73.

8. On Du Bois's work and his relationship with Boas, see Lee D. Baker, *From Savage to Negro: Anthropology and the Construction of Race, 1896–1954* (Berkeley: University of California Press, 1998), pp 99–167. On Du Bois's attack on scientific racism, see Carole M. Taylor, "W.E.B. Du Bois's Challenge to Scientific Racism," *Journal of Black Studies* 11 (1981): 449–60. On Dubois and the NAACP, see David Levering Lewis, *W.E.B. Dubois: Biography of a Race, 1868–1919* (New York: Henry Holt, 1993), pp. 386–434.

9. Vincent P. Franklin, "Black Social Scientists and the Mental Testing Movement, 1920–1940," in *Black Psychology*, ed. Reginald L. Jones, 2d ed. (New York: Harper and Row, 1980), pp. 201–15; Carl Jorgensen, "The African American Critique of White Supremacist Science," *Journal of Negro Education* 64 (1995): 232–42; Richards, *"Race," Racism and Psychology*, pp. 126, 131–33.

10. Biographical details can be found in Benjamin Harris, "Klineberg, Otto," in *American National Biography*, vol. 12, ed. John A. Garraty and Mark C. Carnes (New York: Oxford University Press, 1999), pp. 792–93. An account of the importance of Klineberg's professional career is Richards, *"Race," Racism and Psychology*, pp. 127–31.

11. "Otto Klineberg," in *History of Psychology in Autobiography*, vol. 6, ed. Gardner Linzey (Englewood Cliffs, NJ: Prentice Hall, 1974), p. 166.

12. Otto Klineberg, "An Experimental Study of Speed and Other Factors in 'Racial' Differences," *Archives of Psychology*, 15, 93 (1928): 10.

13. Ibid., p. 25.

14. "Otto Klineberg," p. 167.

15. Klineberg, "Experimental Study of Speed," p. 45.

16. Otto Klineberg, *Negro Intelligence and Selective Migration* (New York: Columbia University Press, 1935), pp. 59–60.

17. Thomas R. Garth, "A Review of Racial Psychology," *Psychological Bulletin* 22 (1925): 359.

18. Thomas R. Garth, *Race Psychology: A Study of Racial Mental Differences* (New York: McGraw-Hill, 1931), p. 83. On the centrality of Garth to the collapse of "race psychology," see Graham Richards, "Reconceptualizing the History of Race Psychology: Thomas Russell Garth (1872–1939) and How He Changed His Mind," *Journal of the History of the Behavioral Sciences* 34 (1998): 15–32.

19. Richards, *"Race," Racism and Psychology*, pp. 90–91.

20. Carl N. Degler, *In Search of Human Nature The Decline and Revival of Darwinism in American Social Thought*, (New York: Oxford University Press, 1991), pp. 175–178.

21. For background on sociologist Robert Park of the Chicago School and his theories, see Stanford M. Lyman, *The Black American in Sociological Thought: A Failure of Perspective* (New York: Capricorn Books, 1972), pp. 27–70; Stanford M. Lyman, *Color, Culture, Civilization: Race and Minority Issues in American Society* (Urbana: University of Illinois Press, 1994), pp. 43–102; Stow Persons, *Ethnic Studies at Chicago, 1905–45* (Urbana: University of Illinois Press, 1987).

22. Robert E. Park, "The Concept of Social Distance" (1924), reprinted in *Race and Culture: The Collected Papers of Robert Ezra Park*, vol. 1 (Glencoe: Free Press, 1950), p. 260.

23. Philip Gleason, "Americans All: World War II and the Shaping of American Identity," *Review of Politics* 43 (October 1981): 495–97.

24. John H. Stansfield, "Race Relations Research and Black Americans between the Two World Wars," *Journal of Ethnic Studies* 3 (Fall 1983): 62.

25. Emory Bogardus, "Social Distance and Its Origins," *Journal of Applied Sociology* 9 (1925): 217.

26. Emory Bogardus, "Measuring Social Distances," *Journal of Applied Sociology* 9 (1925): 303.

27. Biographical details can be found in Ian A. M. Nicholson, "'The Approved Bureaucratic Torpor': Goodwin Watson, Critical Psychology, and the Dilemmas of Expertise, 1930–1945," *Journal of Social Issues* 54 (1998): 29–52; Ian A. M. Nicholson, "The Politics of Scientific Social Reform, 1936–1960: Goodwin Watson and the Society for the Psychological Study of Social Issues," *Journal of the History of the Behavioral Sciences* 33 (1997): 39–60.

28. Goodwin Watson, *The Measurement of Fair-Mindedness* (New York: Teacher's College: Columbia University, 1925), p. 2.

29. Ibid., p. 23.

30. Ibid., p. 41.

31. Ibid., p. 23.

32. The textbook is: Floyd H. Allport, *Social Psychology* (Boston: Houghton Mifflin, 1924). For a brief biography of Floyd Allport see David L. Post, "Floyd H. Allport and the Launching of Modern Social Psychology," *Journal of the History of the Behavioral Sciences* 16 (1980): 369–76. For a view that Allport's experimentalism and his emphasis on the individual have been overemphasized in the historical literature, see Franz Samelson, "Whig and Anti-Whig Histories—And Other Curiosities of Social Psychology," *Journal of the History of the Behavioral Sciences* 36 (2000): 499–506.

33. Jean M. Converse, *Survey Research in the United States: Roots and Emergence, 1890–1960* (Berkeley: University of California Press, 1987), pp. 62–68.

34. Richards, *"Race," Racism and Psychology*, p. 157.

35. Daniel Katz and Floyd H. Allport, *Students' Attitudes: A Report of the Syracuse University Reaction Study* (Syracuse: Craftsman Press, 1931), p. 145.

36. Daniel Katz and Kenneth Braly, "Racial Stereotypes of One Hundred College Students," *Journal of Abnormal and Social Psychology* 28, 3 (October–December 1933): 280.

37. Daniel Katz and Kenneth Braly, "Racial Prejudice and Racial Stereotypes," *Journal of Abnormal and Social Psychology* 30, 2 (July–September 1935): 191–92.

38. Richards, *"Race," Racism and Psychology*, p. 138.

39. See Gardner Murphy, *Personality: A Biosocial Approach to Origins and Structure* (New York: Harper and Brothers, 1947); *Historical Introduction to Modern Psychology* (New York: Harcourt, Brace, and World, 1929).

40. Katherine Pandora, *Rebels within the Ranks: Psychologists' Critique of Scientific Authority and Democratic Realities in New Deal America* (Cambridge: Cambridge University Press, 1997), pp. 28–29, 47–53.

41. Others include Theodore Newcomb, Rensis Likert, and Dorian Cartwright. See Ernest R. Hilgard, "From the Social Gospel to the Psychology of Social Issues: A Reminiscence," *Journal of Social Issues* 42, 1 (1986): 107–10.

42. Pandora, *Rebels within the Ranks*, pp. 53–60.

43. Lois Barclay Murphy, *Gardner Murphy: Integrating, Expanding, and Humanizing Psychology* (Jefferson, NC: McFarland and Company, 1990), p. 109.

44. Gardner Murphy and Lois Barclay Murphy, *Experimental Social Psychology* (New York: Harper and Brothers, 1931), p. 639.

45. Gardner Murphy, "Gardner Murphy," in *A History of Psychology in Autobiography*, vol. 5, ed. Edwin G. Boring and Gardner Linzey (New York: Appleton-Century-Crofts, 1967).

46. Pandora, *Rebels within the Ranks*, provides the most complete argument for this point. But see also Kurt Danzinger, "Making Social Psychology Experimental: A Conceptual History, 1920–1970," *Journal of the History of the Behavioral Sciences* 36 (2000): 329–47; Clare MacMartin and Andrew S. Winston, "The Rhetoric of Experimental Social Psychology, 1930–1960: From Caution to En-

thusiasm," *Journal of the History of the Behavioral Sciences* 36 (2000): 349–64; Henderikus J. Stam, H. Lorraine Radtke, and Ian Lubek, "Strains in Experimental Social Psychology: A Textual Analysis of the Development of Experimentation in Social Psychology," *Journal of the History of the Behavioral Sciences* 36 (2000): 365–82.

47. An excellent discussion of the Horowitzes' work can be found in William E. Cross, Jr., *Shades of Black: Diversity in African-American Identity* (Philadelphia: Temple University Press, 1991), pp. 5–16. My narrative owes much to Cross's work.

48. Bruno Lasker, *Race Attitudes in Children* (New York: Henry Holt, 1929), p. 55.

49. Eugene L. Horowitz, "The Development of Attitude toward the Negro," *Archives of Psychology* 28, 194 (January 1936): 6.

50. Ibid., p. 7.

51. Ibid., p. 9.

52. Ibid., pp. 30, 34–35.

53. Ibid., p. 34.

54. Ruth Horowitz and Lois Barclay Murphy, "Projective Methods in the Psychological Study of Children," *Journal of Experimental Education* 7, 2 (December 1938): 133.

55. Ruth E. Horowitz, "Racial Aspects of Self-Identification in Nursery School Children," *Journal of Psychology* 7 (1939): 97.

56. Cross, *Shades of Black*, p. 9.

57. Mamie Phipps Clark, "Mamie Phipps Clark," in *Models of Achievement: Reflections of Eminent Women in Psychology*, ed. Agnes N. O'Connell and Nancy Felipe Russo (New York: Columbia University Press, 1983), p. 269.

58. For a brief biographical sketch of Kenneth B. Clark, see Charles V. Willie, *Five Black Scholars: An Analysis of Family Life, Education, and Career* (Lanham, MD: University Press of America, 1986), pp. 41–57.

59. Robert V. Guthrie, *Even the Rat Was White: A Historical View of Psychology* (New York: Harper and Row, 1976), pp. 175–89; Thomas F. Sawyer, "Francis Cecil Sumner: His Views and Influence on African American Higher Education," *History of Psychology* 3 (2000): 122–41.

60. Quoted in Nat Hentoff, "The Integrationist," *New Yorker* 58, 23 August 1982, p. 45.

61. Clark, "Mamie Phipps Clark," p. 268. Mamie Clark's work in the Houston law offices demonstrates the extremely small world available to African American professional people in the 1930s. There is little evidence to claim, as Ellen Herman has, that Kenneth Clark was enrolled in the litigation campaign because of Mamie's brief stay at the Houston law offices. See Ellen Herman, *The Romance of American Psychology* (Berkeley: University of California Press, 1995), p. 365.

62. William Cross has pointed out that while the Clarks published five articles on racial identity and preference, there were, in fact, only two data sets: the

one for Mamie's thesis in 1938, and the one obtained in 1940 that resulted in their postwar publications. See Cross, *Shades of Black*, pp. 16–17.

63. Kenneth B. Clark and Mamie P. Clark, "The Development of Consciousness of Self and the Emergence of Racial Identification in Negro Preschool Children," *Journal of Social Psychology* 10 (1939): 594.

64. Ibid., p. 598.

65. Kenneth B. Clark and Mamie P. Clark, "Skin Color as a Factor in Racial Identification of Negro Preschool Children," *Journal of Social Psychology* 11 (1940): 168.

66. Kenneth B. Clark and Mamie P. Clark, "Segregation as a Factor in the Racial Identification of Negro Preschool Children: A Preliminary Report," *Journal of Experimental Education* 8, 2 (December 1939): 163.

67. Cross, *Shades of Black*, p. 21.

68. Clark, "Mamie Phipps Clark," p. 169.

69. Richards, *"Race," Racism, and Psychology*, p. 139.

70. For other treatments of these studies, see Alice Mary O'Connor, "From Lower Class to Underclass: The Poor in American Social Science, 1930–1970" (Ph.D. diss., Johns Hopkins University, 1991), pp. 259–72; Daryl Michael Scott, *Contempt and Pity: Social Policy and the Image of the Damaged Black Psyche, 1880–1996* (Chapel Hill: University of North Carolina Press, 1997), pp. 48–69.

71. "Reid, Ira De Augustine," in *Dictionary of American Biography*, vol. 8, ed. John A. Garraty and Mark C. Carnes (New York: Charles Scribner's Sons, 1988), pp. 521–22.

72. Ira De A. Reid, *In a Minor Key: Negro Youth in Story and Fact* (Washington, DC: American Council on Education, 1940), p. 4.

73. Allison Davis, "Author's Note," in Allison Davis and John Dollard, *Children of Bondage: The Personality Development of Negro Youth in the Urban South* (Washington, DC: American Council on Education, 1940), p. xvi.

74. Davis and Dollard, *Children of Bondage*, p. 256.

75. Daryl Scott has argued that because Davis and Dollard stressed the importance of class, they "minimized the importance of racial discrimination in shaping personality." See Scott, *Contempt and Pity*, p. 35. This is, in my view, an overstatement of Davis and Dollard's position.

76. Davis and Dollard, *Children of Bondage*, p. 245.

77. Richard Robbins, "Johnson, Charles Spurgeon," in *Dictionary of American Biography, Supplement Six, 1956–1960*, ed. John A. Garraty (New York: Charles Scribner's Sons, 1980), pp. 321–22.

78. Charles S. Johnson, *Growing Up in the Black Belt: Negro Youth in the Rural South* (Washington, DC: American Counsel on Education, 1941; reprint, New York: Schocken Books, 1967), p. 257.

79. Ibid., p. 258.

80. Ibid., p. 301.

81. Ibid., p. 288.

82. Ibid., p. 134.

83. E. Franklin Frazier, "The Pathology of Race Prejudice," *Forum* 77 (June 1927): 857.

84. Biographical information can be found in Anthony Platt, *E. Franklin Frazier Reconsidered* (New Brunswick: Rutgers University Press, 1991), pp. 82–85.

85. E. Franklin Frazier, *The Negro Family in the United States* (1939; reprint, New York: Dryden Press, 1948), p. 367.

86. E. Franklin Frazier, *Negro Youth at the Crossways: Their Personality Development in the Middle States* (Washington, DC: American Council on Education, 1940), p. 290.

87. Ibid., pp. 180–81.

88. Robert L. Sutherland, *Color, Class, and Personality* (Washington, DC: American Counsel on Education, 1942; reprint, New York: Greenwood Press, 1972), p. 75.

89. Lorenz J. Finison, "Unemployment, Politics, and the History of Organized Psychology," *American Psychologist* 31 (November 1976): 749.

90. David Krech, "David Krech," in *History of Psychology in Autobiography*, vol. 6, ed. Gardner Linze (Englewood Cliffs, NJ: Prentice Hall, 1974), p. 236.

91. Ibid.

92. Finison, "Unemployment, Politics, and the History of Organized Psychology," p. 753.

93. Ross Stagner, "Reminiscences about the Founding of SPSSI," *Journal of Social Issues* 42, 1 (1986): 35.

94. Murphy, *Gardner Murphy*, p. 138; Finison, "Unemployment, Politics, and the History of Organized Psychology," p. 753.

95. Lorenz Finison, "The Psychological Insurgency: 1936–1945," *Journal of Social Issues* 42, 1 (1986): 28–29.

96. Samelson, "From 'Race Psychology' to 'Studies in Prejudice,'" p. 269.

NOTES TO CHAPTER 3

1. Robin D. G. Kelley, "'We Are Not What We Seem': Rethinking Black Working-Class Opposition in the Jim Crow South," *Journal of American History* 80 (1993): 110.

2. Classic treatments include Richard M. Dalfiume, "The 'Forgotten Years' of the Negro Revolution," *Journal of American History* 55 (1968): 90–106; Lee Finkle, "The Conservative Aims of Militant Rhetoric: Black Protest during World War II," *Journal of American History* 60 (1973): 692–713; Peter J. Kellogg, "Civil Rights Consciousness in the 1940s," *The Historian* 42 (1979): 18–41; Harvard

Sitkoff, "Racial Militancy and Interracial Violence in the Second World War," *Journal of American History* 58 (1971): 661–81.

3. The best treatments of psychologists' activities during World War II are: James Capshew, *Psychology on the March: Science, Practice, and Professional Identity in America, 1929–1969* (Cambridge: Cambridge University Press, 1999), pp. 116–27; Ellen Herman, *The Romance of American Psychology: Political Culture in the Age of Experts* (Berkeley: University of California Press, 1995), pp. 48–81.

4. Biographical details can be found in Katherine Pandora, *Rebels within the Ranks: Psychologists' Critique of Scientific Authority and Democratic Realities in New Deal America* (Cambridge: Cambridge University Press, 1997), pp. 26–28.

5. Gordon W. Allport, *Personality: A Psychological Interpretation* (New York: Henry Holt, 1937). As in his later work in social psychology, Allport conceived of his project in personality psychology as a moral quest; see Ian A. M. Nicholson, "Gordon Allport, Character, and the 'Culture of Personality,' 1897–1937," *History of Psychology* 1 (1998): 52–68.

6. Gordon W. Allport, "An Autobiography," in *The Person in Psychology: Selected Essays by Gordon W. Allport* (Boston: Beacon Press, 1968), p. 396.

7. Gordon Allport, *The Nature of Prejudice* (Reading, MA: Addison Wesley, 1954). On the origins of *The Nature of Prejudice* see Roy J. deCarvalho, "Gordon W. Allport on the Nature of Prejudice," *Psychological Reports* 72 (1993): 301; Frances Cherry, "The Nature of *The Nature of Prejudice*," *Journal of the History of the Behavioral Sciences* 36 (2000): 489–98.

8. Gordon W. Allport, *ABC's of Scapegoating*, rev. ed. (New York: Anti-Defamation League of B'nai B'rith, 1948), p. 56.

9. Capshew, *Psychology on the March*, pp. 116–17, Herman, *Romance of American Psychology*, pp. 48–53.

10. Jean Converse, *Survey Research in the United States: Roots and Emergence, 1890–1960* (Berkeley: University of California Press, 1987), pp. 72–76.

11. Capshew, *Psychology on the March*, pp. 120–21; Blair T. Johnson and Diana R. Nichols, "Social Psychologists' Expertise in the Public Interest: Civilian Morale Research during World War II," *Journal of Social Issues* 54 (1998): 53–77.

12. Resnis Likert, "Negroes and the War: A Study in Baltimore and Cincinnati," Special Report Number 16, Division of Surveys, Office of War Information, July 21, 1942, in Resnis Likert Papers, Box 9, Folder 9–20, Bentley Historical Library, University of Michigan Archives, Ann Arbor.

13. *Civilian Morale: Second Yearbook of the Society for the Psychological Study of Social Issues*, ed. Goodwin Watson (Boston: Houghton Mifflin Company, 1942).

14. Otto Klineberg, "Morale and the Jewish Minority," in *Civilian Morale*, ed. Watson, p. 218.

15. Kenneth B. Clark, "Morale among Negroes," in *Civilian Morale*, ed. Watson, p. 228.

16. Ibid., p. 248.

17. Kenneth B. Clark, "Morale of the Negro on the Home Front: World Wars I and II" *Journal of Negro Education* 12 (Summer 1943): 424–26, 428.

18. Gordon W. Allport, "The Nature of Democratic Morale," in *Civilian Morale*, ed. Watson, p. 9.

19. Harvard Sitkoff, "Racial Militancy and Interracial Violence in the Second World War," *Journal of American History* 58 (December 1971): 673–75.

20. Biographical details can be found in John F. Galliher and James M. Galliher, *Marginality and Dissent in Twentieth-Century Sociology: The Case of Elizabeth Briant Lee and Alfred McClung Lee* (Albany: State University of New York Press, 1995).

21. Betty Lee, quoted in Galliher and Galliher, *Marginality and Dissent in Twentieth-Century Sociology*, p. 75.

22. Alfred McClung Lee and Norman D. Humphrey, *Race Riot* (New York: Dryden Press, 1943), pp. 16, 5.

23. Harvard Sitkoff, "The Detroit Race Riot of 1943," *Michigan History* 53 (Fall 1969): 199–205.

24. Lee and Humphrey, *Race Riot*, pp. 5, 17.

25. Ibid., p. 140.

26. Kenneth B. Clark and James Barker, "The Zoot Effect in Personality: A Race Riot Participant," *Journal of Abnormal and Social Psychology* 40 (1945): 143.

27. Pandora, *Rebels within the Ranks*, p. 61.

28. Kelley, "'We Are Not What We Seem,'" p. 87.

29. Clark and Barker, "Zoot Effect in Personality," p. 147.

30. Kenneth B. Clark Papers, Box 164, Folder "Writings by Clark, Articles, 1942–1949," Manuscript Division, Library of Congress, Washington, D.C.

31. Leonard Dinnerstein, *Anti-Semitism in America* (New York: Oxford University Press, 1994), chap. 7.

32. Ernst Simmel, "Introduction," in *Anti-Semitism: A Social Disease*, ed. Ernst Simmel (New York: International Universities Press, 1946), p. viii.

33. Laura Fermi, *Illustrious Immigrants: The Intellectual Migration from Europe, 1930–41*, 2d ed. (Chicago: University of Chicago Press, 1971), pp. 139–73; Edith Kurzweil, "Psychoanalytic Science: From Oedipus to Culture," in *Forced Migration and Scientific Change: Émigré German-Speaking Scientists and Scholars after 1933*, ed. Mitchell G. Ash and Alfons Söllner (Cambridge: Cambridge University Press, 1996), pp. 139–55.

34. Gordon Allport, "Preface," in *Anti-Semitism*, ed. Simmel, p xi.

35. Mitchell G. Ash and Alfons Söllner, "Introduction: Forced Migration and Scientific Change after 1933," in *Forced Migration and Scientific Change*, ed. Ash and Söllner, pp. 1–19.

36. Nevitt Sanford, "The Approach of the Authoritarian Personality," in *Psychology of Personality: Six Modern Approaches*, ed. J. L. McCary (New York: Logos Press, 1956), p. 261.

37. Martin Jay, *The Dialectical Imagination: A History of the Frankfurt School and the Institute of Social Research, 1923–1950* (Boston: Little, Brown and Company, 1973).

38. Institute for Social Research, "Research Project on Anti-Semitism," *Studies in Philosophy and Social Science* 9 (1941): 124–43.

39. Martin Jay, *Permanent Exiles: Essays on the Intellectual Migration from Germany to America* (New York: Columbia University Press, 1985), pp. 43–44.

40. M. Brewster Smith, "Else Frenkel-Brunswik," in *Women in Psychology*, ed. Agnes N. O'Connell and Nancy Felipe Russo (New York: Greenwood Press, 1990), pp. 88–95.

41. Franz Samelson, "Authoritarianism, from Berlin to Berkeley: On Social Psychology and History," *Journal of Social Issues* 42, 1 (1986): 199.

42. Daniel J. Levinson and R. Nevitt Sanford, "A Scale for the Measurement of Anti-Semitism," *Journal of Psychology* 17 (1944): 339–40.

43. Else Frenkel-Brunswik and R. Nevitt Sanford, "Some Personality Factors in Anti-Semitism," *Journal of Psychology* 20 (1945): 275.

44. To distinguish the American Jewish Committee from the American Jewish Congress, I refer to the AJCommittee and the AJCongress.

45. Ira M. Younker, "Scientific Research on Anti-Semitism in 1944," *The American Jewish Yearbook, 5706, 1945–46* (Philadelphia: Jewish Publication Society of America, 1945), p. 698.

46. American Jewish Committee, *Conference on Research in the Field of Anti-Semitism: Summary of Proceedings and Suggestions for a Program* (New York: American Jewish Committee, March 1945).

47. Younker, "Scientific Research on Anti-Semitism in 1944," p. 697

48. Theodore W. Adorno, Elsa Frankel-Brunswik, Daniel Levinson, and R. Nevitt Sanford, *The Authoritarian Personality* (New York: Harper and Row, 1950).

49. Melville J. Herskovits, *The Myth of the Negro Past* (New York: Harper and Brothers; 1941); Charles S. Johnson, *Patterns of Negro Segregation* (New York: Harper and Brothers, 1943); Richard Sterner, *The Negro's Share* (New York: Harper and Brothers; 1943); Otto Klineberg, ed., *Characteristics of the American Negro* (New York: Harper and Brothers, 1944).

50. Gunnar Myrdal, *An American Dilemma* (New York: Harper and Brothers, 1944), p. xi.

51. Gunnar Myrdal, "Foreword," in *The Negro in America*, ed. Arnold M. Rose (1948; reprint, New York: Harper Torchbook, 1964), p. xii.

52. David W. Southern, *Gunnar Myrdal and Black-White Relations: The Use and Abuse of* An American Dilemma, *1944–1969* (Baton Rouge: Louisiana State University Press, 1987), pp. 71–125.

53. Walter A. Jackson, *Gunnar Myrdal and America's Conscience: Social Engineering and Racial Liberalism, 1938–1987* (Chapel Hill: University of North Car-

olina Press, 1990), chap. 7; Martin Bulmer, "The Apotheosis of Liberalism? *An American Dilemma* after Fifty Years in the Context of the Lives of Gunnar and Alva Myrdal," *Ethnic and Racial Studies* 16 (April 1993): 345–46.

54. Jackson, *Gunnar Myrdal and America's Conscience*, pp. 10–35.

55. Ibid., pp. 109–12. 121–22.

56. Ibid., pp. 140, 161.

57. Myrdal, *American Dilemma*, p. xlviii.

58. Jackson, *Gunnar Myrdal and America's Conscience*, pp. 68–75.

59. Myrdal, *American Dilemma*, pp. 1054–55.

60. Ibid., p. 418.

61. Ibid., p. 516.

62. Ibid., pp. 928–29.

63. Kenneth B. Clark, "Race, Sex, and Democratic Living," in *Human Nature and Enduring Peace: Third Yearbook of the Society for the Psychological Study of Social Issues*, ed. Gardner Murphy (Boston: Houghton Mifflin Company, 1945), p. 358.

64. Lorenz Finison, "The Psychological Insurgency: 1936–1945," *Journal of Social Issues* 42, 1 (1986): 31–33.

65. Ian A. M. Nicholson, "'The Approved Bureaucratic Torpor': Goodwin Watson, Critical Psychology, and the Dilemmas of Expertise, 1930–1945," *Journal of Social Issues* 54 (1998): 43–47; S. Stansfield Sargent and Benjamin Harris, "Academic Freedom, Civil Liberties, and SPSSI," *Journal of Social Issues* 42, 1 (1986): 48.

66. Goodwin Watson, "How Social Engineers Came to Be," *Journal of Social Psychology* 21 (1945): 137.

67. Ronald Lippitt and Marian Radke, "New Trends in the Investigation of Prejudice," *Annals of the American Academy of Political and Social Science* 244 (March 1946): 167.

68. *Journal of Social Issues* 1, 1 (February 1945); 1,2 (May 1945). This focus on prejudice and civil rights would become a hallmark of the *Journal of Social Issues*, as one-half to two-thirds of the material that appeared there related to race and racial prejudice. See Graham Richards, *"Race," Racism and Psychology: Towards a Reflexive History* (London: Routledge, 1997), p. 237.

69. "Preface," *Journal of Social Issues* 1, 3 (August 1945): 1.

NOTES TO CHAPTER 4

1. Gunnar Myrdal, *An American Dilemma* (New York: Harper and Brothers, 1944), p. 1031.

2. For the change in American attitudes regarding race relations, see Philip Gleason, "Americans All: World War II and the Shaping of American Identity,"

Review of Politics 43 (October 1981): 483–518. For the focus on moral exhortation, see Walter A. Jackson, *Gunnar Myrdal and America's Conscience: Social Engineering and Racial Liberalism, 1938–1987* (Chapel Hill: University of North Carolina Press, 1990), chap. 7; Thomas Pettigrew, "Intergroup Contact Hypothesis Reconsidered," in *Contact and Conflict in Intergroup Encounters*, ed. Miles Hewstone and Rupert Brown (London: Basil Blackwell, 1986), pp. 169–195.

3. Robert MacIver, "Preface," in *Group Relations and Group Antagonisms*, ed. Robert M. MacIver (New York: Harper and Brothers, 1944), p. vii.

4. H. H. Giles, "The Status and Programs of Private Intergroup Relations Agencies," *Journal of Negro Education* 20 (1951): 413–14.

5. On this change in Jewish leadership generally, see Lenora E. Berson, *The Negroes and the Jews* (New York: Random House, 1971), pp. 98–107.

6. Edward S. Shapiro, *A Time for Healing: American Jewry since World War II* (Baltimore: Johns Hopkins University Press, 1992), pp. 16–17.

7. Accounts of the formation of the AJCongress can be found in Henry L. Feingold, *A Time for Searching: Entering the Mainstream, 1920–1945* (Baltimore: Johns Hopkins University Press, 1992); Morris Frommer, "The American Jewish Congress: A History, 1914–1950" (Ph.D. diss., Ohio State University, 1978).

8. David Petegorsky, "Report of the Executive Director to the Biennial National Convention of the American Jewish Congress," March 31–April 5, 1948, p. 10, American Jewish Congress Papers, Box 19, American Jewish Historical Society, Waltham, Massachusetts (hereafter AJCongress Papers).

9. Press release, "New Scientific Attack on Anti-Semitism Launched by American Jewish Congress," June 28, 1945, Alfred J. Marrow Papers, Box 20, Folder: "CCI, Pamphlets, Public Relations," Archives for the History of American Psychology, Akron, Ohio (hereafter AJM Papers).

10. Mitchell Ash, "Cultural Contexts and Scientific Change in Psychology: Kurt Lewin in Iowa," *American Psychologist* 47 (1992): 198–207.

11. Alfred J. Marrow, *The Practical Theorist: The Life and Work of Kurt Lewin* (New York: Basic Books, 1969), pp. 123–28.

12. Kurt Lewin, "Experiments in Social Space" (1939), reprinted in Kurt Lewin, *Resolving Social Conflicts: Selected Papers on Group Dynamics*, ed. Gertrud Weiss Lewin (New York: Harper and Brothers, 1948), p. 78.

13. William Graebner, "The Small Group and Democratic Social Engineering, 1900–1950," *Journal of Social Issues* 42 (1986): 137–38.

14. Kurt Lewin, "Cultural Reconstruction," reprinted in Lewin, *Resolving Social Conflicts*, pp. 40–41.

15. Kurt Lewin, "The Place of the Commission on Community Interrelations within the Work of Jewish Organizations," address to the NCRAC, November 16, 1944, Kurt Lewin Papers, Folder 19: "American Jewish Congress, CCI," Archive for the History of American Psychology, Akron, Ohio (hereafter KL Papers).

16. Mitchell G. Ash, "Émigré Psychologists after 1933: The Cultural Coding

of Scientific and Professional Practices," in *Forced Migration and Scientific Change: Émigré German-Speaking Scientists and Scholars after 1933*, ed. Mitchell G. Ash and Alfons Söllner (Cambridge: Cambridge University Press, 1996), pp. 127–32; William Graebner, "Confronting the Democratic Paradox: The Ambivalent Vision of Kurt Lewin," *Journal of Social Issues* 43, 3 (1987): 142.

17. Alfred J. Marrow, *The Practical Theorist: The Life and Work of Kurt Lewin* (New York: Basic Books, 1969), pp. 161–64.

18. Kurt Lewin, "Memorandum on Program for the Commission on Anti-Semitism of the American Jewish Congress" pp. 1, 9, KL Papers, Box M946, Folder 22: "CCI."

19. "Some Basic Issues," December 12, 1944, AJM Papers, Box M1938, Folder 21: "CCI Papers."

20. Goodwin Watson, *Action for Unity* (New York: Harper and Brothers, 1947), p. 64.

21. Stuart Cook, letter to Will Maslow, March 5, 1947, AJM Papers, Box M1938, Folder 14: "1946–1947, CCI Correspondence."

22. On the Committee on Unity, see Gerald Benjamin, *Race Relations and the New York City Commission on Human Rights* (Ithaca: Cornell University Press, 1974), pp. 38–70.

23. Isidor Chein, "Some Considerations in Combating Intergroup Prejudice," *Journal of Educational Sociology* 19 (1946): 412–19, at p. 416.

24. A brief biography of Chein can be found in "Awards for Distinguished Contributions to Psychology in the Public Interest: 1980," *American Psychologist* 36 (1981): 67–70.

25. Isidor Chein, letter to Garner Roney, February 9, 1949, AJM Papers, Box M1938, Folder 15: "1948–1949, CCI Correspondence."

26. For a more complete description of CCI's program of "action research," see Frances Cherry and Catherine Borshuk, "Social Action Research and the Commission on Community Interrelations," *Journal of Social Issues* 54 (1998): 119–42.

27. Ronald Lippitt, "Action Research—Idea and Method," July 17, 1945, AJM Papers, Box M1938, Folder 13: "1943–1945, CCI Correspondence."

28. Barbara Bellow, Milton L. Blum, Kenneth B. Clark, et al., "Prejudice in Seaside," *Human Relations* 1, 1 (1947): 109.

29. Ibid., p. 120.

30. Gerald Markowitz and David Rosner, *Children, Race, and Power: Kenneth and Mamie Clark's Northside Center* (Charlottesville: University Press of Virginia, 1996), p. 81.

31. A brief overview of the attitude/behavior research is Halford H. Fairchild and Patricia Gurin, "Traditions in the Social-Psychological Analysis of Race Relations," *American Behavioral Scientist* 21 (1978): 764–65.

32. R. T. Lapiere, "Attitudes vs. Actions," *Social Forces* 13 (1934): 230–37.

33. Philip Eisenberg, "Current Research in Social Psychology," *Psychologist's League Journal* 2, 5 (November–December 1938): 88.

34. Bernard Kutner, C. Wilkins, and P. R. Yarrow, "Verbal Attitudes and Overt Behavior Involving Racial Prejudice," *Journal of Abnormal and Social Psychology* 47 (1952): 649–52; Gerhart Saenger and E. Golbert, "Customer Reactions to the Integration of Negro Sales Personnel," *International Journal of Opinion and Attitude Research* 4 (1950): 57–76.

35. Marie Jahoda, "The Commission on Community Interrelations of the American Jewish Congress," p. 14, AJM Papers, Box M1938, Folder 21: "CCI Papers."

36. An excellent history of the contact hypothesis is Pettigrew, "Intergroup Contact Hypothesis Reconsidered," pp. 169–95.

37. Stuart W. Cook, "The Program of CCI," December 17, 1948, p. 2, AJM Papers, Box M1938, Folder 15: "1948–1949, CCI Correspondence."

38. On the place of Cook and CCI in the development of the contact hypothesis, see Yehuda Amir, "Contact Hypothesis in Ethnic Relations," *Psychological Bulletin* 71 (May 1969): 320–37.

39. Stuart Cook, *Some Psychological and Sociological Considerations Related to Interracial Housing*, November 1947, p. 2, AJCongress Papers, Box 21, Folder: "CCI, 5/20/49."

40. Robin M. Williams Jr., *The Reduction of Intergroup Tensions* (New York: Social Science Research Council, 1947), p. 91.

41. Samuel A. Stouffer, *The American Soldier* (Princeton: Princeton University Press, 1949).

42. Morton Deutsch and Mary Evans Collins, "Intergroup Relations in Interracial Public Housing: Occupancy Patterns and Racial Attitudes," *Journal of Housing* 7 (April 1950): 127–29; and Morton Deutsch and Mary Evans Collins, *Interracial Housing: A Psychological Evaluation of a Social Experiment* (Minneapolis: University of Minnesota Press, 1951).

43. Daniel M. Wilner, R. P. Walkley, and Stuart W. Cook, "Residential Proximity and Intergroup Relations in Public Housing Projects," *Journal of Social Issues* 8 (1952): 45–69; and Daniel M. Wilner, R. P. Walkley, and Stuart W. Cook, *Human Relations in Interracial Housing: A Study of the Contact Hypothesis* (Minneapolis: University of Minnesota Press, 1955).

44. J. Harding and R. Hogrefe, "Attitudes of White Department Store Employees toward Negro Coworkers," *Journal of Social Issues* 8 (1952): 18–28. For another CCI study on interracial contact in the workplace, see J. D. Minard, "Race Relations in the Pocohontas Coal Field," *Journal of Social Issues* 8 (1952): 29–44.

45. Gordon Allport, *The Resolution of Intergroup Tensions* (New York: National Conference of Christians and Jews, 1952), pp. 22–23.

46. For a thorough description of the Commission on Law and Social Action,

see Stuart Svonkin, *Jews against Prejudice: American Jews and the Fight for Civil Liberties* (New York: Columbia University Press, 1997), chap. 4.

47. Murray Friedman *What Went Wrong? The Creation and Collapse of the Black-Jewish Alliance* (New York: Free Press, 1995), pp. 133–34.

48. M. R. Konvitz, "Introduction," in Alexander H. Pekelis, *Law and Social Action: Selected Essays of Alexander H. Pekelis*, ed. Milton R. Konvitz (Ithaca: Cornell University Press, 1950), p. vii.

49. Morton J. Horowitz, *The Transformation of American Law, 1870–1960: The Crisis of Legal Orthodoxy* (New York: Oxford University Press, 1992), p. 169.

50. Edward A. Purcell, *The Crisis of Democratic Theory: Scientific Naturalism and the Problem of Value* (Lexington: University of Kentucky Press, 1973), pp. 74–75.

51. Karl Llewellyn, "A Realistic Jurisprudence: The Next Step," *Columbia Law Review* 30 (1930): 431–65.

52. An detailed treatment of how social science made inroads into the legal culture is John W. Johnson, *American Legal Culture, 1908–1940* (Westport, CT: Greenwood Press, 1981).

53. See, for example, John Henry Schlegel, *American Legal Realism and Empirical Social Science* (Chapel Hill: University of North Carolina Press, 1995).

54. Pekelis, *Law and Social Action*, p. 3.

55. Ibid., pp. 256–57.

56. Ibid.

57. CLSA memorandum, 1946, AJCongress Papers, Box 33, Folder: "CLSA Memorandum."

58. Note, "Private Attorneys-General: Group Action in the Fight for Civil Liberties," *Yale Law Journal* 58 (1949): 574–98, on pp. 589, 594.

59. Will Maslow, "How CLSA Selects Its Projects," *CSLA Reports*, March 31, 1949, p. 3, AJCongress Papers, Box 40, Folder: "CLSA Reports, 1949."

60. Svonkin, *Jews against Prejudice*, p. 22

61. CLSA memorandum, 1946, AJCongress Papers, Box 33, Folder: "CLSA Memorandum"

62. Maslow, "How CLSA Selects Its Projects."

63. Will Maslow to Justine Polier, May 11, 1948, AJCongress Papers, Box 71, Folder: "Maslow, NY Correspondence."

NOTES TO CHAPTER 5

1. *Plessy v. Ferguson* 163 U.S. 537 (1896), pp. 550–51.

2. Stephen J. Riegel, "The Persistent Career of Jim Crow: Lower Federal Courts and the 'Separate but Equal' Doctrine, 1865–1896," *American Journal of Legal History* 28 (January 1984): 17–40.

3. *Gong Lum v. Rice*, 275 U.S. 78 (1927).

4. Mark V. Tushnet, *The NAACP's Legal Strategy against Segregated Education, 1925–1950* (Chapel Hill: University of North Carolina Press, 1987), p. 27.

5. Genna Rae McNeil, *Groundwork: Charles Hamilton Houston and the Struggle for Civil Rights* (Philadelphia: University of Pennsylvania Press, 1983), pp. 49–56.

6. Tushnet, *NAACP's Legal Strategy*, p. 118; McNeil, *Groundwork*, pp. 76–85.

7. Tushnet, *NAACP's Legal Strategy*, p. 34; McNeil, *Groundwork*, pp. 116–17.

8. Mark V. Tushnet, *Making Civil Rights Law: Thurgood Marshall and the Supreme Court, 1936–1961* (New York: Oxford University Press, 1994), pp. 28–29.

9. *Missouri ex rel. Gaines v. Canada*, 305 U.S. 337 (1938).

10. Tushnet, *NAACP's Legal Strategy*, pp. 87–88.

11. Ibid., pp. 118–19.

12. This account of the case is taken from Charles Wollenberg, *All Deliberate Speed: Segregation and Exclusion in California Schools, 1855–1975* (Berkeley: University of California Press, 1976), pp. 110–21.

13. Tushnet, *Making Civil Rights Law*, pp. 35–36.

14. *Westminster School District of Orange County v. Mendez*, Brief for National Association for the Advancement of Colored People, *amicus curiae*, p. 10, Case Files, Ninth Circuit Court of Appeals, Record Group 276, Box 4464, Folder 11310, National Archives—Pacific Sierra Region, San Bruno, California (hereafter NAACP *Westminster* Brief).

15. Walter G. Daniel and John B. Holden, *Ambrose Caliver: Adult Educator and Civil Servant* (Washington, DC: Adult Education Association of the USA, 1966).

16. NAACP *Westminster* Brief, p. 12

17. Ibid., p. 15.

18. Ibid., p. 17.

19. Ibid., p. 11.

20. Phineas Indritz to Charles Abrams, August 14, 1947, NAACP Papers, Box IIB–133, Folder: "Shelley v. Kramer, McGhee v. Sipes, General, May–Oct. 1947."

21. Tushnet, *Making Civil Rights Law*, pp. 81–86.

22. NAACP *Westminster* Brief, p. 18.

23. Ibid., p. 19.

24. Gunnar Myrdal, *An American Dilemma* (New York: Harper and Brothers, 1944), p. 605.

25. Richard Sterner, *The Negro's Share: A Study of Income, Consumption, Housing, and Public Assistance* (New York: Harper and Brothers, 1943), chaps. 9 and 10.

26. Charles S. Johnson, *Patterns of Segregation* (New York: Harper and Brothers, 1943), pp. 243 and 231.

27. Ibid., p. 292.

28. Ibid., pp. 178–85.

29. Ibid., p. 321.

30. The NAACP-LDEF had rather hurriedly enlisted Loren Miller as local counsel to submit their brief for the *Westminster* when, midway through the process, Carter realized that neither he nor Marshall had been admitted to the Ninth Circuit. Robert Carter to Loren Miller, September 14, 1946, NAACP Papers, Box IIB–136, Folder: "California—*Mendez v. Westminster School District of Orange County, 1946–47.*"

31. Carey McWilliams, *The Education of Carey McWilliams* (New York: Simon and Schuster, 1979), pp. 76–107.

32. Carey McWilliams, *Brothers under the Skin*, rev. ed. (Boston: Little, Brown and Company, 1943).

33. Carey McWilliams, *A Mask for Privilege: Anti-Semitism in America* (Boston: Little, Brown, and Company, 1948).

34. Carey McWilliams, "Race Discrimination and the Law," *Science and Society* 9 (1945): 2.

35. *Westminster School District v. Mendez*, Brief for the American Jewish Congress, *amicus curiae*, 1946, p. 3, Case Files, Ninth Circuit Court of Appeals, Record Group 276, Box 4464, Folder 11310, National Archives—Pacific Sierra Region, San Bruno, California (hereafter CLSA Brief).

36. *Plessy v. Ferguson*, 163 U.S. 537 (1896).

37. CLSA Brief, p. 21.

38. Ibid., p. 22.

39. Ibid., p 4.

40. Ibid., p. 5

41. Ibid., pp. 14–15

42. Wollenberg, *All Deliberate Speed*, p. 132.

43. The article was Howard Hale Long, "Some Psychogenic Hazards of Segregated Education of Negroes," *Journal of Negro Education* (1935): 336–50.

44. Memorandum to the Public Relations Department, April 24, 1947, NAACP Papers, Series IIB, Box B136, Folder: "California—*Mendez v. Westminster School District of Orange County, 1946–47,*" Manuscript Division, Library of Congress, Washington, D.C. (hereafter NAACP Papers).

45. William Hastie to Thurgood Marshall, October 25, 1946, NAACP Papers, Series IIB, Box B136, Folder: "California—*Mendez v. Westminster School District of Orange County, 1946–47.*" Also see Tushnet, *NAACP's Legal Strategy*, p. 120.

46. Thurgood Marshall to Carl Murphy, December 20, 1946, NAACP Papers, Series IIB, Box B136, Folder, "California—*Mendez v. Westminster School District of Orange County, 1946–47.*"

47. Jack Greenberg, *Crusaders in the Courts* (New York: Basic Books, 1994), p. 35; Tushnet, *Making Civil Rights Law*, p. 89.

48. Annette H. Peyser, "The Use of Sociological Data to Indicate the Unconstitutionality of Racial Segregation," Kenneth B. Clark Papers, Box 63, Folder:

"Background Reports, undated" Manuscript Division, Library of Congress, Washington, D.C. (hereafter KBC Papers).

49. Robert L. Carter to Claude G. Metzler, December 6, 1946, NAACP Papers, Series IIB, Box B136, Folder, "California—*Mendez v. Westminster School District of Orange County*, 1946–47."

50. Tracy S. Kendler, "Contributions of the Psychologist to Constitutional Law," *American Psychologist* 10 (1950): 505–10.

51. The cover letter and the survey are reprinted in: Max Deutscher and Isidor Chein, "The Psychological Effects of Enforced Segregation: A Survey of Social Science Opinion," *Journal of Psychology* 26 (1948): 286–87.

52. Isidor Chein, "What Are the Psychological Effects of Segregation under Conditions of Equal Facilities?" (paper read at the Nineteenth Annual Meeting of the Eastern Psychological Association, April 16–17, 1948), KBC Papers, Box 32, Folder: "American Jewish Congress Reports, 1946–49." A version of this paper was published as Isidor Chein, "What Are the Psychological Effects of Segregation under Conditions of Equal Facilities?" *International Journal of Opinion and Attitude Research* 3 (Summer 1949): 229–34.

53. Chein, "What Are the Psychological Effects of Segregation?" p. 259.

54. See, for example, "Rogers on Expert Testimony," NAACP Papers, Series IIB, Box 138, Folder: "Schools, Kansas, Topeka, *Brown v. Board of Education*, Expert Witnesses, 1951."

55. Deutscher and Chein, "Psychological Effects of Enforced Segregation," p. 259.

56. Will Maslow to Thurgood Marshall, April 14, 1947, and Will Maslow to Thurgood Marshall, April 28, 1947, both in NAACP Papers, Series IIB, Box 204, Folder: "University of Texas, *Sweatt v. Painter*, Correspondence, Jan.–June 1948."

57. George W. Stocking Jr., "Redfield, Robert," in *Dictionary of American Biography, Supplement Six, 1956–1960*, ed. John A. Garraty (New York: Charles Scribner's Sons, 1980), pp. 532–34.

58. Robert Redfield, "Race and Human Nature: An Anthropologist's View" (1944), reprinted in *The Social Uses of Social Science: The Papers of Robert Redfield*, vol. 2, edited by Margaret Park Redfield (Chicago: University of Chicago Press, 1963), p. 142.

59. Memorandum by Louis Wirth, May 1, 1947, Louis Wirth Papers, University of Chicago Archives, Regenstein Library, Chicago, Illinois.

60. Clement E. Vose, *Caucasians Only: The Supreme Court, the NAACP, and the Restrictive Covenant Cases* (Berkeley: University of California Press, 1959), pp. 159–63.

61. See his pretrial notes for *Briggs* a few years later, in Robert Redfield Papers, Box 23, Folder 4, University of Chicago Archives, Regenstein Library, Chicago, Illinois (hereafter RR Papers).

62. Pretrial notes, RR papers, Box 33, Folder 7.

63. Redfield's testimony in *Sweatt* was part of the record of *Briggs v. Elliot*, 98 F. Supp. 529 (1951). All references are to Redfield's testimony as printed in the *Briggs* transcript. See Redfield testimony, pp. 166–67, copy in Tom C. Clark Papers, Tarleton Law Library, University of Texas, Austin, Texas.

64. For example, see the trial testimony of M. Brewster Smith in *Davis et al. v. County School Board of Prince Edward County*, 103 F. Supp. 337 (1952), Case File 1333, Box 126, Volume 2, pp. 292–93, Civil Case Files, 1938–1958; Richmond Division, Records of the U.S. District Court to the Eastern District of Virginia, Record Group 21, National Archives—Mid Atlantic Region, Philadelphia, Pennsylvania.

65. *Sweatt v. Painter*, 210 S.W. 2d 442 (1947).

66. *Sipuel v. Oklahoma State Regents*, 332 U.S. 631 (1948). See also *Fisher v. Hurst*, 333 U.S. 147 (1948); Tushnet, *NAACP's Legal Strategy*, pp. 120–23; George Lynn Cross, *Blacks in White Colleges: Oklahoma's Landmark Cases* (Norman: University of Oklahoma Press, 1975), pp. 35–80.

67. "*Sipuel v. Board of Regents University of Oklahoma et al.*: Possible Theories Which May Be Used in Brief and Amendment," NAACP Papers, Series IIB, Box 202, Folder: "University of Oklahoma, *Sipuel v. Board of Regents of the University of Oklahoma*, 1946–48."

68. Thurgood Marshall to Earl G. Harrison, April 20, 1948, NAACP Papers, Series IIB, Box 202, Folder: "University of Oklahoma, *Sipuel v. Board of Regents of the University of Oklahoma*, 1946–48."

69. "Persons Who Testified on Sipuel Case Hearing," NAACP Papers, Series IIB, Box 202, Folder: "University of Oklahoma, Correspondence, Jan.–May 1948."

70. Press release, NAACP Papers, Series IIB, Box 202, Folder: "University of Oklahoma, Correspondence, Jan.–May 1948."

71. Robert Redfield to Thurgood Marshall, June 11, 1948, RR Papers, Box 23, Folder 4.

72. Stuart Cook to David Petegorsky, May 24, 1948, American Jewish Congress Papers, Box 19, Folder "CCI, 1948–49," American Jewish Historical Society, Waltham Massachusetts (hereafter AJCongress Papers).

73. *McLaurin v. Board of Regents, University of Oklahoma*, 87 F. Supp. 528 (1948); Cross, *Blacks in White Colleges*, pp. 85–105.

74. Annette Peyser to M. Brewster Smith, March 25, 1952, M. Brewster Smith Papers, Box M605, Folder: "NAACP," Archives for the History of American Psychology, Akron, Ohio.

75. Annette H. Peyser, "The Use of Sociological Data to Indicate the Unconstitutionality of Racial Segregation," KBC Papers, Box 63, Folder: "Background Reports, Undated." This document is undated, but internal evidence suggests it is the 1948 address.

76. Brief of the NAACP-LDEF, *Sweatt v. Painter*, 339 U.S. 629 (1950), pp. 24–25.

77. Ibid., pp. 27–28.

78. *McLaurin v. Oklahoma State Regents for Higher Education*, 339 U.S. 637 (1950); *Sweatt v. Painter*, 339 U.S. 629 (1950).

79. Tushnet, *NAACP's Legal Strategy*, pp. 130–32.

80. Stuart Cook to Alfred Marrow, June 5, 1947, Alfred J. Marrow Papers, Box M1938, Folder 14: "1946–1947 CCI Correspondence," Archives for the History of American Psychology, Akron, Ohio (hereafter AJM Papers).

81. Stuart Cook to Alfred Marrow, August 11, 1950, AJCongress Papers, Box 70, Folder: "Dr. Stuart Cook."

82. John Harding to Marie Jahoda, April 9, 1952, AJM Papers, Box M1938, Folder 17: "1952–1953 CCI Correspondence."

83. Isidor Chein to Marie Jahoda, April 9, 1952, AJM Papers, Box M1938, Folder 17: "1952–1953 CCI Correspondence."

84. Marie Jahoda, "The Commission on Community Interrelations of the American Jewish Congress," 1952, pp. 14, 15, AJM Papers, Box M1938, Folder 21: "CCI Papers."

85. Ibid., p. 18.

86. Ibid., p. 20.

NOTES TO CHAPTER 6

1. A fifth case is often grouped with these four: *Bolling v. Sharpe* 347 U.S. 497 (1954). *Bolling* attacked school segregation by the federal government in the District of Columbia. This was not a NAACP-LDEF case, however, and did not use social-scientific research; therefore, I do not consider it in this work.

2. Edward A. Richards, ed., *Proceedings of the MidCentury White House Conference on Children and Youth* (Raleigh, NC: Health Publications Institute, 1951), pp. 12–26. The most complete treatment of the 1950 conference is Katherine Kerr, "Race and the Making of American Liberalism, 1912–1965" (Ph.D. diss., Johns Hopkins University, 1995), pp. 221–64.

3. Melvin A. Glasser to Samuel Flowerman, May 16, 1950, and Samuel Flowerman to Kenneth Clark, May 29, 1950, both in Kenneth B. Clark Papers, Box 109, Folder 1 of 2: "MidCentury White House Conference on Children and Youth, Correspondence, Jan.–Aug 1950," Manuscript Division, Library of Congress, Washington, D.C. (hereafter KBC Papers).

4. Clark's report was chapter 6 of *Personality in the Making: The Fact-Finding Report of the MidCentury White House Conference on Children and Youth*, ed. Helen Leland Witmer and Ruth Kotinsky (New York: Harper and Brothers, 1952), p. 145.

5. Else Frenkel-Brunswik, Daniel J. Levinson, and R. Nevitt Sanford, "The Antidemocratic Personality," in *Readings in Social Psychology*, ed. Theodore M.

Newcomb and Eugene L. Hartley (New York: Henry Holt and Company, 1947), pp. 531–41.

6. *Personality in the Making*, pp. 148–49.

7. Ibid., p. 153.

8. Kenneth B. Clark, quoted in Richard Kluger, *Simple Justice: The History of Brown v. Board of Education and Black America's Struggle for Equality* (New York: Vintage, 1975), p. 321.

9. Kenneth B. Clark, oral history with Columbia University, July 17, 1989, p. 113, KBC Papers, Box 192, Folder: "Writings by Clark, Oral History, Draft II, 1976–89.

10. Kluger, *Simple Justice*, p. 321.

11. Mark Tushnet, *Making Civil Rights Law* (New York: Oxford University Press, 1994), p. 157; Jack Greenberg, *Crusaders in the Courts* (New York: Basic Books, 1994), p. 124.

12. William E. Cross, *Shades of Black: Diversity in African-American Identity* (Philadelphia: Temple University Press, 1991), p. 16.

13. Kenneth B. Clark to Robert Carter, February 15, 1951, KBC Papers, Box 61, Folder: "NAACP, General Correspondence, 1951–52" 1/6.

14. Kenneth B. Clark to Robert Carter, March 7, 1951, and Robert Carter to Kenneth B. Clark, March 7, 1951, KBC Papers, Box 61, Folder: "NAACP, General Correspondence, 1951–52" 1/6.

15. Clark to Carter, March 7, 1951, KBC Papers, Box 61, Folder 1 of 6: "NAACP, General Correspondence, 1951–52."

16. Theodore M. Newcomb, Gardner Murphy, and Lois Barclay Murphy, *Experimental Social Psychology*, 2d ed. (New York: Harper and Brothers, 1937).

17. George Hartmann and Theodore M. Newcomb, eds., *Industrial Conflict* (New York: Cordon, 1939).

18. See interview by the United States Civil Service Commission, Theodore M. Newcomb Papers, Box 1, Folder: "Federal Investigation of Political Activities," University of Michigan Archives, Bentley Historical Library, Ann Arbor, Michigan.

19. Biographical sketches include: Ernest R. Hilgard, *Psychology in America: A Historical Survey* (San Diego: Harcourt, Brace, Jovanovich, 1987), pp. 597–98; Theodore M. Newcomb, "Theodore M. Newcomb," in *History of Psychology in Autobiography*, vol. 6, ed. Gardner Linzey (Englewood Cliffs, NJ: Prentice Hall, Press, 1974).

20. Theodore M. Newcomb, *Social Psychology* (New York: Dryden Press, 1950), pp. 609, 610.

21. Kluger, *Simple Justice*, pp. 337–38.

22. David Krech and Richard S. Crutchfield, *Theory and Problems of Social Psychology* (New York: McGraw-Hill, 1948), p. 471.

23. Ibid., pp. 512, 513.

24. Ibid., p. 516.

25. Robert Carter to Kenneth B. Clark, March 20, 1951, KBC Papers Box 61, Folder 1 of 6: "NAACP, General Correspondence, 1951–52." On Allport's involvement, also see Kluger, *Simple Justice*, pp. 336–37.

26. Marion Radke, Helen Trager, and H. Davis, "Social Perceptions and Attitudes of Children," *Genetic Psychology Monographs* 40 (1949): pp. 327–447.

27. Thurgood Marshall to Robert Redfield, April 12, 1951, Robert Redfield Papers, Box 23, Folder 4, University of Chicago Archives, Regenstein Library, Chicago, Illinois (hereafter RR Papers).

28. RR Papers, Box 23, Folder 4.

29. Robert Lynd, *Knowledge for What?* (Princeton: Princeton University Press, 1939); Lois Barclay Murphy *Gardner Murphy* (Jefferson, NC: McFarland, 1990), pp. 114, 186.

30. Greenberg, *Crusaders in the Courts*, p. 127.

31. Arnold Rose, "The Influence of Legislation on Prejudice" (1949), reprinted in *Race Prejudice and Discrimination: Readings in Intergroup Relations in the United States*, ed. Arnold Rose (New York: Alfred A. Knopf, 1951), p. 554.

32. Arnold Rose to Jack Greenberg, June 7, 1951, Arnold M. Rose Papers, University of Minnesota Archives, Walter Library, Minneapolis, Minnesota.

33. Kluger, *Simple Justice*, p. 419.

34. Lawrence J. Friedman, *Menninger: The Family and the Clinic* (Lawrence: University of Kansas Press, 1990), p. 181; Kluger, *Simple Justice*, pp. 416–19.

35. Murphy, *Gardner Murphy*, pp. 85, 138.

36. On Reid, see Kluger, *Simple Justice*, p. 439. On Sanford and Cantril, see Jack Greenberg, Trial Memorandum, October 11, 1951, NAACP Papers, Box 139–IIB, Folder: "Schools, Kansas, Topeka, *Brown v. Board of Education (Belton v. Gebhart, et al.)*, Legal Papers, notes, 1951–52."

37. Kluger, *Simple Justice*, pp. 440–42.

38. Annette Peyser to Stuart Cook, February 19, 1952, Stuart W. Cook Papers, Box M2324, Folder: "*Brown v. Board of Education*—Early Material," Archives for the History of American Psychology, Akron Ohio.

39. On the Department of Social Relations see Hilgard, *Psychology in America*, pp. 599–602.

40. M. Brewster Smith, "The Shaping of American Social Psychology: A Personal Perspective from the Periphery," *Personality and Social Psychology Bulletin* 9 (June 1983): 168.

41. See handwritten notes "Information Booth, 9:30 Sunday Morning," KBC Papers, Box 66, Folder: "NAACP School Segregation Cases, States, Documents re Individual, Virginia, 1951–53, n.d."

42. Sander Gilman, *Jewish Self-Hatred: Anti-Semitism and the Hidden Language of the Jews* (Baltimore: Johns Hopkins University Press, 1986), pp. 286–306.

43. Kurt Lewin, "Self-Hatred among Jews," *Contemporary Jewish Record* 4

(June 1941): 225, 229–30. Historian Daryl Michael Scott, "The logic of Lewin's view of subordinate-dominate group relations was that Jewish people who were physically separated from gentiles would not suffer from self-hate." See Scott's *Contempt and Pity: Social Policy and the Image of the Damaged Black Psyche, 1880–1996* (Chapel Hill: University of North Carolina Press, 1997), p. 26. Scott's conclusion about Lewin's logic assumes that it was possible in the modern United States for Jews to be "physically separate" from Gentiles, a possibility that Lewin flatly rejected. For Lewin, group isolation was not the solution to self-hate, and his entire career in the United States was dedicated to lowering discriminatory barriers to free social movement of individuals.

44. Isidor Chein, "Group Membership and Group Belonging," paper presented at the International Congress on Mental Health, KBC Papers, Box 32, Folder 4 of 4: "American Jewish Congress Reports, undated" 4/4.

45. Isidor Chein, "Securing Our Children against Prejudice," paper presented at the Fifty-third Annual Meeting of the National Conference of Jewish Communal Service, Chicago, Illinois, June 1–5, 1952, KBC Papers, Box 196, Folder: "Writings by Others, Articles, 1948 June–1952 June." On the contrast between Bettelheim and Lewin's theories, see Gilman, *Jewish Self-Hatred*, pp. 304–8.

46. David Krech to Richard Kluger, December 17, 1973, David Krech Papers, Box M554, Folder: "Krech Corr. 1973," Archives for the History of American Psychology, Akron, Ohio.

NOTES TO CHAPTER 7

1. The claim that the doll tests were actually cited by the Supreme Court in the *Brown* opinion is common. See, for example, Hadley Arkes, "The Problem of Kenneth Clark," *Commentary* 58 (November 1974): 37–46; Harold Cruse, *Plural but Equal: A Critical Study of Blacks and Minorities and America's Plural Society* (New York: William Morrow, 1987), pp. 72–74; Roy L. Brooks, *Integration or Separation? A Strategy for Racial Equality* (Cambridge: Harvard University Press, 1996), pp. 12–16.

2. "Trial Memorandum," p. 7, Robert Redfield Papers, Box 23, Folder 4, University of Chicago Archives, Regenstein Library, Chicago, Illinois (hereafter RR Papers).

3. Richard Kluger, *Simple Justice: The History of* Brown v. Board of Education *and Black America's Struggle for Equality* (New York: Vintage, 1975), pp. 347–48.

4. Jack Greenberg, *Crusaders in the Courts* (New York: Basic Books, 1994), p. 127.

5. "Trial Memorandum," p. 7, RR Papers, Box 23, Folder 4.

6. Thurgood Marshall, "An Evaluation of Recent Efforts to Achieve Racial Integration in Education through Resort to the Courts," *Journal of Negro Education* 21 (1952): 322.

7. Trial Memorandum," p. 8, RR Papers, Box 23, Folder 4.

8. Marion Radke, Helen Trager, and H. Davis, "Social Perceptions and Attitudes of Children," *Genetic Psychology Monographs* 40 (1949): 336–37.

9. Trial testimony of Helen Trager, *Briggs v. Elliott*, pp. 142, 143. Tom C. Clark Papers, Tarleton Law Library, University of Texas, Austin, Texas (hereafter TCC Papers).

10. Transcript of the Record of *Gebhart v. Belton*, pp. 87a–88a, TCC Papers.

11. Trial testimony of John J. Kane, *Brown v. Board of Education*, p. 176, TCC Papers.

12. Trial testimony of Louisa Holt, *Brown v. Board of Education*, p. 172, TCC Papers.

13. See, for example, "Rogers on Expert Testimony," NAACP Papers, Series IIB, Box 138, Folder: "Schools, Kansas, Topeka, *Brown v. Board of Education*, Expert Witnesses, 1951," Manuscript Division, Library of Congress, Washington, D.C., (hereafter NAACP Papers).

14. Isidor Chein to Will Maslow, December 21, 1954, Kenneth B. Clark Papers, Box 31, Folder: "American Jewish Congress, Correspondence, 1945–66, n.d.," Manuscript Division, Library of Congress, Washington, D.C. (hereafter KBC Papers).

15. Judge Dobie to Isidor Chein, *Davis et al. v. County School Board of Prince Edward County*, Case File 1333, Box 126, Volume 2, p. 273, Civil Case Files, 1938–1958; Richmond Division, Records of the U.S. District Court to the Eastern District of Virginia, Record Group 21, National Archives—Mid Atlantic Region, Philadelphia, Pennsylvania.

16. Trial testimony of Louisa Holt, *Brown v. Board of Education*, p. 170, TCC Papers.

17. Trial testimony of Isidor Chein, *Davis et al. v. County School Board of Prince Edward County*, 103 F. Supp. 337 (1952), p. 358.

18. Trial testimony of M. Brewster Smith, *Davis et al. v. County School Board of Prince Edward County*, 103 F. Supp. 337 (1952), pp. 296–329.

19. Transcript of the Record of *Briggs v. Elliott*, p. 133, TCC Papers.

20. Annette Peyser to M. Brewster Smith, February 20, 1952, M. Brewster Smith Papers, Box M605, Folder: "NAACP," Archives for the History of American Psychology, Akron, Ohio (hereafter MBS papers).

21. Trial testimony of M. Brewster Smith in *Davis et al. v. County School Board of Prince Edward County*, 1952, Case File 1333, Box 126, Volume 2, p. 273, Civil Case Files, 1938–1958; Richmond Division, Records of the U.S. District Court to the Eastern District of Virginia, Record Group 21, National Archives—Mid Atlantic Region, Philadelphia, Pennsylvania. (hereafter Smith, *Davis* Testimony).

22. Kluger, *Simple Justice*, pp. 484–85.

23. Smith, *Davis* Testimony, pp. 292–93.

24. Ibid., pp. 294–295.

25. Robert V. Guthrie, "Mamie Phipps Clark," in *Women in Psychology: A Bio-Bibliographic Sourcebook*, ed. Agnes N. O'Connell and Nancy Felipe Russo (New York: Greenwood Press, 1990), pp. 69–70. See also Gerald Markowitz and David Rosner, *Children, Race, and Power: Kenneth and Mamie Clark's Northside Center* (Charlottesville: University Press of Virginia, 1996).

26. On Lewin's influence on the Clarks, see William E. Cross, *Shades of Black* (Philadelphia: Temple University Press, 1991), pp. 28–38.

27. Kenneth B. Clark, "Candor about Negro-Jewish Relations," *Commentary* 1 (February 1946): 12.

28. Kenneth B. Clark and Mamie P. Clark, "Racial Identification and Preferences in Negro Children," in *Readings in Social Psychology*, ed. Theodore M. Newcomb and Eugene L. Hartley, (New York: Henry Holt and Company, 1947; 2d ed., 1952), p. 169.

29. Kluger, *Simple Justice*, p. 318.

30. Clark and Clark "Racial Identification and Preference," p. 175.

31. Ibid., p. 178.

32. Kenneth B. Clark and Mamie P. Clark, "Emotional Factors in Racial Identification and Preference in Negro Children," *Journal of Negro Education* 19, 3 (Summer 1950): 342.

33. Ibid., p. 346.

34. Ibid., p. 350.

35. Kluger, *Simple Justice*, pp. 328–31.

36. Transcript of the Record of *Briggs v. Elliott*, p. 86, TCC Papers.

37. Ibid., pp. 88, 89.

38. Ibid., p. 92.

39. Louis Redding to Kenneth B. Clark, August 12, 1951, and Kenneth B. Clark to Louis Redding, August 20, 1951, KBC Papers, Box 15, Folder: "General Correspondence, 1951, June–December."

40. Kenneth B. Clark to Louis Redding, September 19, 1951, KBC Papers, Box 15, Folder, "General Correspondence, 1951, June–December."

41. Clark and Clark, "Racial Identification and Preference," p. 175.

42. "Preliminary Report: Tests of Racial Preference of Adolescent Negro Subjects in Wilmington, Delaware," KBC Papers, Box 66, Folder: "NAACP School Segregation Cases, States, Documents re Individuals, Delaware, 1954."

43. Ruth Horowitz and Lois Barclay Murphy, "Projective Methods in the Psychological Study of Children," *Journal of Experimental Education* 7, 2 (December 1938): 133–40.

44. "Preliminary Report: Tests of Racial Preference of Adolescent Negro Subjects in Wilmington, Delaware," KBC Papers.

45. Transcript of the Record of *Belton v. Gebhart*, pp. 170–171, TCC Papers.

46. Clark and Clark, "Racial Identification and Preference," p.172.

47. Handwritten notes, KBC Papers, Box 66, Folder: "NAACP, School Segregation Cases, States, Documents re Individuals, Virginia, 1951–52, n.d."

48. Trial testimony of Kenneth B. Clark in *Davis et al. v. County School Board of Prince Edward County*, 1952, Case File 1333, Box 126, Volume 5, p. 404–5, Civil Case Files, 1938–1958, Richmond Division, Records of the U.S. District Court to the Eastern District of Virginia, Record Group 21, National Archives—Mid Atlantic Region, Philadelphia, Pennsylvania (hereafter Clark, *Davis* testimony).

49. Ibid., pp. 426–27.

50. Clark and Clark, "Racial Identification and Preference," p. 177.

51. Clark, *Davis* testimony, p. 448.

52. Kluger, *Simple Justice*, p. 355.

53. Ibid., pp. 343–44.

54. See handwritten notes "Information Booth, 9:30 Sunday Morning," KBC Papers, Box 66, Folder: "NAACP School Segregation Cases, States, Documents re Individuals, Virginia, 1951–52, n.d."

55. Trial testimony of Isidor Chein in *Davis et al. v. County School Board of Prince Edward County*, 1952, Case File 1333, Box 126, Volume 2, pp. 322–23, 273, Civil Case Files, 1938–1958, Richmond Division, Records of the U.S. District Court to the Eastern District of Virginia, Record Group 21, National Archives—Mid Atlantic Region, Philadelphia, Pennsylvania (hereafter Chein, *Davis* Testimony).

56. Ibid., p. 352.

57. Ibid., p. 364.

58. Judge Dobie, in Chein, *Davis* Testimony, p. 362.

59. Trial testimony of William H. Kelly and John Nelson Buck in *Davis et al. v. County School Board of Prince Edward County*, 1952, Case File 1333, Box 126, Volume 5, pp. 856–83 (Kelly) and pp. 884–910 (Buck), Civil Case Files, 1938–1958, Richmond Division, Records of the U.S. District Court to the Eastern District of Virginia, Record Group 21, National Archives—Mid Atlantic Region, Philadelphia, Pennsylvania.

60. William H. Tucker, *The Science and Politics of Racial Research* (Urbana: University of Illinois Press, 1994), pp. 153–57; Andrew S. Winston, "Science in the Service of the Far Right: Henry E. Garrett, the IAAEE, and the Liberty Lobby," *Journal of Social Issues* 54 (1998): 179–210.

61. Trial testimony of Henry E. Garrett in *Davis et al. v. County School Board of Prince Edward County*, 1952, Case File 1333, Box 126, Volume 5, p. 919, Civil Case Files, 1938–1958, Richmond Division, Records of the U.S. District Court to the Eastern District of Virginia, Record Group 21, National Archives—Mid Atlantic Region, Philadelphia, Pennsylvania.

62. Ibid., pp. 920–21.

63. Ibid., pp. 924, 922.

64. Ibid., p. 926.

65. Ibid., p. 927–28.

66. Ibid., p. 943.

67. Ibid., pp. 954–55.

68. M. Brewster Smith to Annette Peyser, March 6, 1952, MBS Papers, Box M605, Folder: "NAACP."

69. Robert Carter to M. Brewster Smith, March 11, 1952, MBS Papers, Box M605, Folder: "NAACP."

70. M. Brewster Smith to Annette Peyser, March 31, 1952, MBS Papers, Box M605, Folder: "NAACP."

71. M. Brewster Smith to Robert Carter, March 13, 1952, MBS Papers, Box M605, Folder: "NAACP."

72. Stuart Cook, "Attitudes and Attitude-Related Behavior," paper presented at the Eighty-ninth Convention of the American Psychological Association, Los Angeles, August 24–28, 1981, p. 5., in Stuart W. Cook Papers, Box M2342, Folder 16, Archives for the History of American Psychology, Akron, Ohio.

73. Isidor Chein to Robert Carter, March 31, 1952, KBC Papers, Box 61, Folder 1 of 6: "NAACP, General Correspondence, 1951–52."

74. *Davis et al. v. County School Board of Prince Edward County*, 103 F. Supp. 337 (1952).

75. *Belton v. Gebhart*, 87 A. 2d 862 (1952).

76. In the United States District Court for the District of Kansas, "Finding of Fact," NAACP Papers, Box 138–IIB, Folder: "Schools, Kansas, Topeka, *Brown v. Board of Education*, Legal Papers, 1951–53."

77. Judge Walter A. Huxman quoted in Hugh A. Speer, *The Case of the Century*, (Washington, D.C.: Office of Education, Department of Health, Education and Welfare, 1968), p. 27. I also note that Huxman made his finding in the one trial where Kenneth Clark did not appear. Hence, legally, the finding of fact could not have been based on the doll tests—further evidence of the relative unimportance of the doll tests to the decision in *Brown*.

NOTES TO CHAPTER 8

1. Kenneth B. Clark to William Delano, February 19, 1952, Kenneth B. Clark Papers, Box 15, Folder: "General Correspondence, 1952, January–March" Manuscript Division, Library of Congress, Washington, D.C. (hereafter KBC Papers).

2. William Cross, *Shades of Black* (Philadelphia: Temple University Press, 1991), p. 29.

3. "Grade School Segregation: The Latest Attack on Racial Discrimination," *Yale Law Journal* 61, 5 (May 1952): 737.

4. Robert Carter to Kenneth B. Clark, October 31, 1951, KBC Papers, Box 61, Folder 1 of 6: "NAACP, General Correspondence, 1951–52."

5. Eugene Hartley to Theodore Newcomb, November 27, 1945, Theodore M. Newcomb Papers, Box 6, Folder: "SPSSI, 1941–1945," University of Michigan Archives, Bentley Historical Library, Ann Arbor, Michigan.

6. "Report of the Committee on Intergroup Relations," January 20, 1952, Society for the Psychological Study of Social Issues Papers, Box 197, Folder: "Intergroup Relations Committee 2," Archives for the History of American Psychology, Akron Ohio (hereafter SPSSI Papers).

7. Gerhart Saenger to subcommittee members, December 4, 1951, SPSSI Papers, Box 197, Folder: "Intergroup Relations Committee 2."

8. Robert Carter to Kenneth B. Clark, January 11, 1952, KBC Papers, Box 61, Folder 1 of 6: "NAACP, General Correspondence, 1951–52."

9. "The Social Scientific Argument against Segregation in the Schools," p. 2, KBC Papers, Box 61, Folder 1 of 6: "NAACP General Correspondence, 1951–52."

10. Memo from Gerhart Saenger, June 11, 1952, KBC Papers, Box 97, Folder 1 of 11: "Society for the Psychological Study of Social Issues, Memoranda, Reports, Minutes, etc., 1951–54."

11. Kenneth B. Clark, quoted in Hugh Speer, *The Case of the Century: A Historical and Social Perspective on* Brown v. Board of Education of Topeka *with Present and Future Implications* (Washington, DC: Office of Education, U.S. Department of Health, Education and Welfare, 1968), p. 222.

12. Draft of Social Science Statement, KBC Papers, Box 63, Folder 2 of 2: "Appendix to Appellant's Brief 'The Effect of Segregation and Consequences of Desegregation: A Social Science Statement,' 22 Sept. 1952, Drafts."

13. "Appendix to Brief for Appellants: The Effects of Segregation and the Consequence of Desegregation—A Social Science Statement," pp. 1–2, reprinted in *Landmark Briefs and Arguments of the Supreme Court of the United States: Constitutional Law*, ed. Philip B. Kurland and Gerhard Casper. (Arlington, VA: University Publications of America, 1975).

14. Draft of Social Science Statement, KBC Papers.

15. "Appendix to Brief for Appellants: The Effects of Segregation and the Consequences of Desegregation—A Social Science Statement," pp. 13–15.

16. Draft of Social Science Statement, KBC Papers. Historian Darryl Scott argues that Chein's theories on group self-hatred were vulnerable because Lewin held that Jewish self-hatred increased "after the Ghetto period of Jewish history." See Daryl Michael Scott, *Contempt and Pity: Social Policy and the Image of the Damaged Black Psyche, 1880–1996* (Chapel Hill: University of North Carolina Press, 1997), p. 128. It is ironic, therefore, that Chein addressed this very point in a deleted draft of the Social Statement.

17. Appendix to Brief for Appellants: The Effects of Segregation and the Consequences of Desegregation—A Social Science Statement," pp. 3–11.

18. Ibid., pp. 12–17.

19. Richard Kluger, *Simple Justice: The History of* Brown v. Board of Education *and Black America's Struggle for Equality* (New York: Vintage, 1975), p. 555–56.

20. Stuart Cook to Gerhart Saenger, February 7, 1952, SPSSI Papers, Box 197, Folder: "Intergroup Relations Committee 2."

21. On SSSP, see John F. Galliher and James M. Galliher, *Marginality and Dissent in Twentieth-Century American Sociology: The Case of Elizabeth Briant Lee and Alfred McClung Lee* (Albany: State University of New York Press, 1995), pp. 98–105.

22. Alfred McClung Lee to Kenneth B. Clark, September 8, 1952, KBC Papers, Box 61, Folder 1 of 6: "NAACP General Correspondence, 1951–52."

23. Harry Estill Moore to Kenneth B. Clark, September 19, 1952, KBC Papers, Box 61, Folder 1 of 6: "NAACP General Correspondence, 1951–52."

24. Isidor Chein to David Krech, September 15, 1952, David Krech Papers, Box M554.5, Folder: "Correspondence," Archives of the History of American Psychology, Akron, Ohio.

25. Charlotte G. Babcock to Kenneth B. Clark, September 22, 1952, and Kenneth B. Clark to Charlotte G. Babcock, September 26, 1952, KBC Papers, Box 61, Folder 1 of 6: "NAACP General Correspondence, 1951–52."

26. Jerome Bruner to Kenneth B. Clark, September 22, 1952, KBC Papers, Box 61, Folder 1 of 6: "NAACP General Correspondence, 1951–52."

27. Robert Redfield to Kenneth B. Clark, September 24, 1952, Robert Redfield Papers, Box 23, Folder 4, University of Chicago Archives, Regenstein Library, Chicago, Illinois.

28. Kenneth B. Clark to Jerome Bruner, September 26, 1952; on Frazier and McLean see Kenneth B. Clark to E. Franklin Frazier, September 15, 1952, and Kenneth B. Clark to Helen McLean September 15, 1952; Gordon to Kenneth B. Clark, September 16, 1952, and Kenneth B. Clark to Gordon, September 25, 1952, all in KBC Papers, Box 61, Folder 1 of 6: "NAACP General Correspondence, 1951–52."

29. Kluger, *Simple Justice*, p. 537.

30. Leon Friedman, ed., *Argument: The Oral Argument before the Supreme Court in* Brown v. Board of Education of Topeka, *1952–1955* (New York: Chelsea House Publishers, 1969), p. 59.

31. Thurgood Marshall to Kenneth B. Clark, January 20, 1953, and Kenneth B. Clark to Thurgood Marshall, January 23, 1953, KBC Papers Box 61, Folder 2 of 6: "NAACP General Correspondence, 1953."

32. Kenneth B. Clark, "The Social Scientist as an Expert Witness in Civil Rights Litigation," pp. 9–10, KBC Papers, Box 55, Folder: "Speeches by Clark, 1946 Jan.–1953 Feb."

33. M. Brewster Smith to Annette Peyser, March 31, 1952, M. Brewster Smith Papers, Box M605, Folder: "NAACP," Archives for the History of American Psychology, Akron, Ohio.

34. Isidor Chein to Will Maslow, December 21, 1954, KBC Papers, Box 31, Folder: "American Jewish Congress, Correspondence, 1945–66, n.d."

35. On Rose's role, see Kenneth B. Clark to Arnold M. Rose, February 20, 1953; Arnold M. Rose to Kenneth B. Clark, March 6, 1953; and Kenneth B. Clark

to Arnold M. Rose, March 17, 1953, all in Arnold M. Rose Papers, University of Minnesota Archives, Walter Library, Minneapolis, Minnesota. The brief appeared as "The Effects of Segregation and Consequences of Desegregation: A Social Science Statement," *Minnesota Law Review* 37 (May 1953): 427–38.

36. Mark V. Tushnet, *Making Civil Rights Law* (New York: Oxford University Press, 1994), pp. 194–95.

37. Miscellaneous Orders, 345 U.S. 972, 1953.

38. Document titled "May the Court Enter a Gradual Decree Where the Violation of Constitutional Rights Is Asserted?" NAACP Papers, Box IIB–141, Folder: "Schools, Kansas, Topeka, *Brown v. Board of Education* (and other cases), 2nd Reargument, Background Materials, Greenberg, Jack, and Pinsky, David, 1953," Manuscript Division, Library of Congress, Washington, D.C.

39. Memo from Robert Carter to Kenneth B. Clark, June 22, 1953, p. 6, KBC Papers, Box 65, Folder 1 of 2: "Reargument, 1st Social Science Answer to Question IV, December 1953, Drafts and Related Documents."

40. "Steps in Attaining Answers to Question IV," KBC Papers, Box 65, Folder 1 of 2: "Rearguments, 1st Social Science Answer to Question IV, December 1953, Drafts and Related Documents."

41. Jack Greenberg, *Crusaders in the Courts* (New York: Basic Books, 1994), p. 179.

42. "Digest of Discussion concerning the Ford Foundation Study," KBC Papers, Box 65, Folder 2 of 2: "Rearguments, 1st Social Science Answer to Question IV, December 1953, Drafts and Related Documents."

43. Gordon Allport to Kenneth B. Clark, August 4, 1953, Gordon W. Allport Papers, Box 23, Folder: "Ca–Cn, 1951–53," Harvard University Archives, Cambridge, Massachusetts.

44. Floyd Allport to Kenneth B. Clark, August 18, 1953, KBC Papers, Box 65, Folder: "Rearguments, 1st Social Science Answer to Question IV, Dec. 1953, Correspondence, 1953."

45. Daniel Wilner to Kenneth B. Clark, August 28, 1953, KBC Papers, Box 65, Folder: "Rearguments, 1st Social Science Answer to Question IV, Dec. 1953, Correspondence, 1953."

46. Isidor Chein to Kenneth B. Clark, August 5, 1953, KBC Papers, Box 65, Folder: "Rearguments, 1st Social Science Answer to Question IV, Dec. 1953, Correspondence, 1953."

47. Theodore Newcomb to Kenneth B. Clark, August 10, 1953, KBC Papers, Box 65, Folder: "Rearguments, 1st Social Science Answer to Question IV, Dec. 1953, Correspondence, 1953."

48. Kenneth B. Clark, "Desegregation: An Appraisal of the Evidence," *Journal of Social Issues* 9 (1953): 6.

49. Ibid., pp. 13–34.

50. Ibid., p. 54.

51. Greenberg, *Crusaders in the Courts*, pp. 188–89.

52. Kluger, *Simple Justice*, pp. 657–67.

53. Greenberg, *Crusaders in the Courts*, p. 193.

54. *Brown v. Topeka Board of Education*, 347 U.S. 483 (1954).

55. Greenberg, *Crusaders in the Courts*, p. 199.

56. Paul R. Kimmel, "SPSSI and *Brown v. Board of Education*," *SPSSI Newsletter*, no. 194 (July 1994): 16.

57. "Statement of the Meaning of the Supreme Court Decision," recorded at WNBC, May 28, 1954, KBC Papers, Box 194, Folder: "Statements and Testimony, 1949–51."

58. Ben Keppel, *The Work of Democracy* (Cambridge, MA: Harvard University Press, 1994), pp. 116–17.

59. David W. Southern, *Gunnar Myrdal and Black-White Relations* (Baton Rouge: Louisiana State University Press, 1987), pp. 155–224

60. *Saturday Evening Post* 226, June 19, 1954, p. 10.

61. Roy Wilkins to Kenneth B. Clark, June 17, 1954, KBC Papers, Box 61, Folder 3 of 6: "NAACP, General Correspondence, Jan.–June, 1954"; Kenneth B. Clark to Editor of the *Saturday Evening Post*, June 21, 1954, KBC Papers, Box 16, "General Correspondence, 1954, June."

62. "Jurisprudence," *New York University Law Review* 30 (January 1955): 157–58, 160.

63. Ibid., pp. 157–58.

64. Ibid., pp. 161–65.

65. Ibid., p. 166.

66. Will Maslow to Kenneth B. Clark, May 19, 1955, KBC Papers, Box 31, Folder: "American Jewish Congress, Correspondence, 1945–66, n.d."

67. M. Brewster Smith to Kenneth B. Clark, KBC Papers, Box 166, Folder 2 of 2: "Writings by Clark, Articles, 1955, Sept.–Oct."

68. "The Sense of Irrelevance," semi-final draft, KBC Papers, Box 166, Folder 2 of 2: "Writings by Clark, Articles, 1955, Sept.–Oct."

69. See, for example, Alexandra Pekelis to Kenneth B. Clark, February 26, 1946, KBC Papers, Folder: "Jewish-Negro Relations, Correspondence, 1945–46"; and handwritten notes discussing Clark and Chein's relationship with Pekelis, KBC Papers, Box 42, Folder: "Desegregation: Notes and Outlines, 1954–55, n.d."

70. "The Sense of Irrelevance, The Quest for Legal Certainty," pp. 16, 9, KBC Papers, Box 166, Folder 2 of 2: "Writings by Clark, Articles, 1955, Sept.–Oct."

71. Ibid., p. 12.

72. Ibid., p. 14.

73. Ibid., pp. 11–13.

74. Isidor Chein to Will Maslow, December 21, 1954, KBC Papers, Box 31, Folder: "American Jewish Congress, Correspondence, 1945–66, n.d."

75. Edmond Cahn, "Jurisprudence," *New York University Law Review* 31 (January 1956): 184–185.

NOTES TO CHAPTER 9

1. Harry S. Ashmore, *The Negro and the Schools* (Chapel Hill: University of North Carolina Press, 1954). Also see Harry S. Ashmore, *Civil Rights and Wrongs: A Memoir of Race and Politics, 1944–1994* (New York: Pantheon, 1994), pp. 98–112.

2. "Summary of Relevant Material from *The Negro and the Schools*," Kenneth B. Clark Papers, Box 65, Folder: "Reargument, 2nd Social Science Memoranda re Question IV, April 1955 for the Legal Division of the NAACP, 23 July 1954," Manuscript Division, Library of Congress, Washington, D.C. (hereafter KBC Papers).

3. Thurgood Marshall to Staff, September 27, 1954, KBC Papers, Box 61, Folder 4 of 6: "NAACP General Correspondence, July–December 1954."

4. Robert Carter to Legal Staff, KBC Papers, Box 65, Folder: "Reargument, 2nd Social Science Memoranda re Question IV, April 1955, Correspondence, 1954, n.d."

5. Kenneth B. Clark to Gordon Allport, June 28, 1954, Gordon W. Allport Papers, Box 23, Folder: "Ca–Cn, 1954–55," Harvard University Archives, Cambridge, Massachusetts (hereafter GWA Papers).

6. "Conference of Social Scientists for the Legal Division of the NAACP," Friday, June 23, 1954, Arnold M. Rose Papers, University of Minnesota Archives, Walter Library, Minneapolis, Minnesota (hereafter AMR Papers).

7. "Summary and Integration of Discussion and Conclusions of the July 23, 1954 Conference of Social Scientists," KBC Papers, Box 65, Folder: "Reargument, 2nd Social Science Memoranda re Question IV, April 1955, Conference of Social Scientists to the Legal Division of the NAACP, 23 July 1954."

8. Gordon Allport to Kenneth B. Clark, July 3, 1954, AMR Papers.

9. "Summary and Integration of Discussion and Conclusions."

10. Ibid., pp. 4, 5.

11. Ibid.

12. Allport to Clark, July 3, 1954, AMR Papers.

13. "Summary and Integration of Discussion and Conclusions," pp. 4, 5; and handwritten notes, KBC Papers, Box 65, Folder: "2nd Social Science Memoranda re Question IV, April 1955, Conference of Social Scientists for the Legal Division of NAACP, 23 July 1954."

14. Allport to Clark, July 3, 1954, AMR Papers.

15. "Summary and Integration of Discussion and Conclusions," pp. 9, 12.

16. Fragment from Theodore M. Newcomb, July 26, 1954, KBC Papers, Box

65, Folder: "Reargument 2nd Social Science Memoranda re Question IV, April 1955, Correspondence, 1954, n.d."

17. The text in quotation marks is taken from question 4 as worded by the Supreme Court. "Preliminary Draft: Social Science Memo Re: Question IV," p. 12, KBC Papers, Box 65, Folder: "Reargument, 2nd Social Science Memoranda re Question IV, April 1955, Correspondence, 1954, n.d."

18. Kenneth B. Clark to Gordon Allport, August 10, 1954, GWA Papers, Box 23, Folder: "Ca–Cn, 1954–57."

19. Kenneth Clark to Mamie Clark, August 9, 1954, KBC Papers, Box 65, Folder: "Reargument, 2nd Social Science Memoranda re Question IV, April 1955, Correspondence, 1954, n.d."

20. Robert Merton to Theodore Newcomb, August 25, 1954, Theodore M. Newcomb Papers, Box 5, Folder: "APA, General Correspondence, 1954," University of Michigan Archives, Bentley Historical Library, Ann Arbor, Michigan.

21. Gardner Murphy to Kenneth B. Clark, August 16, 1954, KBC Papers, Box 65, Folder: "Reargument, 2nd Social Science Memoranda re Question IV, April 1955, Correspondence, 1954, n.d."

22. Gordon Allport to Kenneth B. Clark, August 17, 1954, KBC Papers, Box 61, Folder: "NAACP General Correspondence, July–Dec. 1954."

23. Arnold Rose to Kenneth B. Clark, August 12, 1954, KBC Papers, Box 65, Folder: "Reargument, 2nd Social Science Memoranda re Question IV, April 1955, Correspondence, 1954, n.d."

24. Newcomb to Clark, August 13, 1954, KBC papers, Box 65, Folder: "Reargument 2nd Social Science Memoranda re Question IV, April 1955, Correspondence, 1954, n.d."

25. Kenneth B. Clark to Stuart W. Cook, August 9, 1954, Stuart W. Cook Papers, Box M2362, Folder 8: "Correspondence: *Brown v. Board of Education*," Archives for the History of American Psychology, Akron, Ohio (hereafter SWC Papers).

26. Various handwritten notes, SWC Papers, Box M2362, Folder 6.

27. Robert Carter memorandum, September 29, 1954, KBC Papers, Box 61, Folder: "NAACP General Correspondence, July–December 1954."

28. Richard Kluger, *Simple Justice: The History of* Brown v. Board of Education *and Black America's Struggle for Equality* (New York: Vintage, 1975), pp. 720–24.

29. Lewis M. Killian recounted his experiences in "Working for the Segregationist Establishment," *Journal of Applied Behavioral Science*, 25, 4 (1989): 487–98.

30. Bob Johnson to Thurgood Marshall et. al., October 8, 1954, KBC papers, Box 61, Folder 1 of 6: "NAACP General Correspondence, July–Dec., 1954."

31. "Memorandum re: Florida Amicus Brief in School Segregation Cases," KBC Papers, Box 66, Folder: "NAACP School Segregation Cases, States, Documents re Individuals, Florida (re Amicus Curie Brief) 1955, n.d."

32. Killian, "Working for the Segregationist Establishment," pp. 498, 492. Harry Ashmore reported a similar experience when he worked as a consultant with the state of Florida on the brief. See Ashmore, *Civil Rights and Wrongs*, p. 107.

33. John F. Galliher and James M. Galliher, *Marginality and Dissent in Twentieth-Century American Sociology* (Albany: State University of New York Press, 1995), p. 118.

34. Lewis Killian, "The Social Scientist's Role in the Preparation of the Florida Desegregation Brief," *Social Problems* 3 (1956): 211, 214, 212.

35. Killian, "Working for the Segregationist Establishment," p. 496.

36. "Second Draft, Social Science Memo Re Question IV," pp. 6, 7, KBC Papers, Box 65, Folder: "Reargument, 2nd Social Science Memoranda re Question IV, April 1955, Correspondence, 1954, n.d."

37. Ibid., pp. 6, 7.

38. Ibid., pp. 26, 27.

39. See memo from June Shagaloff to Thurgood Marshall, "Terse Summary of Footnotes re Social Science Materials," April 8, 1955, NAACP Papers, Box IIB–141, Folder: "Schools, Kansas, Topeka, *Brown v. Board of Education* (and other cases), 2nd Reargument, Background Materials, Medical and Psychological Reports, 1955 and undated," Manuscript Division, Library of Congress, Washington, D.C.

40. Mark V. Tushnet, *Making Civil Rights Law* (New York: Oxford University Press, 1994), pp. 218–19.

41. Ibid., pp. 314–15.

42. Leon Friedman, ed., *Argument: The Oral Argument before the Supreme Court in* Brown v. Board of Education of Topeka, *1952–1955* (New York: Chelsea House, 1969), pp. 525, 531.

43. *Brown v. Topeka Board of Education*, 349 U.S. 294 (1955).

NOTES TO CHAPTER 10

1. "Proposed Community Education Activity for Improved Inter-Race Relations," Kenneth B. Clark Papers, Box 61, Folder: "NAACP General Correspondence, 1953," 2 of 6, Manuscript Division, Library of Congress, Washington, D.C. (hereafter KBC Papers).

2. June Shagaloff, "A Study of Community Acceptance of Desegregation in Two Selected Areas," *Journal of Negro Education* 23, 3 (Summer 1954): 330–38.

3. "Proposed Community Education Activity."

4. John F. Galliher and James F. Galliher, *Marginality and Dissent in Twentieth-Century American Sociology: The Case of Elizabeth Briant Lee and Alfred McClung Lee* (Albany: State University of New York Press, 1995), pp. 97–109.

5. Alfred McClung Lee to Gordon Allport, April 30, 1954, Gordon W. Allport Papers, Box 31, Folder: "Lee, Alfred McClung," Harvard University Archives, Cambridge, Massachusetts (hereafter GWA Papers).

6. Gordon W. Allport to Alfred McClung Lee, May 4, 1954, GWA Papers, Box 31, Folder: "Lee, Alfred McClung."

7. Alfred McClung Lee to Gordon W. Allport, May 18, 1954, GWA Papers, Box 31, Folder: "Lee, Alfred McClung."

8. "Proposed Community Action Research in Harmonious Desegregation," Robert Redfield Papers, Box 23, Folder 4, University of Chicago Archives, Regenstein Library, Chicago, Illinois (hereafter RR Papers).

9. Robert Redfield to Alfred McClung Lee, May 5, 1954, RR Papers, Box 23, Folder 4.

10. Alfred McClung Lee to Robert Redfield, May 18, 1954, RR Papers, Box 23, Folder 4.

11. Alfred McClung Lee to Gordon W. Allport, June 7, 1954, GWA Papers, Box 31, Folder: "Lee, Alfred McClung"

12. On NAACP-LDEF finances, see Jack Greenberg, *Crusaders in the Courts* (New York: Basic Books; 1994), pp. 152–55.

13. Ibid., p. 201.

14. Anna Frank to Thurgood Marshall, memorandum on "The Work of the Committee of Social Science Consultants," KBC Papers, Box 61, Folder: "NAACP General Correspondence, July–December 1954," 4 of 6.

15. "Proposed Community Action Research to Further Harmonious Desegregation," GWA Papers, Box 31, Folder: "Lee, Alfred McClung."

16. Robert Redfield to Alfred McClung Lee, August 13, 1954, and Alfred McClung Lee to Robert Redfield, August 19, 1954, RR Papers, Box 20, Folder 12.

17. Alfred McClung Lee, *Fraternities without Brotherhood: A Study of Prejudice on the American Campus* (Boston: Beacon Press, 1955).

18. Memorandum: "A Proposed Coordinating Center to Make Available Existing Research on Racial Integration in the Schools," KBC Papers, Box 61, Folder: "Committee of 100, 1954–56."

19. Anna Capks Frank to Thurgood Marshall, memorandum on "The Work of the Committee of Social Science Consultants," KBC Papers, Box 61, Folder: "NAACP General Correspondence, July–December 1954," 4 of 6.

20. Walter A. Jackson, *Gunnar Myrdal and America's Conscience* (Chapel Hill: University of North Carolina Press, 1990), pp. 264–67.

21. Stuart Cook to Emily Kimball, March 7, 1957, Stuart W. Cook Papers, Box M2328, Folder 4: "Desegregation Correspondence," Archives for the History of American Psychology, Akron, Ohio.

22. Frank to Marshall, memorandum on "The Work of the Committee of Social Science Consultants."

23. Ibid.

24. Press release, "Social Science Consultants to Aid Desegregation Programs," KBC Papers, Box 62, Folder, "NAACP General Correspondence, 1955–1958," 5 of 6.

25. For example, CSSC met at the Fourth Annual Joint Conference of SSSP, March 2, 1956; see Alfred McClung Lee to Gordon W. Allport, January 9, 1956, GWA Papers, Box 31, Folder: "La–Ln 1954–57"; Alfred McClung Lee to Kenneth B. Clark, February 3, 1956, KBC Papers, Box 61, Folder: "Committee of Social Science Consultants, NAACP Legal Defense and Education Fund, 1955–56, n.d."

26. "Purpose and Functions of the Committee and Coordinator" December 28, 1955, Theodore M. Newcomb Papers, Box 5, Folder: "APA General Correspondence, 1955," University of Michigan Archives, Bentley Historical Library, Ann Arbor, Michigan.

27. Alfred McClung Lee to Gordon W. Allport, December 30, 1955, GWA Papers, Box 31, Folder: "La–Ln 1954–57."

28. Thurgood Marshall to Kenneth B. Clark, April 26, 1957, KBC Papers, Box 61, Folder: "Committee of Social Science Consultants, NAACP Legal Defense and Education Fund, 1955–57, n.d."

29. Kenneth B. Clark to Thurgood Marshall, memorandum regarding "Meeting of Small Group of Social Scientists Who Have Worked with the NAACP in the Past," June 3, 1957, KBC Papers, Box 61, Folder: "Committee of Social Science Consultants, NAACP Legal Defense and Education Fund, 1955–57, n.d."

30. M. Brewster Smith to Oliver Hill and Spottswood Robinson, April 3, 1952, M. Brewster Smith Papers, Box M605, Folder: "NAACP," Archives for the History of American Psychology, Akron, Ohio.

31. Kenneth B. Clark to Bernard Kutner, September 1953, KBC Papers, Box 16, Folder: "General Correspondence, 1953, July–September."

32. Kenneth B. Clark to Bigham Dai, May 13, 1954, KBC Papers, Box 97, Folder: "Society for the Psychological Study of Social Issues, *Journal of Social Issues*, Comment on 'Desegregation' Issue, 1954."

33. Kenneth B. Clark to B. M. Hindman, June 16, 1954, Box 97, Folder: "Society for the Psychological Study of Social Issues, *Journal of Social Issues*, Comment on 'Desegregation' Issue, 1954."

34. Kenneth B. Clark, *Prejudice and Your Child* (Boston: Beacon Press, 1955).

35. Press release, KBC Papers, Box 33, Folder: "Beacon Press, Boston, Mass., Correspondence, 1955–69, n.d."

36. Ben Keppel, *The Work of Democracy* (Cambridge, MA: Harvard University Press, 1995), p. 125.

37. Ernest van den Haag, *Education as an Industry* (New York: Augustus M. Kelley, 1956), pp. 147, 148, 151.

38. Ralph Ross and Ernest van den Haag, *The Fabric of Society* (New York: Harcourt, Brace and Company, 1957), pp. 165–66.

39. Kenneth B. Clark to Alfred McClung Lee, March 16, 1955, KBC Papers, Box 17, Folder: "General Correspondence, March 1955."

40. Kenneth B. Clark, "The Desegregation Cases: Criticism of the Social Scientist's Role," *Villanova Law Review* 5 (1960): 224–247.

41. Ernest van den Haag, "Social Science Testimony in the Desegregation Cases: A Reply to Professor Kenneth Clark," *Villanova Law Review* 6 (1960): 69–79.

42. William H. Tucker, *The Science and Politics of Racial Research* (Urbana: University of Illinois Press, 1994), pp. 151–52, 167, 182, 211–13, 252. On Van den Haag's testimony in defense of segregation, see John P. Jackson Jr., "The Triumph of the Segregationists? A Historiographical Inquiry into Psychology and the *Brown* Litigation," *History of Psychology* 3 (2000): 239–61.

43. Kenneth B. Clark, *Dark Ghetto: Dilemmas of Social Power* (New York: Harper and Row, 1965). On Clark's activities in the 1960s, see Keppel, *Work of Democracy*, pp. 133–75. On Kenneth and Mamie's work at Northside, see Gerald Markowitz and David Rosner, *Children, Race, and Power: Kenneth and Mamie Clark's Northside Center* (Charlottesville: University Press of Virginia, 1996).

44. Mary Harrington Hall, "A Conversation with Kenneth B. Clark," *Psychology Today* 2 (June 1968): 21.

45. Kenneth B. Clark, "Racial Progress and Retreat: A Personal Memoir," in *Race in America: The Struggle for Equality*, ed. Herbert Hill and James E. Jones Jr. (Madison: University of Wisconsin Press, 1993), p. 18.

NOTES TO CHAPTER 11

1. Michael J. Klarman, "How *Brown* Changed Race Relations: The Backlash Thesis," *Journal of American History* 81 (1994): 81–118; Michael J. Klarman, "*Brown*, Racial Change, and the Civil Rights Movement," *Virginia Law Review* 80 (1994): 7–150; Gerald Rosenberg, *Hollow Hope: Can Courts Bring about Social Change?* (Chicago: University of Chicago Press, 1991).

2. Isidor Chein, "*Brown vs. Bakke*," paper presented at the Eighty-seventh Annual Convention of the American Psychological Association, September 1979, Stuart W. Cook Papers, Box M2363, Folder 12, Archives for the History of American Psychology, Akron, Ohio. Also see Stuart Cook's defenses of social scientists' actions in *Brown:* "The 1954 Social Science Statement and School Desegregation: A Reply to Gerard," in *Eliminating Racism: Profiles in Controversy*, ed. Phyllis A. Katz and Dalmas A. Taylor (New York: Plenum Press, 1988): 237–56; "Experimenting on Social Issues: The Case of School Desegregation," *American Psychologist* 40 (1985): 452–60; "Social Science and School Desegregation: Did We Mislead the Supreme Court?" *Personality and Social Psychology Bulletin* 5 (1979): 420–37.

3. Frederic Wertham, "Nine Men Speak to You," *The Nation* 178, June 12, 1954, p. 498.

4. Hadley Arkes, "The Problem of Kenneth Clark," *Commentary* 58 (November 1974): 37–46.

5. Walter G. Stephan, "School Desegregation: An Evaluation of the Predictions Made in *Brown v. Board of Education*, *Psychological Bulletin* 85, 2 (March 1978): 217–38. H. B. Gerard, "School Desegregation: The Social Science Role," *American Psychologist* 39 (1983): 869–77.

6. In his response to van den Haag, Clark noted that van den Haag made the same mistake about the drawings that Cahn did. Van den Haag merely claimed in turn that the mistake was irrelevant to his argument. In fact, what the mistake might demonstrate is that van den Haag did not read Clark's testimony in the *Briggs* trial but merely read Cahn, whose argument van den Haag then repeated.

7. For example, see William M. Banks, *Black Intellectuals: Race and Responsibility in American Life* (New York: Norton, 1996), p. 146.

8. Kenneth B. Clark, "Desegregation: The Role of the Social Sciences," *Teachers College Record* 62 (1960): 2.

9. "A Blasphemous Use of the Name of John Dewey," John Dewey Memorial Lecture, Chicago, Illinois, February 26, 1971, Kenneth B. Clark Papers, Box 160, Folder: "Speeches by Clark, 1971, Jan.–Aug.," Manuscript Division, Library of Congress, Washington, D.C.

10. Clark never identified the study in question, but in all likelihood it was Howard Hale Long's 1935 article on "Some Psychogenic Hazards of Segregated Education," which had been a mainstay of NAACP-LDEF briefs since 1946. It never appeared in any brief after Clark was brought on board in 1951.

Bibliography

MANUSCRIPT SOURCES CITED

American Jewish Historical Society, Waltham, Massachusetts
American Jewish Congress Papers

Archives for the History of American Psychology, Akron, Ohio
Stuart W. Cook Papers
David Krech Papers
Kurt Lewin Papers
Alfred J. Marrow Papers
M. Brewster Smith Papers
Society for the Psychological Study of Social Issues Papers

Harvard University Archives, Cambridge, Massachusetts
Gordon W. Allport Papers

Manuscript Division, Library of Congress, Washington, D.C.
Kenneth B. Clark Papers
NAACP—National Association for the Advancement of Colored People Papers

Tarleton Law Library, University of Texas, Austin, Texas
Tom C. Clark Papers

University of Chicago Archives, Regenstein Library, Chicago, Illinois
Robert Redfield Papers
Louis Wirth Papers

University of Michigan Archives, Bentley Historical Library, Ann Arbor, Michigan
Resnis Likert Papers
Theodore M. Newcomb Papers

University of Minnesota Archives, Walter Library, Minneapolis, Minnesota
Arnold M. Rose Papers

COURT CASES CITED

Belton v. Gebhart, 87 A. 2d 862 (1952).
Briggs v. Elliott, 98 F. Supp. 529 (1951).
Brown v. Topeka Board of Education, 98 F. Supp. 797 (1951).
Brown v. Topeka Board of Education, 347 U.S. 483 (1954).
Brown v. Topeka Board of Education, 349 U.S. 294 (1955).
Davis et al. v. County School Board of Prince Edward County, 103 F. Supp. 337 (1952).
Fisher v. Hurst, 333 U.S. 147 (1948).
Gong Lum v. Rice, 275 U.S. 78 (1927).
McLaurin v. Board of Regents, University of Oklahoma, 87 F. Supp. 528 (1948).
McLaurin v. Oklahoma State Regents for Higher Education, 339 U.S. 637 (1950).
Missouri ex rel. Gaines v. Canada, 305 U.S. 337 (1938).
Plessy v. Ferguson, 163 U.S. 537 (1896).
Sipuel v. Oklahoma State Regents, 332 U.S. 631 (1948).
Sweatt v. Painter, 210 S.W. 2d 442 (1947).
Sweatt v. Painter, 339 U.S. 629 (1950).
Westminster School District of Orange County v. Mendez, 161 F. 2d 774 (1947).

PUBLISHED WORKS CITED

Unauthored Articles

"Award for Distinguished Contributions to the International Advancement of Psychology: Otto Klineberg." *American Psychologist* 47 (1992): 860–61.
"Awards for Distinguished Contributions to Psychology in the Public Interest: 1980." *American Psychologist* 36 (1981): 67–70.
"The Effects of Segregation and Consequences of Desegregation: A Social Science Statement." *Minnesota Law Review* 37 (May 1953): 427–38.
"Grade School Segregation: The Latest Attack on Racial Discrimination." *Yale Law Journal* 61, 5 (May 1952): 730–44.
"Private Attorneys-General: Group Action in the Fight for Civil Liberties." *Yale Law Journal* 58 (1949): 574–98.

Authored Works

Adorno, T., W. Else Frenkel-Brunswik, Daniel Levinson, and R. Nevitt Sanford. *The Authoritarian Personality*. New York: Harper and Row, 1950.
Aichele, Gary J. *Legal Realism and Twentieth Century American Jurisprudence: The Changing Consensus*. New York: Garland Publishing Company, 1990.
Allport, Floyd H. *Social Psychology*. Boston: Houghton Mifflin, 1924.
Allport, Gordon W. *ABC's of Scapegoating*. Rev. ed. New York: Anti-Defamation League of B'nai B'rith, 1948.

Allport, Gordon W. "The Nature of Democratic Morale." In *Civilian Morale: Second Yearbook of the Society for the Psychological Study of Social Issues*, edited by Goodwin Watson, p. 9. Boston: Houghton Mifflin Company, 1942.

———. *The Nature of Prejudice*. Reading, MA: Addison Wesley, 1954.

———. *The Person in Psychology: Selected Essays by Gordon W. Allport*. Boston: Beacon Press, 1968.

———. *Personality: A Psychological Interpretation*. New York: Henry Holt, 1937.

———. "Preface." In *Anti-Semitism: A Social Disease*, edited by Ernst Simmel, pp. vii–xii. New York: International Universities Press, 1946.

———. *The Resolution of Intergroup Tensions: A Critical Appraisal of Methods*. New York: National Conference of Christians and Jews, 1952.

American Jewish Committee. *Conference on Research in the Field of Anti-Semitism: Summary of Proceedings and Suggestions for a Program*. New York: American Jewish Committee, March 1945.

Amir, Yehuda. "Contact Hypothesis in Ethnic Relations." *Psychological Bulletin* 71 (May 1969): 320–37.

"Appendix to Brief for Appellants: The Effects of Segregation and the Consequences of Desegregation—A Social Science Statement." In *Landmark Briefs and Arguments of the Supreme Court of the United States: Constitutional Law*, edited by Philip B. Kurland and Gerhard Casper, pp. 43–61. Arlington, VA: University Publications of America, 1975.

Arkes, Hadley. "The Problem of Kenneth Clark." *Commentary* 58 (November 1974): 37–46.

Ash, Mitchell G. "Cultural Contexts and Scientific Change in Psychology: Kurt Lewin in Iowa." *American Psychologist* 47 (1992): 198–207.

———. "Émigré Psychologists after 1933: The Cultural Coding of Scientific and Professional Practices." In *Forced Migration and Scientific Change: Émigré German-Speaking Scientists and Scholars after 1933*, edited by Mitchell G. Ash and Alfons Söllner, pp. 117–38. Cambridge: Cambridge University Press, 1996.

———. "Historicizing Mind Science: Discourse, Practice, Subjectivity." *Science in Context* 5 (1992): 193–207.

Ash, Mitchell G., and Alfons Söllner. "Introduction: Forced Migration and Scientific Change after 1933." In *Forced Migration and Scientific Change: Émigré German-Speaking Scientists and Scholars after 1933*, edited by Mitchell G. Ash and Alfons Söllner, pp. 1–19. Cambridge: Cambridge University Press, 1996.

Ashmore, Harry S. *Civil Rights and Wrongs: A Memoir of Race and Politics 1944–1994*. New York: Pantheon, 1994.

———. *The Negro and the Schools*. Chapel Hill: University of North Carolina Press, 1954.

Baker, Lee D. *From Savage to Negro: Anthropology and the Construction of Race, 1896–1954*. Berkeley: University of California Press, 1998.

Banks, William M. *Black Intellectuals: Race and Responsibility in American Life.* New York: Norton, 1996.

Barkan, Elazar. *The Retreat of Scientific Racism: Changing Concepts of Race in Britain and the United States between the World Wars.* Cambridge: Cambridge University Press, 1992.

Bellow, Barbara, Milton L. Blum, Kenneth B. Clark, Margot Haas, Edward Haydon, Russell Hogrefe, Jane Holzberg, Philip Katch, Lillian Wald Kay, Regina Loewenstein, Mary MacDuff, and Iliana Schreiber. "Prejudice in Seaside: A Report of an Action-Research Project." *Human Relations* 1, 1 (1947): 98–120.

Benjamin, Gerald. *Race Relations and the New York City Commission on Human Rights.* Ithaca: Cornell University Press, 1974.

Berson, Lenora E. *The Negroes and the Jews.* New York: Random House, 1971.

Bogardus, Emory S. "Measuring Social Distances." *Journal of Applied Sociology* 9 (1925): 299–308.

———. "Social Distance and Its Origins." *Journal of Applied Sociology* 9 (1925): 216–26.

Brown, JoAnne. *The Definition of a Profession: The Authority of Metaphor in the History of Intelligence Testing, 1890–1930.* Princeton: Princeton University Press, 1992.

Bulmer, Martin. "Apotheosis of Liberalism? *An American Dilemma* after Fifty Years in the Context of the Lives of Gunnar and Alva Myrdal." *Ethnic and Racial Studies* 16 (April 1993): 345–57.

Cahn, Edmond. "Jurisprudence." *New York University Law Review* 30 (January 1955): 150–69.

———. "Jurisprudence." *New York University Law Review* 31 (January 1956): 182–95.

Capshew, James H. "Networks of Leadership: A Quantitative Study of SPSSI Presidents, 1936–1986." *Journal of Social Issues* 42 (1986): 75–106.

———. *Psychology on the March: Science, Practice, and Professional Identity in America, 1929–1969.* Cambridge: Cambridge University Press, 1999.

Chein, Isidor. "Some Considerations in Combating Intergroup Prejudice." *Journal of Educational Sociology* 19 (1946): 412–19.

———. "What Are the Psychological Effects of Segregation Under Conditions of Equal Facilities?" *International Journal of Opinion and Attitude Research* 3 (Summer 1949): 229–34.

Cherry, Frances. "The Nature of *The Nature of Prejudice*." *Journal of the History of the Behavioral Sciences* 36 (2000): 489–98.

Cherry, Frances, and Catherine Borshuk. "Social Action Research and the Commission on Community Interrelations." *Journal of Social Issues* 54 (1998): 119–42.

Clark, Kenneth B. "Candor about Negro-Jewish Relations." *Commentary* 1 (February 1946): 8–14.

Clark, Kenneth B. *Dark Ghetto: Dilemmas of Social Power.* New York: Harper and Row, 1965.

———. "Desegregation: An Appraisal of the Evidence." *Journal of Social Issues* 9 (1953): 1–77.

———. "The Desegregation Cases: Criticism of the Social Scientist's Role." *Villanova Law Review* 5 (1960): 224–247.

———. "Desegregation: The Role of the Social Sciences." *Teachers College Record* 62 (1960): 1–17.

———. "Morale among Negroes." In *Civilian Morale: Second Yearbook of the Society for the Psychological Study of Social Issues,* edited by Goodwin Watson, pp. 228–48. Boston: Houghton Mifflin Company, 1942.

———. "Morale of the Negro on the Home Front: World Wars I and II." *Journal of Negro Education* 12 (Summer 1943): 417–28.

———. "Race, Sex, and Democratic Living." In *Human Nature and Enduring Peace: Third Yearbook of the Society for the Psychological Study of Social Issues,* edited by Gardner Murphy. Boston: Houghton Mifflin Company, 1945.

———. "Racial Progress and Retreat: A Personal Memoir." In *Race in America: The Struggle for Equality,* edited by Herbert Hill and James E. Jones Jr. 3–18 Madison: University of Wisconsin Press, 1993.

———. "The Social Scientist As an Expert Witness in Civil Rights Litigation." *Social Problems* 1 (1953): 5–9.

Clark, Kenneth B., and James Barker. "The Zoot Effect in Personality: A Race Riot Participant." *Journal of Abnormal and Social Psychology* 40 (1945): 143–47.

Clark, Kenneth B., and Mamie P. Clark. "The Development of Consciousness of Self and the Emergence of Racial Identification in Negro Preschool Children." *Journal of Social Psychology* 10 (1939): 591–99.

———. "Emotional Factors in Racial Identification and Preference in Negro Children." *Journal of Negro Education* 19, 3 (Summer 1950): 341–50.

———. "Racial Identification and Preferences in Negro Children." In *Readings in Social Psychology,* edited by Theodore M. Newcomb and Eugene L. Hartley. New York: Henry Holt and Company, 1947. 2d ed., 1952.

———. "Segregation as a Factor in the Racial Identification of Negro Preschool Children: A Preliminary Report." *Journal of Experimental Education* 8, 2 (December 1939): 161–65.

———. "Skin Color as a Factor in Racial Identification of Negro Preschool Children." *Journal of Social Psychology* 11 (1940): 159–69.

Clark, Mamie Phipps. "Mamie Phipps Clark." In *Models of Achievement: Reflections of Eminent Women in Psychology,* edited by Agnes N. O'Connell and Nancy Felipe Russo, pp. 267–76. New York: Columbia University Press, 1983.

Converse, Jean M. *Survey Research in the United States: Roots and Emergence, 1890–1960.* Berkeley: University of California Press, 1987.

Cook, Stuart W. "Experimenting on Social Issues: The Case of School Desegregation." *American Psychologist* 40 (1985): 452–60.

———. "The 1954 Social Science Statement and School Desegregation: A Reply to Gerard." In *Eliminating Racism: Profiles in Controversy*, edited by Phyllis A. Katz and Dalmas A. Taylor, pp. 237–56. New York: Plenum Press, 1988.

———. "Social Science and School Desegregation: Did We Mislead the Supreme Court?" *Personality and Social Psychology Bulletin* 5 (1979): 420–37.

Cravens, Hamilton. "History of the Social Sciences." In *Historical Writing on American Science: Perspectives and Prospects*, edited by Sally Gregory Kohlstedt and Margaret W. Rossiter. 183–207 Baltimore: Johns Hopkins University Press, 1986.

———. *The Triumph of Evolution: The Heredity-Environment Controversy, 1900–1941.* 1978. Reprint, Baltimore: Johns Hopkins University Press, 1988.

Cross, George Lynn. *Blacks in White Colleges: Oklahoma's Landmark Cases.* Norman: University of Oklahoma Press, 1975.

Cross, William E. *Shades of Black: Diversity in African-American Identity.* Philadelphia: Temple University Press, 1991.

Cruse, Harold. *Plural but Equal: A Critical Study of Blacks and Minorities and America's Plural Society.* New York: William Morrow, 1987.

Dalfiume, Richard M. "The 'Forgotten Years' of the Negro Revolution." *Journal of American History* 55 (1968): 90–106.

Daniel, Walter G., and John B. Holden. *Ambrose Caliver: Adult Educator and Civil Servant.* Washington, DC: Adult Education Association of the USA, 1966.

Danziger, Kurt. *Constructing the Subject: Historical Origins of Psychological Research.* Cambridge and New York: Cambridge University Press, 1990.

———. "Making Social Psychology Experimental: A Conceptual History, 1920–1970." *Journal of the History of the Behavioral Sciences* 36 (2000): 329–47.

Davis, Allison, and John Dollard. *Children of Bondage: The Personality Development of Negro Youth in the Urban South.* Washington, DC: American Council on Education, 1940.

deCarvalho, Roy J. "Gordon W. Allport on the Nature of Prejudice." *Psychological Reports* 72 (1993): 299–308.

Degler, Carl N. *In Search of Human Nature: The Decline and Revival of Darwinism in American Social Thought.* New York: Oxford University Press, 1991.

Deutsch, Morton, and Mary Evans Collins. "Intergroup Relations in Interracial Public Housing: Occupancy Patterns and Racial Attitudes." *Journal of Housing* 7 (April 1950): 127–29.

———. *Interracial Housing: A Psychological Evaluation of a Social Experiment.* Minneapolis: University of Minnesota Press, 1951.

Deutscher, Max, and Isidor Chein. "The Psychological Effects of Enforced Segregation: A Survey of Social Science Opinion." *Journal of Psychology* 26 (1948): 259–87.

Diner, Hasia R. *In the Almost Promised Land: American Jews and Blacks, 1915–1935.* Westport, CT: Greenwood Press, 1977.

Dinnerstein, Leonard. *Antisemitism in America.* New York: Oxford University Press, 1994.

Eisenberg, Philip. "Current Research in Social Psychology." *Psychologist's League Journal* 2, 5 (November–December 1938): 87–90, 98.

Fairchild, Halford H., and Patricia Gurin. "Traditions in the Social-Psychological Analysis of Race Relations." *American Behavioral Scientist* 21 (1978): 757–78.

Feingold, Henry L. *A Time for Searching: Entering the Mainstream, 1920–1945.* Baltimore: Johns Hopkins University Press, 1992.

Fermi, Laura. *Illustrious Immigrants: The Intellectual Migration from Europe, 1930–41.* 2d ed. Chicago: University of Chicago Press, 1971.

Finison, Lorenz J. "An Aspect of the Early History of the Society for the Psychological Study of Social Issues: Psychologists and Labor." *Journal of the History of Behavioral Sciences* 15 (1979): 29–37.

———. "Unemployment, Politics, and the History of Organized Psychology." *American Psychologist* 31 (November 1976): 747–55.

———. "Unemployment, Politics, and the History of Organized Psychology II: The Psychologists League, the WPA, and the National Health Program." *American Psychologist* 33 (1978): 471–77.

Finkle, Lee. "The Conservative Aims of Militant Rhetoric: Black Protest during World War II." *Journal of American History* 60 (1973): 692–713.

Franklin, John Hope. "On the Evolution of Scholarship in Afro-American History." In *The State of Afro-American History*, edited by Darlene Clark Hine, pp. 13–22. Baton Rouge: Louisiana State University Press, 1986.

Franklin, Vincent P. "Black Social Scientists and the Mental Testing Movement, 1920–1940." In *Black Psychology*, edited by Reginald L. Jones, pp. 201–15. 2d ed. New York: Harper and Row, 1980.

Frazier, E. Franklin. *The Negro Family in the United States.* 1939 Reprint. New York: Dryden Press, 1948.

———. *The Negro in the United States.* New York: Macmillan Co., 1949.

———. *Negro Youth at the Crossways: Their Personality Development in the Middle States.* Washington, DC: American Council on Education, 1940.

———. "The Pathology of Race Prejudice." *Forum* 77 (June 1927): 856–62.

Frenkel-Brunswik, Else, and R. Nevitt Sanford. "Some Personality Factors in Anti-Semitism." *Journal of Psychology* 20 (1945): 271–91.

Frenkel-Brunswik, Else, Daniel J. Levinson, and R. Nevitt Sanford. "The Antidemocratic Personality." In *Readings in Social Psychology*, edited by Theodore Newcomb and Eugene L. Hartley. New York: Henry Holt and Company, 1947.

Friedman, Leon, ed. *Argument: The Oral Argument before the Supreme Court in Brown v. Board of Education of Topeka, 1952–1955.* New York: Chelsea House, 1969.

Friedman, Murray. *What Went Wrong? The Creation and Collapse of the Black-Jewish Alliance.* New York: Free Press, 1995.

Frommer, Morris. "The American Jewish Congress: A History, 1914–1950." Ph.D. diss., Ohio State University, 1978.

Furner, Mary O. *Advocacy and Objectivity: A Crisis in the Professionalization of American Social Science, 1865–1905.* Lexington: University of Kentucky Press, 1975.

Galliher, John F., and James M. Galliher. *Marginality and Dissent in Twentieth-Century American Sociology: The Case of Elizabeth Briant Lee and Alfred Mc-Clung Lee.* Albany: State University of New York Press, 1995.

Garth, Thomas R. *Race Psychology: A Study of Racial Mental Differences.* New York: McGraw-Hill, 1931.

———. "A Review of Racial Psychology." *Psychological Bulletin* 22 (1925): 343–64.

Gerard, Harold B. "School Desegregation: The Social Science Role." *American Psychologist* 38 (1983): 869–77.

Giles, H. H. "The Status and Programs of Private Intergroup Relations Agencies." *Journal of Negro Education* 20 (1951): 408–24.

Gilkerson, John S. "Domestication of 'Culture' in Interwar America." In *The Estate of Social Knowledge*, edited by JoAnne Brown and David K. van Keuren, pp. 153–74. Baltimore: Johns Hopkins University Press, 1991.

Gilman, Sander. *Jewish Self-Hatred: Anti-Semitism and the Hidden Language of the Jews.* Baltimore: Johns Hopkins University Press, 1986.

Glass, Bentley. "Geneticists Embattled: Their Stand against Rampant Eugenics and Racism in America during the 1920s and 1930s." *Proceedings of the American Philosophical Society* 130 (1986): 130–54.

Gleason, Philip. "Americans All: World War II and the Shaping of American Identity." *Review of Politics* 43 (October 1981): 483–518.

———. *Speaking of Diversity: Language and Ethnicity in Twentieth Century America.* Baltimore: Johns Hopkins University Press, 1992.

Goebel, Julius. *History of the School of Law, Columbia University.* New York: Columbia University Press, 1955.

Goldberg, Steven. *Culture Clash: Law and Science in America.* New York: New York University Press, 1994.

Graebner, William. "Confronting the Democratic Paradox: The Ambivalent Vision of Kurt Lewin." *Journal of Social Issues* 43, 3 (1987): 141–46.

———. "The Small Group and Democratic Social Engineering, 1900–1950." *Journal of Social Issues* 42 (1986): 137–54.

Greenberg, Jack. *Crusaders in the Courts: How a Dedicated Band of Lawyers Fought for the Civil Rights Revolution.* New York: Basic Books, 1994.

Guthrie, Robert V. *Even the Rat Was White: A Historical View of Psychology.* New York: Harper and Row, 1976.

Hall, Mary Harrington. "A Conversation with Kenneth B. Clark." *Psychology Today* 2 (June 1968): 19–25.

Handler, Richard. "Boasian Anthropology and the Critique of American Culture." *American Quarterly* 42 (1990): 252–73.

Harding, J., and R. Hogrefe. "Attitudes of White Department Store Employees toward Negro Coworkers." *Journal of Social Issues* 8 (1952): 18–28.

Hartmann, George, and Theodore M. Newcomb, eds. *Industrial Conflict.* New York: Cordon, 1939.

Hentoff, Nat. "The Integrationist." *New Yorker* 58, 23 August 1982, pp. 37–73.

Herman, Ellen. *The Romance of American Psychology: Political Culture in the Age of Experts.* Berkeley: University of California Press, 1995.

Herskovits, Melville J. *Franz Boas: The Science of Man in the Making.* New York: Charles Scribner's Sons, 1953.

———. *The Myth of the Negro Past.* New York: Harper and Brothers, 1941.

Hilgard, Ernest R. "From the Social Gospel to the Psychology of Social Issues: A Reminiscence." *Journal of Social Issues* 42, 1 (1986): 107–10.

———. *Psychology in America: A Historical Survey.* San Diego: Harcourt, Brace, Jovanovich, 1987.

Hollinger, David. *Postethnic America: Beyond Multiculturalism.* New York: Basic Books, 1995.

Horowitz, Eugene L. "The Development of Attitude toward the Negro." *Archives of Psychology* 28, 194 (January 1936): 1–45.

Horowitz, Eugene L., and Ruth E. Horowitz. "Development of Social Attitudes in Children." *Sociometry* 1 (1938): 301–38.

Horowitz, Morton J. *The Transformation of American Law, 1870–1960: The Crisis of Legal Orthodoxy.* New York: Oxford University Press, 1992.

Horowitz, Ruth. "Racial Aspects of Self-Identification in Nursery School Children." *Journal of Psychology* 7 (1939): 91–99.

Horowitz, Ruth, and Lois Barclay Murphy. "Projective Methods in the Psychological Study of Children." *Journal of Experimental Education* 7, 2 (December 1938): 133–40.

Hyatt, Marshall. *Franz Boas, Social Activist: The Dynamics of Ethnicity.* New York: Greenwood Press, 1990.

Institute for Social Research. "Research Project on Anti-Semitism." *Studies in Philosophy and Social Science* 9 (1941): 124–43.

Jackson, John P., Jr. "The Triumph of the Segregationists? A Historiographical Inquiry into Psychology and the *Brown* Litigation." *History of Psychology* 3 (2000): 239–61.

Jackson, Walter A. *Gunnar Myrdal and America's Conscience: Social Engineering and Racial Liberalism, 1938–1987.* Chapel Hill: University of North Carolina Press, 1990.

Jay, Martin. *The Dialectical Imagination: A History of the Frankfurt School and the*

Institute of Social Research, 1923–1950. Boston: Little, Brown and Company, 1973.

———. *Permanent Exiles: Essays on the Intellectual Migration from Germany to America*. New York: Columbia University Press, 1985.

Johnson, Charles S. *Growing Up in the Black Belt: Negro Youth in the Rural South*. Washington, DC: American Council on Education, 1941. Reprint. New York: Schocken Books, 1967.

———. *Patterns of Negro Segregation*. New York: Harper and Brothers, 1943.

Johnson, John W. *American Legal Culture, 1908–1940*. Westport, CT: Greenwood Press, 1981.

Jorgensen, Carl. "The African American Critique of White Supremacist Science." *Journal of Negro Education* 64 (1995): 232–42.

Katz, Daniel, and Floyd H. Allport. *Students' Attitudes: A Report of the Syracuse University Reaction Study*. Syracuse: Craftsman Press, 1931.

Katz, Daniel, and Kenneth Braly. "Racial Prejudice and Racial Stereotypes." *Journal of Abnormal and Social Psychology* 30, 2 (July–September 1935): 175–93.

———. "Racial Stereotypes of One Hundred College Students." *Journal of Abnormal and Social Psychology* 28, 3 (October–December 1933): 280–90.

Kelley, Robin D. G. "'We Are Not What We Seem': Rethinking Black Working-Class Opposition in the Jim Crow South." *Journal of American History* 80 (1993): 75–112.

Kellogg, Peter J. "Civil Rights Consciousness in the 1940s." *The Historian* 42 (1979): 18–41.

Kendler, Tracy S. "Contributions of the Psychologist to Constitutional Law." *American Psychologist* 5 (1950): 505–10.

Kennedy, Shawn G. "Stuart W. Cook, 79, Psychologist Who Revealed Effects of Racism." *New York Times*, March 29 1993, sec. B, p. 11.

Keppel, Ben. *The Work of Democracy: Ralph Bunche, Kenneth B. Clark, Lorraine Hansberry, and the Cultural Politics of Race*. Cambridge, MA: Harvard University Press, 1995.

Kerr, Katherine. "Race and the Making of American Liberalism, 1912–1965." Ph.D. diss., Johns Hopkins University, 1995.

Killian, Lewis M. "The Social Scientist's Role in the Preparation of the Florida Desegregation Brief." *Social Problems* 3 (1956): 211–14.

———. "Working for the Segregationist Establishment." *Journal of Applied Behavioral Science* 25, 4 (1989): 487–98.

Kimmel, Paul R. "SPSSI and *Brown v. Board of Education*." *SPSSI Newsletter*, no. 194 (July 1994): 5, 16.

Klarman, Michael J. "*Brown*, Racial Change, and the Civil Rights Movement." *Virginia Law Review* 80 (1994): 7–150.

———. "How *Brown* Changed Race Relations: The Backlash Thesis." *Journal of American History* 81 (1994): 81–118.

Klineberg, Otto. "An Experimental Study of Speed and Other Factors in 'Racial' Differences." *Archives of Psychology* 15, 93 (1928): 1–107.

———. "Morale and the Jewish Minority." In *Civilian Morale: Second Yearbook of the Society for the Psychological Study of Social Issues*, edited by Goodwin Watson, pp. 218–27. Boston: Houghton Mifflin Company, 1942.

———. *Negro Intelligence and Selective Migration*. New York: Columbia University Press, 1935.

———. "Otto Klineberg." In *History of Psychology in Autobiography*, vol. 6, edited by Gardner Linzey, pp. 163–82. Englewood Cliffs, NJ: Prentice Hall, 1974.

———. *Race Differences*. New York: Harper and Brothers, 1935.

———., ed. *Characteristics of the American Negro*. New York: Harper, 1944.

Kluger, Richard. *Simple Justice: The History of* Brown v. Board of Education *and Black America's Struggle for Equality*. New York: Vintage, 1975.

Krech, David. "David Krech." In *History of Psychology in Autobiography*, vol. 6 edited by Gardner Linzey, pp. 221–50. Englewood Cliffs, NJ: Prentice Hall, 1974.

Krech, David, and Richard S. Crutchfield. *Theories and Problems of Social Psychology*. New York: McGraw-Hill, 1948.

Kurzweil, Edith, "Psychoanalytic Science: From Oedipus to Culture." In *Forced Migration and Scientific Change: Émigré German-Speaking Scientists and Scholars after 1933*, edited by Mitchell G. Ash and Alfons Söllner, pp. 139–55. Cambridge: Cambridge University Press, 1996.

Kutner, Bernard, C. Wilkins, and P. R. Yarrow. "Verbal Attitudes and Overt Behavior Involving Racial Prejudice." *Journal of Abnormal and Social Psychology* 47 (1952): 649–52.

Lapiere, R. T. "Attitudes vs. Actions." *Social Forces* 13 (1934): 230–237.

Lee, Alfred McClung. *Fraternities without Brotherhood: A Study of Prejudice on the American Corps*. Boston: Beacon Press, 1955.

Lee, Alfred McClung, and Norman D. Humphrey. *Race Riot*. New York: Dryden Press, 1943.

Levinson, Daniel J., and R. Nevitt Sanford. "A Scale for the Measurement of Anti-Semitism." *Journal of Psychology* 17 (1944): 339–70.

Lewin, Kurt. *Resolving Social Conflicts: Selected Papers on Group Dynamics*. Edited by Gertrud Weiss Lewin. New York: Harper and Brothers, 1948.

———. "Self-Hatred among Jews." *Contemporary Jewish Record* 4 (June 1941): 219–32.

Lewin, Kurt, and Ronald Lippitt. "An Experimental Approach to the Study of Autocracy and Democracy: A Preliminary Note." *Sociometry* 1 (1938): 292–300.

Lewis, David Levering. *W.E.B. Du Bois: Biography of a Race, 1868–1919*. New York: Henry Holt, 1993.

Lewis, Earl. "To Turn as on a Pivot: Writing African Americans into a History of Overlapping Diasporas." *American Historical Review* 100 (1995): 765–87.

Lieberman, Leonard. "Gender and the Deconstruction of the Race Concept." *American Anthropologist* 99 (1997): 545–58.

Lippitt, Ronald. "Preface." *Journal of Social Issues* 13, (1945): 1.

Lippitt, Ronald, and Marian Radke. "New Trends in the Investigation of Prejudice." *Annals of the American Academy of Political and Social Science* 244 (March 1946): 167–76.

Llewellyn, Karl. "A Realistic Jurisprudence: The Next Step." *Columbia Law Review* 30 (1930): 431–65.

Long, Howard Hale. "Some Psychogenic Hazards of Segregated Education of Negroes." *Journal of Negro Education* 4 (1935): 336–50.

Lyman, Stanford M. *The Black American in Sociological Thought: A Failure of Perspective.* New York: Capricorn Books, 1972.

———. *Color, Culture, Civilization: Race and Minority Issues in American Society.* Urbana: University of Illinois Press, 1994.

Lynd, Robert. *Knowledge for What?* Princeton: Princeton University Press, 1939.

MacIver, Robert M., ed. *Group Relations and Group Antagonisms.* New York: Harper and Brothers, 1944.

MacMartin, Clare, and Andrew S. Winston. "The Rhetoric of Experimental Social Psychology, 1930–1960: From Caution to Enthusiasm." *Journal of the History of the Behavioral Sciences* 36 (2000): 349–64.

Mann, Robert. *The Walls of Jericho.* New York: Harcourt Brace, 1996.

Markowitz, Gerald, and David Rosner. *Children, Race, and Power: Kenneth and Mamie Clark's Northside Center.* Charlottesville: University Press of Virginia, 1996.

Marrow, Alfred J. *The Practical Theorist: The Life and Work of Kurt Lewin.* New York: Basic Books, 1969.

Marshall, Thurgood. "An Evaluation of Recent Efforts to Achieve Racial Integration through Resort to the Courts." *Journal of Negro Education* 21 (1952): 316–27.

McNeil, Genna Rae. *Groundwork: Charles Hamilton Houston and the Struggle for Civil Rights.* Philadelphia: University of Pennsylvania Press, 1983.

McWilliams, Carey. *Brothers under the Skin.* Rev. ed. Boston: Little, Brown and Company, 1951.

———. *The Education of Carey McWilliams.* New York: Simon and Schuster, 1979.

———. *A Mask for Privilege: Anti-Semitism in America.* Boston: Little, Brown and Company, 1948.

———. "Race Discrimination and the Law." *Science and Society* 9 (1945): 1–22.

Minard, J. D. "Race Relations in the Pocohontas Coal Field." *Journal of Social Issues* 8 (1952): 29–44.

Morawski, Jill G., and Gail A. Hornstein. "Quandary of the Quacks: The Struggle for Expert Knowledge in American Psychology, 1890–1940." In *The Estate of*

Social Knowledge, edited by JoAnne Brown, and David K. van Keuren 106–133. Baltimore: Johns Hopkins University Press, 1991.

Murphy, Gardner. "Gardner Murphy." In *A History of Psychology in Autobiography*, vol. 5, edited by Edwin G. Boring and Gardner Linzey 253–82. New York: Appleton-Century-Crofts, 1967.

———. *Personality: A Biosocial Approach to Origins and Structure*. New York: Harper and Brothers, 1947.

Murphy, Gardner, and Lois Barclay Murphy. *Experimental Social Psychology*, 2d ed. New York: Harper and Brothers, 1937.

Murphy, Lois Barclay. *Gardner Murphy: Integrating, Expanding, and Humanizing Psychology*. Jefferson, NC: McFarland and Company, 1990.

Murray, Albert. "White Norms, Black Deviance." In *The Death of White Sociology*, edited by Joyce A. Ladner, pp. 96–113. New York: Vintage, 1973.

Myrdal, Gunnar. *An American Dilemma: The Negro Problem and Modern Democracy*. New York: Harper and Brothers, 1944.

Newcomb, Theodore M. *Social Psychology*. New York: Dryden Press, 1950.

———. "Theodore M. Newcomb." In *A History of Psychology in Autobiography*, vol. 6, edited by Gardner Linzey 365–392. Englewood Cliffs, NJ: Prentice Hall, 1974.

Nicholson, Ian A. M. "'The Approved Bureaucratic Torpor': Goodwin Watson, Critical Psychology, and the Dilemmas of Expertise, 1930–1945." *Journal of Social Issues* 54 (1998): 29–52.

———. "Gordon Allport, Character, and the 'Culture of Personality,' 1897–1937." *History of Psychology* 1 (1998): 52–68.

———. "The Politics of Scientific Social Reform, 1936–1960: Goodwin Watson and the Society for the Psychological Study of Social Issues." *Journal of the History of the Behavioral Sciences* 33 (1997): 39–60.

O'Connor, Alice Mary. "From Lower Class to Underclass: The Poor in American Social Science, 1930–1970." Ph.D. diss., Johns Hopkins University, 1991.

O'Donnell, J. M. *The Origins of Behaviorism: American Psychology, 1870–1920*. New York: New York University Press, 1985.

Pandora, Katherine. *Rebels within the Ranks: Psychologists' Critique of Scientific Authority and Democratic Realities in New Deal America*. Cambridge: Cambridge University Press, 1997.

Park, Robert E. *Race and Culture: The Collected Papers of Robert Ezra Park*. Glencoe: Free Press, 1950.

Patterson, James T. *Grand Expectations: The United States, 1945–1974*. New York: Oxford University Press, 1996.

Pekelis, Alexander H. *Law and Social Action: Selected Essays of Alexander H. Pekelis*. Edited by Milton R. Konvitz. Ithaca: Cornell University Press, 1950.

Peller, Gary. "Race against Integration." *Tikkun* 6 (1991): 54–7.

Persons, Stow. *Ethnic Studies at Chicago, 1905–45*. Urbana: University of Illinois Press, 1987.

Pettigrew, Thomas. "The Intergroup Contact Hypothesis Reconsidered." In *Contact and Conflict in Intergroup Encounters*, edited by Miles Hewstone and Rupert Brown 169–195. London: Basil Blackwell, 1986.

Platt, Anthony. *E. Franklin Frazier Reconsidered*. New Brunswick: Rutgers University Press, 1991.

Post, David L. "Floyd H. Allport and Launching of Modern Social Psychology." *Journal of the History of the Behavioral Sciences* 16 (1980): 369–76.

Provine, Will B. "Geneticists and the Biology of Race Crossing." *Science* 182 (1973): 790–96.

Purcell, Edward A. *The Crisis of Democratic Theory: Scientific Naturalism and the Problem of Value*. Lexington: University of Kentucky Press, 1973.

Radke, Marion, Helen Trager, and H. Davis. "Social Perceptions and Attitudes of Children." *Genetic Psychology Monographs* 40 (1949): 336–37.

Redfield, Robert. "Race and Human Nature: An Anthropologist's View" (1944). Reprinted in *The Social Uses of Social Science: The Papers of Robert Redfield*, vol. 2, edited by Margaret Park Redfield, pp. 137–45. Chicago: University of Chicago Press, 1963.

Reid, Ira De A. *In a Minor Key: Negro Youth in Story and Fact*. Washington DC: American Council on Education, 1940.

"Reid, Ira De Augustine." In *Dictionary of American Biography*, vol. 8, edited by John A. Garraty and Mark C. Carnes, pp. 521–22. New York: Charles Scribner's Sons, 1988.

Richards, Edward A., ed. *Proceedings of the MidCentury White House Conference on Children and Youth*. Raleigh, NC: Health Publications Institute, 1951.

Richards, Graham. "Of What Is History of Psychology a History?" *British Journal for the History of Science* 20 (1987): 201–11.

———. *"Race," Racism and Psychology: Towards a Reflexive History*. London: Routledge, 1997.

———. "Reconceptualizing the History of Race Psychology: Thomas Russell Garth (1872–1939) and How He Changed His Mind." *Journal of the History of the Behavioral Sciences* 34 (1998): 15–32.

Riegel, Stephen J. "The Persistent Career of Jim Crow: Lower Federal Courts and the 'Separate but Equal' Doctrine, 1865–1896." *American Journal of Legal History* 28 (January 1984): 17–40.

Robbins, Richard. "Johnson, Charles Spurgeon." In *Dictionary of American Biography, Supplement Six, 1956–1960*, edited by John A. Garraty, pp. 321–22. New York: Charles Scribner's Sons, 1980.

Rose, Arnold M. ed. *The Negro in America*.

———, ed. *Race Prejudice and Discrimination: Readings in Intergroup Relations in the United States*. New York: Alfred A. Knopf, 1951.

Rosenberg, Gerald. *Hollow Hope: Can Courts Bring about Social Change?* Chicago: University of Chicago Press, 1991.

Ross, Ralph, and Ernest van den Haag. *The Fabric of Society*. New York: Harcourt, Brace, and Company, 1957.

Saenger, Gerhart, and E. Golbert. "Customer Reactions to the Integration of Negro Sales Personnel." *International Journal of Opinion and Attitude Research* 4 (1950): 57–76.

Samelson, Franz. "Authoritarianism, from Berlin to Berkeley: On Social Psychology and History." *Journal of Social Issues* 42, 1 (1986): 191–208.

———. "From 'Race Psychology' to 'Studies in Prejudice': Some Observations on the Thematic Reversal in Social Psychology." *Journal of the History of the Behavioral Sciences* 14 (July 1978): 265–78.

———. "Whig and Anti-Whig Histories—And Other Curiosities of Social Psychology." *Journal of the History of the Behavioral Sciences* 36 (2000): 499–506.

Sanford, Nevitt. "The Approach of the Authoritarian Personality." In *Psychology of Personality: Six Modern Approaches*, edited by J. L. McCary. New York: Logos Press, 1956.

Sargent, S. Stansfield, and Benjamin Harris. "Academic Freedom, Civil Liberties, and SPSSI." *Journal of Social Issues* 42, 1 (1986): 43–68.

Sawyer, Thomas F. "Francis Cecil Sumner: His Views and Influence on African American Higher Education." *History of Psychology* 3 (2000): 122–41.

Schlegel, John Henry. *American Legal Realism and Empirical Social Science*. Chapel Hill: University of North Carolina Press, 1995.

Scott, Daryl Michael. *Contempt and Pity: Social Policy and the Image of the Damaged Black Psyche, 1880–1996*. Chapel Hill: University of North Carolina Press, 1997.

Shagaloff, June. "A Study of Community Acceptance of Desegregation in Two Selected Areas." *Journal of Negro Education* 23, 3 (Summer 1954): 330–38.

Shapiro, Edward S. *A Time for Healing: American Jewry since World War II*. Baltimore: Johns Hopkins University Press, 1992.

Simmel, Ernst. "Introduction." In *Anti-Semitism: A Social Disease*, edited by Ernst Simmel, pp. xvii–xxiv. New York: International Universities Press, 1946.

Sitkoff, Harvard. "The Detroit Race Riot of 1943." *Michigan History* 53 (Fall 1969): 183–206.

———. "Racial Militancy and Interracial Violence in the Second World War." *Journal of American History* 58 (December 1971): 661–81.

Smedley, Audrey. *Race in North America: Origin and Evolution of a Worldview*. Boulder, CO: Westview Press, 1999.

Smith, Henry Clay. "Allport, Gordon Willard." In *Dictionary of American Biography, Supplement Eight*, edited by John A. Garraty and Mark C. Carnes, pp. 7–9. New York: Charles Scribner's Sons, 1988.

Smith, M. Brewster. "The Shaping of American Social Psychology: A Personal Perspective from the Periphery." *Personality and Social Psychology Bulletin* 9 (June 1983): 165–80.

Smith, M. Brewster. "Stuart W. Cook (1913–1993)." *American Psychologist* 49 (1994): 521.

Smith, Mark. *Social Science in the Crucible: The American Debate over Objectivity and Purpose, 1918–1941.* Durham, NC: Duke University Press, 1994.

Southern, David W. *Gunnar Myrdal and Black-White Relations: The, Use and Abuse of* An American Dilemma, *1944–1969.* Baton Rouge: Louisiana State University Press, 1987.

Speer, Hugh A. *The Case of the Century: A Historical and Social Perspective of* Brown v. Board of Education of Topeka *with Present and Future Implications.* Washington, DC: Office of Education, U.S. Department of Health, Education and Welfare, 1968.

Stagner, Ross. "Reminiscences about the Founding of SPSSI." *Journal of Social Issues* 42, 1 (1986): 35–42.

Stam, Henderikus J., Lorraine Radtke, and Ian Lubek. "Strains in Experimental Social Psychology: A Textual Analysis of the Development of Experimentation in Social Psychology." *Journal of the History of the Behavioral Sciences* 36 (2000): 365–82.

Stampp, Kenneth. *The Peculiar Institution: Slavery in the Ante-Bellum South.* New York: Vintage Books, 1956.

Stansfield, John H. "Race Relations Research and Black Americans between the World Wars." *Journal of Ethnic Studies* 3 (Fall 1983): 61–93.

Steinberg, Stephen. *Turning Back: The Retreat from Racial Justice in American Thought and Policy.* Boston: Beacon Press, 1995.

Stephan, Walter G. "School Desegregation: An Evaluation of Predictions Made in *Brown v. Board of Education.*" *Psychological Bulletin* 85, 2 (March 1978): 217–38.

Sterner, Richard. *The Negro's Share: A Study of Income, Consumption, Housing, and Public Assistance.* New York: Harper and Brothers, 1943.

Stocking, George W., Jr. *Race, Culture, and Evolution: Essays in the History of Anthropology.* Chicago: University of Chicago Press, 1968.

———. "Redfield, Robert." In *Dictionary of American Biography, Supplement Six, 1956–1960,* edited by John A. Garraty, pp. 532–34. New York: Charles Scribner's Sons, 1980.

Sutherland, Robert L. *Color, Class, and Personality.* Washington, DC: American Council on Education, 1942. Reprint. New York: Greenwood Press, 1972.

Svonkin, Stuart. *Jews against Prejudice: American Jews and the Fight for Civil Liberties.* New York: Columbia University Press, 1997.

Taylor, Carole M. "W.E.B. Dubois's Challenge to Scientific Racism." *Journal of Black Studies* 11 (1981): 449–60.

Tucker, William H. *The Science and Politics of Racial Research.* Urbana: University of Illinois Press, 1994.

Tushnet, Mark V. *Making Civil Rights Law: Thurgood Marshall and the Supreme Court, 1936–1961.* New York: Oxford University Press, 1994.

————. *The NAACP's Legal Strategy against Segregated Education, 1925–1950.* Chapel Hill: University of North Carolina Press, 1987.

Twining, William. *Karl Llewellyn and the Realist Movement.* London: Weidenfeld and Nicholson, 1973.

van den Haag, Ernest. *Education as an Industry.* New York: Augustus M. Kelley, 1956.

————. "Social Science Testimony in the Desegregation Cases: A Reply to Professor Kenneth Clark." *Villanova Law Review* 6 (1960): 69–79.

Vose, Clement E. *Caucasians Only: The Supreme Court, the NAACP, and the Restrictive Covenant Cases.* Berkeley: University of California Press, 1959.

Watson, Goodwin. *Action for Unity.* New York: Harper and Brothers, 1947.

————. "How Social Engineers Came to Be." *Journal of Social Psychology* 21 (1945): 135–41.

————. *Measurement of Fair-Mindedness.* New York: Teacher's College, Columbia University, 1925.

Wertham, Frederic. "Nine Men Speak to You." *The Nation* 178, June 12, 1954, pp. 497–99.

Williams, Robin M., Jr. *The Reduction of Intergroup Tensions: A Survey of Research on Problems of Ethnic, Racial, and Religious Group Relations.* New York: Social Science Research Council, 1947.

Willie, Charles V. *Five Black Scholars: An Analysis of Family Life, Education, and Career.* Lanham, MD: University Press of America, 1986.

Wilner, Daniel M., R. P. Walkley, and Stuart W. Cook. *Human Relations in Interracial Housing: A Study of the Contact Hypothesis.* Minneapolis: University of Minnesota Press, 1955.

————. "Residential Proximity and Intergroup Relations in Public Housing Projects." *Journal of Social Issues* 8 (1952): 45–69.

Winston, Andrew S. "Science in the Service of the Far Right: Henry E. Garrett, the IAAEE, and the Liberty Lobby." *Journal of Social Issues* 54 (1998): 179–210.

Witmer, Helen Leland, and Ruth Kotinsky, eds. *Personality in the Making: The Fact-Finding Report of the MidCentury White House Conference on Children and Youth.* New York: Harper and Brothers, 1952.

Wollenberg, Charles. *All Deliberate Speed: Segregation and Exclusion in California Schools, 1855–1975.* Berkeley: University of California Press, 1976.

Younker, Ira M. "Scientific Research on Anti-Semitism in 1944." In *The American Jewish Yearbook, 5706, 1945–46.* Philadelphia: Jewish Publication Society of America, 1945.

Index

Adorno, Theodor, 53–54
African American culture, pathology of, 3, 5, 18, 34–40, 57
Allport, Floyd, 25–26, 44, 164, 171
Allport, Gordon W., 7, 44–45, 47, 50, 52, 74, 117, 121, 164, 171, 184–188, 202–203, 215
American Civil Liberties Union, 119
American Council on Education, 34–40, 86, 119, 138
American Council on Race Relations, 85, 96, 99
American Dilemma, An (Myrdal), 54–58, 63, 102, 118, 162, 205
American Jewish Committee, 52–54, 65, 111, 121, 156, 177–178; American Jewish Congress, 9, 12, 59, 63–78, 79, 82–83, 101–106, 146, 204, 206, 215; Department of Scientific Research, 54, 111; Studies in Prejudice series, 54, 111–112, 209
American Psychological Association, 1, 40–41, 147
Anti-Defamation League of B'nai B'rith, 65
Anti-Semitism, 19, 45, 51–54, 65, 67, 76–78, 88, 112
Ash, Mitchell, 6
Ashmore, Harry, 170–171, 182, 191
Assimilation, 3, 23, 57
Atlanta University, 19–20, 38
Attitude: origin of the study of, 26–34; relationship with behavior, 71–72, 118, 134, 216–217
Authoritarian Personality (Adorno, Frenkel-Brunswik, Levinson, Sanford), 54, 111–112, 119, 135

Babcock, Charlotte G., 163
Baker, Newton, 55

Barker, James, 50
Belk, Bettie, 119
Belton v. Gebhart, 110, 140
Benedict, Ruth, 18–19
Bernard, Viola, 156
Bettelheim, Bruno, 123
Blumer, Herbert, 202
Boas, Franz, 18–20, 31
Bogardus, Emory, 23–24, 26, 27
Bond, Horace Mann, 20
Braly, Kenneth, 26–28, 30
Brameld, Theodore, 174
Briggs v. Elliott, 13, 110, 113, 117, 123, 125–128, 142
Brigham, Carl, 23
Brookover, Wilbur B., 119
Bruner, Jerome S., 116, 120, 163–164
Brunswik, Egon, 53
Buck, John N., 147
Bulmer, Martin, 55
Bunche, Ralph, 55

Caliver, Ambrose, 84–85, 87
Cantril, Hadley, 119
Carnegie Corporation, 55
Carnegie Foundation, 203, 205
Carter, Robert L., 83–88, 91–92, 110, 113–114, 125–128, 149, 155–157, 169, 183, 186, 189
Caste, 35–36
Chein, Isidor, 1, 2, 7, 69, 104–106, 120–123, 131–132, 146–150, 156, 158, 160–164, 171, 177, 180, 184, 202, 207, 217; survey of social scientific opinion of segregation, 93–96, 100, 102–103, 118–119, 139, 148–149, 160–161, 165–167, 174, 222
Child Welfare Research Station, 66

About the Author

John P. Jackson, Jr., received his Ph.D. in the History of Science and Technology from the University of Minnesota in 1997. His research interests include the history of the scientific study of race, the interaction of science with the American legal system, and the history of psychology. He teaches at the University of Colorado and lives in Boulder with his wife and two children.

www.ingramcontent.com/pod-product-compliance
Lightning Source LLC
Chambersburg PA
CBHW032117020426
42334CB00016B/983